Advance Praise for

The Human-Powered Home

This is a visionary book! For anyone looking for ideas to transition to a future less dependent on fossil fuels, *The Human-Powered Home* is a rich source of inspiration. With meticulous research, humor, and encouragement, Tamara Dean empowers readers with information, resources, and tools to create human-powered appropriate technology in their lives. Everyone I've shown the book to has loved it!

— SANDOR ELLIX KATZ, author of *Wild Fermentation: The Flavor, Nutrition, and Craft of Live-Culture Foods* and *The Revolution Will Not Be Microwaved: Inside America's Underground Food Movements*

The Human-Powered Home is full of stuff you haven't come across before — and that may come in handy in a future when 'plug it in' may not always be a viable strategy. We do have all these limbs and muscles — it's kind of a relief to be reminded how much they can accomplish.

— BILL MCKIBBEN, author of *Deep Economy*

Lively and informative, *The Human Powered Home* made me want to go out and pedal my own blender.

— ELIZABETH KOLBERT, staff writer, *New Yorker* and author of *Field Notes from a Catastrophe: Man, Nature, and Climate Change*

I got great enjoyment from Tamara Dean's book. It covers the entire spectrum of human power from its history, its inventors, to plans for making devices. It celebrates self-sufficiency and human ingenuity, and is an inspiration to anyone trying to cut down on the use of earth's more precious resources.

— TREVOR BAYLIS, inventor of the clockwork radio and flashlight, founder of Baylis Brands plc.

The HUMAN-POWERED HOME

CHOOSING MUSCLES OVER MOTORS

Tamara Dean

NEW SOCIETY PUBLISHERS

Cataloging in Publication Data:
A catalog record for this publication is available from
the National Library of Canada.

Cover design by Diane McIntosh.
Cover images: Bicep curl - istock/Neal Domenico; all others - www.clipart.com

Printed in Canada. First printing September 2008.

Paperback ISBN: 978-0-86571-601-8

Inquiries regarding requests to reprint all or part of *The Human-Powered Home*
should be addressed to New Society Publishers at the address below.
To order directly from the publishers, please call toll-free
(North America) 1-800-567-6772, or order online at www.newsociety.com
Any other inquiries can be directed by mail to:

New Society Publishers
P.O. Box 189, Gabriola Island, BC V0R 1X0, Canada
(250) 247-9737

New Society Publishers' mission is to publish books that contribute in fundamental ways to building an ecologically sustainable and just society, and to do so with the least possible impact on the environment, in a manner that models this vision. We are committed to doing this not just through education, but through action. This book is one step toward ending global deforestation and climate change. It is printed on Forest Stewardship Council-certified acid-free paper that is **100% post-consumer recycled** (100% old growth forest-free), processed chlorine free, and printed with vegetable-based, low-VOC inks, with covers produced using FSC-certified stock. Additionally, New Society purchases carbon offsets based on an annual audit, operating with a carbon-neutral footprint. For further information, or to browse our full list of books and purchase securely, visit our website at: www.newsociety.com

Books for Wiser Living recommended by Mother Earth News

Today, more than ever before, our society is seeking ways to live more conscientiously. To help bring you the very best inspiration and information about greener, more sustainable lifestyles, Mother Earth News is recommending select New Society Publishers' books to its readers. For more than 30 years, Mother Earth has been North America's "Original Guide to Living Wisely," creating books and magazines for people with a passion for self-reliance and a desire to live in harmony with nature. Across the countryside and in our cities, New Society Publishers and Mother Earth are leading the way to a wiser, more sustainable world.

NEW SOCIETY PUBLISHERS
www.newsociety.com

Recycled
Supporting responsible use
of forest resources
FSC
www.fsc.org Cert no. SW-COC-1271
© 1996 Forest Stewardship Council

CONTENTS

ACKNOWLEDGMENTS

Thanks to:

Jonathan Teller-Elsberg, for his wonderful ideas, including the book's title, and his unflagging enthusiasm; without him, this book would not exist.

B.C. Brown and Ann Shaffer, for friendly consultation from the start.

Judy Wilmes, for help with procurement.

Nick Reitenour, for his talent and patience in transforming my sketches and photos into illustrations.

David Gordon Wilson, who set the bar for improved human-powered devices a generation ago and who has inspired me and so many of the inventors featured in this book.

The following human-power enthusiasts, for generously sharing their inventions, expertise, and photos: Richard Andrews, Dave Askins, George Austin, Roxana Baechle, Kevin Blake, Jock Brandis, Frederick Breeden, Carrie Brown, Ray Browning, Colin Bulthaup, David Butcher, Nate Byerley, Bill Carter, Scott Cooper, Graham Corbett, Frank Daller, Max Davis, Ali Dwyer, Job Ebenezer, Richard Ehrlich, Alex Gadsden, Bill Gerosa, Steven Gray, Albert Hartman, Laurie Hoffmann, Eric Hollenbeck, Rick Hutcheson, Gwyn Jones, Colin Kerr, Sheila Kerr, Roy Kornbluh, Anne Kusilek, Jennie Lane, Dave Miller, Jim Miller, Jason Moore, Ingrid Niehaus, Bart Orlando, Raj Pandian, Woody Roy Parker, Larry Pizzi, Ben Polito, Lee Ravenscroft, Jeff Rose, Michael Sacco, Shelley Salsburey, Steve Schmeck, Larry Shannon, Amy Smith, Henry Sodano, David Sowerwine, Jim Sylivant, Victoria Tai, David Temple, Marissa Valdez, Mike Viney, Ken Weimar, Alex Weir, Dick Wightman, and Rory Woods.

The kind staff at museums, libraries, newspapers, universities, and companies who helped with research and obtaining images to reprint in the book.

Carol Rawleigh, for her close and thoughtful editing.

Chris Plant and Ingrid Witvoet at New Society Publishers, who immediately embraced the project and shepherded it through publication.

EJ Hurst and Ginny Miller, for their dedicated publicity and marketing efforts; Sue

Custance, for managing the book's production and cover design; Greg Green, for his excellent work with the layout and figures; and others at New Society Publishers who collaborated in bringing the book to the world.

Deepest gratitude to my partner David, whose contributions are reflected throughout this book, for tinkering, instigating, encouraging—and occasionally, providing the human power.

FOREWORD

by David Gordon Wilson

As I write this draft in April 2008 it seems that Tamara Dean's book is an exact fit for the time. Global warming has become accepted as a highly probable consequence of human interference with the Earth's systems; the prices of oil and gasoline have never been higher; obesity has been recognized as a serious health threat across the "first world"; and we have failed to improve the poverty, malnutrition and access to good water of most of the third world. The proposals, the reviews of successful and failed developments, and comments in this book can make positive contributions in all these areas.

To bring about change in such difficult fields seems like a fantasy. Yet Tamara Dean's book could be another *Silent Spring*. People do change. When I first came to the US in 1955 race relations were appalling and seemingly could not be improved. The situation in 2008 is not perfect, but conditions have undergone a massive transformation. Also in those days just about everyone smoked. I tried to get some rights for nonsmokers at MIT and elsewhere, and my friends said "Give it up, Dave! Look around — everyone wants to smoke!"

And they were right: students and faculty smoked in class, and doctors smoked even when with their patients. Rather suddenly, the US changed abruptly from being a country where our freedoms included freedom to smoke almost anywhere to one having just about the most restrictive policies on smoking in the world. The major changes in these two different areas buoy me up when I contemplate seemingly intractable problems involving people's behavior, expectations and deeply held beliefs about their rights. If the problems are explained honestly and directly, even the most hide-bound of us can change.

Tamara Dean wants to bring about changes in the way we use the energy of our muscles, and I am with her all the way. As an engineer I am embarrassed by the way we abandoned the development of human-powered tools and other devices as soon as the electric motor and internal-combustion engine came along. It annoys me that when I rake leaves or clip my hedge I am using far less power than my body could comfortably produce, but I am forced to use very old forms of shears and lawn rakes that constrain my output to being a small fraction of what my neighbors can produce with electric shears and powered leaf gatherers. I know that it doesn't have to be that way: I have made a human-powered plough with which I can clear our driveway of snow in much less time than our neighbors take with their gasoline-powered snowblowers. I have been challenging generations of MIT students to produce better human-powered lawnmowers and brush-shredders and the like, and some have produced delightful devices. But as Tamara Dean shows, creating better systems is not trivial. Our fossil-energy-powered competition has evolved over many decades of successive improvements, during which time human-powered devices have languished.

Therefore please read this book with high ambitions and expectations to bring about changes in our lives and in those of others, so that we can look forward to a future of greatly reduced adverse impacts on our environment, and of better health here and in places where impoverished people are presently scraping out a thin living. We could change the world!

INTRODUCTION

What if I could harness this energy?

For many of us the question arose during a long stint on an exercise bike or treadmill. Sweating, straining, generating heat, we felt our bodies as engines. Yet the engine's output was wasted. Surely our effort was worth something! What if we could direct it toward a useful purpose, such as generating electricity, blending a smoothie, or turning a piece of wood? Besides keeping us fit, wouldn't it also help to reduce our dependence on polluting fossil fuels?

Most of us probably didn't follow the idea beyond supposition. If we'd made the calculations we would have discovered that the maximum power we could generate during our 1-hour workout would equal about one penny's worth of electricity, or the same potential that's in roughly 2 teaspoons of gasoline. We might have given up on the idea of human-powering our TV or blender. As it can't save much money or greatly reduce fossil fuel emissions, why bother?

The answer, given the enthusiasm of the dozens of human-power inventors and fans I've interviewed, centers on one vital notion: empowerment. People like Rob Roy, who pedal-powers his home's water pump, aren't beholden to the electric company. If the power goes out in Rob's area, he can still fill his water tank, and his family can still bathe and drink from the tap. Anne Kusilek, who operates a quilt finishing business using only treadle sewing machines, continues working and doesn't even notice when her home loses power. The band Shake Your Peace toured Utah on bikes and used pedal-powered amplifiers, freeing themselves of engines and extension cords. Human power is portable and available on demand. No matter how small the output, it's empowering to discover how much we can do without the utility company, or the noisy, smelly motor, or the plug.

Also striking was the number of people who described the unique connection to their processes or products that resulted from using human power. For instance, a chef realized that he could better gauge the quality of his chutneys and sauces when he mixed them in a bike-powered blender, because he could sense their thickness from the resistance to his pedaling. The same goes for Frederick Breeden of Just Soap, who mixes soaps and salves in a large bicycle-powered blender. He told me if the soap is mixed too long, it will be spoiled, and as long as he's pedal-powering a batch he can feel when it's time to stop. An electric machine wouldn't offer such control. Similarly, a potter told me he never used motorized wheels because he valued the way that operating a kick wheel connected him to the pot he was throwing.

Using human power, our exertion makes visceral what we take for granted from the grid. It raises our awareness. Some science museum exhibits allow visitors to pedal-power a 60-watt incandescent light bulb. Feeling what an effort this takes teaches us that real work — by something, somewhere — has occurred to light our rooms when we flip the switch. Museums might also allow visitors to pedal-power a compact fluorescent bulb that's just as bright as a 60-watt incandescent bulb but requires only 14 watts. Noticing the comparative ease in our quadriceps, we understand how much less power a compact fluorescent bulb uses.

Replacing motors with muscles can even be considered a political act. Gandhi urged his fellow Indians to spin and weave their own cloth, endorsing local self-reliance as a means to defy the British textile industry, which had crushed cottage industries and changed the nature of Indian society. He called this self-sufficiency "swadeshi." Through swadeshi he believed India could gain its independence. Each day he sat at his spinning wheel and practiced it himself. Perhaps we can claim hand-cranking our coffee mill each morning or pedal-powering our laptop in the evening as our personal swadeshi.

Others, like David Butcher, human-power their appliances partly to improve their health. David began tinkering with pedal-powered devices 30 years ago. In the last 2 years he's made riding his Pedal Powered Prime Mover — which can drive virtually any appliance, from a bread-making machine to a washing machine — part of his daily routine. As a result, he's lost 30 pounds, lowered his resting heart rate, and quadrupled his power output. He plans to continue developing human-powered devices and his muscles.

Not surprisingly, researchers have discovered that countries in which people use the most labor-saving devices also have the highest obesity rates. One study concluded that by not washing our dishes by hand, hanging our laundry to dry, and walking up stairs rather than taking the elevator, for example, we burn about 111 fewer Calories per day.[1] Another study compared all activities typical of a mid-1800s lifestyle to a sedentary 21st-century lifestyle and calculated a 500–1,000 Calories per day difference. These researchers suggested that the currently prescribed 30 minutes of daily aerobic exercise might actually be ⅓ of the exertion our body needs to remain healthy.[2]

I confess that none of these reasons — empowerment, awareness, politics or health — drew my partner David and I to making human-powered devices initially. Instead, it was the challenge of figuring out what we could cobble together in a pinch.

Several years ago we were building a straw bale shed. We'd been mixing earthen plaster by foot in a stock tank, but by this method each batch took at least an hour to make, never mind how long it took to apply. We thought we'd found the solution in a cheap, old cement mixer we bought at an auction. But even after some repair, the dusty motor smoked and wheezed to a halt. Days later we found an exercise bike marked "Free" on an elderly neighbor's lawn. With some ingenuity we put the two together and made a bicycle-powered cement mixer, which lasted exactly as long as we needed it to plaster the rest of our building. (The exercise bike was never meant to work so hard, and in our final week of work one of its welded joints gave out.)

Making do, or using what's available, drives the use of human-powered devices in many developing countries. For example, pedal-powered electrical generators and LED lights replace kerosene lamps in rural areas of Nepal, where electricity is either unavailable or too expensive. Pumps powered by merry-go-rounds bring clean drinking water to villages in sub-Saharan Africa. In Mexico and Guatemala, bike-powered machines grind corn, depulp coffee beans, and shell macadamia nuts. In Mali and the Philippines, a pedal-powered peanut sheller makes processing and eating peanuts more economical. Human-powered devices are a form of intermediate technology — contraptions more sophisticated than hoes, for example, but simpler and less expensive than tractors. Reducing manual labor, improving nutrition, freeing time for more profitable pursuits, and enabling groups to establish small businesses, they serve real health and economic needs.

As recently as 150 years ago, human-powered devices were the norm in every nation. This book begins by describing the evolution of human-powered devices from Archimedes' screw to electricity-generating boots. It explains how bicycles influenced woodworking tools and how gun manufacturing related to treadle sewing machines. The book does not, however, explore human-powered transportation. Many other authors have published excellent, thorough works on the history, principles and various uses of bicycles, velomobiles and flycycles.

The second chapter describes the physics and physiology behind human power. You'll learn how many watts one human can practically generate and how our muscles deliver that power. Chapter 2 also examines the drive types, frames and applications of human-powered machines in use around the globe today. It includes tips on maximizing the efficiency and comfort of the device you're building, plus hints on how to scrounge parts. This is the heart of the book for those who want to understand and design their own human-powered devices.

The remaining chapters offer plans for making specific human-powered devices grouped by area of use. For example, in the "Human-Powered Devices for the Kitchen" chapter you'll find instructions for making a pedal-powered blender. Chapter 4, "Human-Powered Devices for Lawn and Garden," includes a plan for making a treadle-powered water pump. In Chapter 6, "Human-Powered Devices for Recreation and Emergency Preparedness," you'll learn how to pedal-power your TV or laptop. For each plan I've provided a list of materials and necessary tools, plus clear, step-by-step instructions and accompanying illustrations to guide you. I've also noted each design's ease of construction, relative cost to make, time to make, and ease of operation. Finally, because improvisation is so much a part of invention, I've added lists of workable variations to the instructions.

All of the machines in the plans can be built from scavenged materials with common tools and parts from a hardware store. None requires special mechanical or metalworking skills. However, if you know how to weld or own a metal lathe, for example, you can craft more sophisticated versions of any device. I encourage you to improvise and modify the plans to enhance your machine's strength, longevity, aesthetics or personal comfort.

On the other hand, if you prefer to purchase off-the-shelf products, the last four chapters also feature commercially available human-powered devices and, where possible, include reviews of their effectiveness. For example, in Chapter 4 you'll find a comparison of human-powered push lawn mowers. Chapter 6 features several types of human-powered electricity generators, from costly bicycle-based systems to small hand-cranked mobile phone chargers.

What inspired me most while researching and writing this book was talking with individuals who had that idea — *What if I could harness this energy?* — one day, and then set about making it happen. Each was delighted to describe his or her invention and graciously shared technical details and photos. These are the people highlighted in vignettes interspersed throughout the book. Even if you don't long to construct or operate a human-powered device in your home, I hope you'll be captivated by the creativity and energy that went into making them.

A NOTE ON THE PLANS

This book's step-by-step instructions for making your own human-powered devices are meant to be guides, not absolutes. I aimed to keep the plans simple and to use conveniently available materials. You might choose different materials or techniques that better suit your situation. For instance, if you want to optimize the gear ratio of a machine for your personal output, you can replace a belt drive with a chain drive that incorporates variable gearing, as on a bicycle. If you have welding skills and tools, you can use those to make sturdier frames. In many cases, you can also make substitutions for parts in the plans — for example, replacing ½-inch plywood with ¾-inch plywood or heavy duty shelving supports for perforated angle iron — without impacting the machine's functioning. By all means, improvise and improve on what's presented here. Take to heart the tips from dozens of experienced human-powered machine inventors, most of which are found in Chapter 2. Small things, like using nylon lock-type nuts to minimize the effects of vibration over time, can make a big difference.

Also, a word about safety. At all times while making and operating human-powered devices, follow common sense, including, but not limited to, the safety precautions I've mentioned in the plans. For example, keep fingers, long hair, loose clothing or jewelry clear of bike chains, pulleys or pistons where they could get caught, potentially causing you harm. Be especially careful when operating power tools or when dealing with electricity. Neither the author nor publisher can be held responsible for damages to people or equipment resulting from your experimentation with human-powered devices.

Finally, take to heart the advice I heard most frequently from experienced inventors: though your first design might not work perfectly, or at all, keep trying until you get it right.

CHAPTER 1

THE EVOLUTION
OF HUMAN-POWERED DEVICES

Looking far into the past, we are reminded that every tool was human-powered. Rock and stick served as hammer and lever. Other simple machines — wedge, pulley, wheel, inclined plane and screw — followed. Next came compound machines, and then finally the tools of precision manufacturing, which could fabricate the machines that helped people apply muscle power more efficiently. But the evolution of human-powered devices hasn't been swift or logical. Centuries passed during which technology seemed to stand still. Inventions such as the hand crank languished before we realized their potential. Others we discovered, then forgot for many centuries before rediscovering them. And while it seems obvious that we would have abandoned human power as soon as we harnessed oxen, that's not the case. From antiquity until the Industrial Revolution, human power remained an adaptable, portable and (especially until the practice of slavery was abolished) economical option. The use of muscles as prime movers began to taper off in the 1600s. Still, it was the best solution for

many artisans, farmers and small fabricators even into the 20th century.

This chapter does not attempt to cover every human-powered device through history. It does, however, highlight some key innovations, from rotary mills to biomolecular motors. It explains the impact of the bicycle on other human-powered devices (but as the book does not include human-powered transportation, it doesn't linger there). Because human power continues to prove practical for those living in developing countries where electricity and other power sources are expensive, if available at all, this chapter also devotes several pages to human power in appropriate technology.

Early Human Power

All the human-powered devices featured in this book incorporate rotary motion. However, generating rotary motion, even in short bursts, took a long time for humans to figure out. *Homo sapiens* has been around for close to 200,000 years. But we didn't invent the wheel until almost 6,000 years ago, according to archaeological records found in what was Mesopotamia, now Iraq.

Not long after the invention of the wheel came the potter's wheel, the first human-powered household device our ancestors knew. In fact, some archaeologists claim that the potter's wheel preceded the type of wheel that was designed for transporting things (and further, that its invention was fueled by the desire to make smoother drinking goblets). The potter's wheel dates back to sometime around 3,500 BC. Curiously, its design changed little from then until the 19th century.

No record exists to indicate how the potter's wheel evolved, but historians theorize that it was preceded by a kind of turntable that allowed one to easily shape all sides of a pot without having to move the pot itself. To make it turn more easily, a pivot point was cre-

ated in the center of the rotating disk's underside, similar to the point on a toy top. Then a matching socket was carved into the center of a second disk, which would remain stationary below the rotating disk. Wheels were probably made of wood, stone or clay, but of course only the weightiest stone specimens survive. Excavators have sometimes mistaken early potter's wheels for grinding wheels.

It's believed that from at least 8,000 BC, people knew one other way of causing a tool to rotate. They wrapped a belt or cord around a spindle (or stick). Pulling back and forth on the ends of the belt or cord caused the spindle to turn, thus converting reciprocating arm motion into rotary motion. That's the concept behind bow drills, used for boring holes, and it's also the principle behind early lathes. The first lathes, recorded in Egyptian tomb drawings from about 300 BC, required two people to operate. One held the gouging tool against the spinning stock and the other drew a belt wrapped around the stock back and forth. Archaeological evidence, including turned spokes, hubs, mallets, bowls and jewelry pieces, shows that Romans and Vikings were also skilled turners.

Spring pole lathes, such as the one in Figure 1.1, were favored by Europeans. Evidence of their use dates to a 13th-century stained-glass illustration in Chartres Cathedral that depicts a woman seated at one. Spring pole lathes can be operated by one person and rely on the tension in a sapling or a similar, pliable length of wood. A frame supports the thicker end of the sapling above the operator. The sapling's narrow end extends outward. A cord connected to the tip of the narrow end is

Figure 1.1 Spring Pole Lathe

wound around a piece of wood to be shaped (the turning stock), and then attached to a treadle below. Pressing on the pedal spins the stock as the operator cuts. When the operator releases the treadle, the spring pulls the cord back up. (Unlike treadle lathes, which came later, pole lathes don't allow for continuous cutting.)

Yet the one invention that made nearly every device in this book possible, the hand crank, was still centuries away. In the course of human history, this humble, mechanical component took a very long time to materialize. In the words of historian Lynn White, Jr., "The crank is profoundly puzzling not only historically but psychologically: the human mind seems to shy away from it."[1]

Some historians credit Egyptian drills with the first hand cranks, but more recent retrospectives have discounted that conclusion. Another misconception about hand cranks applies to Archimedes' screw. Archimedes' screw was a human-powered water lifter. It consisted of a large auger, or spiral, within a cylinder. One end of the cylinder was submerged in a water source, and the other end was raised to a collection point. Turning the screw (either within the casing or along with the casing) scooped and lifted water from its source to the collection point. In Renaissance and contemporary representations of Archimedes' screw, such as the one in Figure 1.2, cranks are shown as the screw's driving mechanism. However, historians point out that this is probably an edit made with hindsight. Ancient drawings and scripts indicate that the original Archimedes' screw was turned by treading on the cylindrical casing.[2]

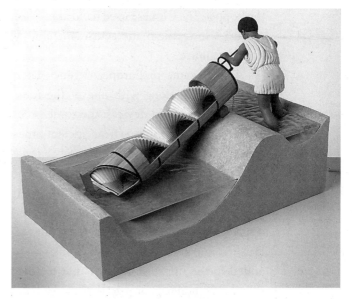

Figure 1.2 Archimedes' Screw Water Lifter

In fact, the first evidence of a hand crank appears in a model found in a Chinese tomb that dates to no later than AD 200. In this model, a man is pounding grain, and nearby sits a hopper with a handle sticking out from below the opening. The handle was the crank for a winnower, used to rotate a fan that would blow the chaff off the rice poured into

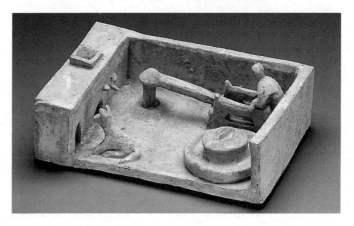

Figure 1.3 Hand Crank Evident in Han Dynasty Tomb Model

the hopper. The Chinese used hand cranks for centuries in textile manufacture, metallurgy and agriculture.

Cranks came to Europeans much later, likely evolving along with one of the most common household devices: the stone grain grinder, or quern. Querns from ancient times consisted of a stone base and another large stone that fit on top of the base. Bases contained a slight depression into which grain seed was poured. As the operator moved the upper stone over the lower one, the grain was crushed into meal. Over time, handles were added to the upper stone. The first handles were horizontal bars or pegs that allowed one to slide the stone back and forth over the base. By the 8th century BC, handles had moved to the center of the upper stone, enabling the user to rotate the stone rather than slide it back and forth. Rotary querns, it is theorized, then led to rotary grindstones with central shafts (now moved to a horizontal axis) and attached cranks.[3] The first recorded reference to this grindstone and crank appears in *The Utrecht Psalter*, an illuminated manuscript dating to between 816 and 834 BC.

Europeans, however, didn't recognize the worth of the crank, or else kept their appreciation quiet for a long time. Cranks don't appear again in their manuscripts until the 12th century. Then a few assorted references surface during the following three centuries, including hand cranks on hurdy gurdies. It wasn't until the early 1400s when certain evidence of a compound hand crank appears on a carpenter's brace in illustrations of that period. A compound crank refers to the type of crankshaft recognizable on bicycles, for example.

This arrangement allows better leverage and greater torque transfer than simply attaching a handle to the outer edge of a wheel.

Our muscles' natural back-and-forth motion had now been converted to rotary motion. But because force is applied in bursts, on the downstroke, the rotary motion that resulted was uneven. Flywheels, or weighty disks, added to axles of devices evened out the force. (Read more about the flywheel effect in Chapter 2.) The Neolithic potter's wheel could be considered a flywheel because the weight of the stone helped to keep it spinning even when someone wasn't pushing it. But the earliest record of a flywheel incorporated as part of a machine comes in the late 11th century. The monk Theophilus Presbyter described using flywheels on a pigment grinder with a rotary pestle and on the spindle of a boring device.[4] From the mid-15th century onward,

Figure 1.4 Spinning Wheel

flywheels proliferated together with hand-cranked devices.

Three elements of early human-powered devices — a treadle, a continuous belt and a flywheel — were first combined in the spinning wheel. People have spun, or twisted, raw fiber such as cotton or wool into thread, since prehistoric times. However, until the Middle Ages in Europe and probably a few centuries earlier in India, spinning was accomplished using one's hands and a stick or a simple drop spindle. Then came wheels connected via belt to a spindle. In these 13th-century devices, the first illustration of which comes from Baghdad, the wheels were hand-turned. In the late 1400s, a treadle was added to drive the wheel. This addition allowed spinners to sit while working and left the hands free for manipulating yarn. For centuries, home spinning wheels, such as the one shown in Figure 1.4, differed little from this Renaissance-era design.

So far this chapter's examples of early human-powered devices have required the strength of no more than two people. However, group efforts were also harnessed. For example, human-powered cranes were used to build Roman monuments as early as AD 100. They also built the Gothic cathedrals of Central Europe. The cranes relied on several men walking inside drums that were 12-to-25-feet high (a giant version of today's hamster wheels). A rope connected the wheels to a pulley at the top of a boom. As the men walked, the wheel turned, pulled the rope, and raised materials attached to the rope's end.

In 2006 a group of people in Prague built a human-powered crane based on a Medieval design. The crane was then used for its original purpose, to build (or in this case, rebuild) a castle. One carpenter who worked on the project said that it would have been impossible for a contemporary crane to reach the castle, which was at the top of a hill and accessible only by a narrow road. He also said that with the crane, which has two tread wheels, two men could lift 2 tons of material.[5] Human-powered cranes similar to the full-scale

Figure 1.5 Human-Powered Crane

reproduction pictured in Figure 1.5 were used at waterfronts to unload goods from docked ships and in quarries to raise stone. Since antiquity, combined human power has also powered ships, pulled carts, excavated canals and roads, and turned large millstones to grind grain, among other things.

However, humans have always sought more powerful and less exhausting alternatives to using their own muscles. Oxen were yoked as early as 7,000 years ago. Slow and relatively clumsy, they excelled at plowing fields, but weren't good at operating machinery. Horses would have been a better choice, but humans couldn't fully exploit them before figuring out how to shoe and harness the horses. On a horse, the ox's harness choked and prevented the animal from exerting its full strength. One historian explained, "In a good harness the horse can pull roughly fifteen times as strongly as a man, but in a harness of the type used for oxen it could pull barely four times as much. At the same time, a horse cost roughly four times as much to feed as a man, who had the advantage of being much more adaptable. In such circumstances, there was no great incentive to replace men by horses as a source of power."[6]

Later, wind and water replaced many of the tasks powered by humans and animals. But simply knowing how to capture alternate power sources didn't make using them economical. For example, although ancient Greeks and Romans could build water-driven mills, they weren't motivated to invest in them until slave labor became scarce.

Materials, too, limited what our forebears could achieve. No matter what powered them, early machines were less efficient and durable than the machines that came after the 17th century. Nearly all were constructed of wood, which is particularly vulnerable to friction, stress and the elements. It warps and wears down. A rotary device depends on precisely engineered bearings and wheels to turn smoothly, but making these out of wood — and getting them to stay true — is difficult. Further, gears that interlock exactly transfer the most power, but until they were made of metal and achieved a certain minimum tolerance, they couldn't fulfill their potential. That would have to wait for precision engineering — for example, the tooling and casting that emerged as part of the Industrial Revolution.

The Industrial Revolution

In his discussion of the Industrial Revolution, H. G. Wells wrote:

> The power of the old world was human power; everything depended ultimately upon the driving power of human muscle, the muscle of ignorant and subjugated men. A little animal muscle, supplied by draft oxen, horse traction and the like, contributed. Where a weight had to be lifted, men lifted it; where a rock had to be quarried, men chipped it out; where a field had to be ploughed, men and oxen ploughed it; the Roman equivalent of the steamship was the galley with its bank of sweating rowers. A vast proportion of mankind in the early civilizations were employed in purely mechanical drudgery.[7]

The machines of the Industrial Revolution, he argued, had displaced the drudges (though only where economical). Now average workers were required to be discerning and educated to remain employed. Wells connected the necessary education of the middle class with the social and political changes that inevitably followed. Certainly, the roles of muscle power and brain power on the job changed during this period. This section explores some of the significant advances between the 18th century and the 20th century that affected the application of human power or allowed human power to alter history.

For the sake of discussion, the Industrial Revolution is often said to have begun when James Watt unveiled his improved steam engine around 1770. However, the period wasn't defined only by greater horsepower. (In fact, early steam engines offered no more power than a water wheel or windmill.) Instead, it was characterized by rapid technological inventions in several fields, which brought with them political and cultural shifts. Traditional sources of energy, including human power, remained viable throughout this period. Historian R. J. Forbes wrote, "For many industries...the obstacles to the use of power were cost and physical availability rather than the mechanical difficulty of application. The capital involved was large relative to the amount of power generated, so that power-using devices were not generally preferred to the mechanisms actuated by the workman."[8]

Prior to Watt's steam engine, another device credited with fueling the Industrial Revolution is Jethro Tull's seed drill, invented in 1701. Though horse-powered, not human-powered, his machine, which allowed regular, reliable seed planting, set into motion a series of significant technological repercussions. From the same amount of land farmers harvested greater yields. In the world of textiles, this meant that more cotton became available, which heightened demands on cotton processors. And after 1733 weavers were increasing their rate of work with the use of the new flying shuttle. But bottlenecks in spinning fiber into thread limited their output.

Soon, however, spinning would catch up. In 1764, James Hargreaves, an illiterate British carpenter and weaver, invented the spinning jenny. Shown in Figure 1.6, it turned spinning on its side, making the operation horizontal. More important, it was the first machine capable of spinning more than one skein of yarn or thread at once. And it was human-powered, turned by a hand crank. Accounts of how the machine was named differ. Some say it was named after Hargreaves's daughter or wife, but church registers show that neither his wife nor any of his offspring were named Jenny. In fact, *jenny* was an abbreviation for *engine*.

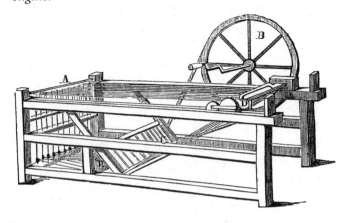

Figure 1.6 Spinning Jenny

Compulsory Human Power

Since antiquity, humans have coerced others into generating power. Slaves and prisoners served as oarsmen for early European war vessels or were conscripted as miners, toolmakers or textile workers. In Britain, forced labor became part of a prisoner's penance when King George III signed into law the Penitentiary Act in 1779. Also known as the Hard Labour Bill, this act sanctioned "labour of the hardest and most servile kind in which drudgery is chiefly required…, such as treading in a wheel, or drawing in a capstan, for turning a mill or other machine or engine, sawing stone, polishing marble, beating hemp, rasping logwood, chopping rags, making cordage, or any other hard and laborious service." Religious activists and reformers supported the policy. They reasoned that idleness led to sin, and that while busy, prisoners would have plenty of quiet time to consider their misdeeds (talking was strictly forbidden).[9]

The first such treadmill was installed at the Suffolk County jail in 1819. It was invented by William Cubitt, a millwright and civil engineer better known for designing bridges and railways. His was the first-known machine conceived "specifically to harness the collective muscle power of jailed criminals."[10] The treadmill, shaped something like a steamship's paddle wheel, was de-scribed as a "big iron frame of steps around a revolving cylinder."[11] Prisoners held on to a bar while stepping on the treads that were 8 to 10 inches apart. Some treadmills were connected to grain grinders. However, others, also known as endless ladders or treadwheels, simply spun in the air or turned a wheel that jutted from the top of the prison and most likely acted as a crime deterrent as it reminded passersby of the drudgery taking place inside.

The most famous prison treadmiller was author Oscar Wilde, who was sentenced in 1895 to 2 years of hard labor for "gross indecency." After his sentence, he emerged thin and bankrupt, but not too broken to move to France and later write a famous poem about his experience, "The Ballad of Reading Gaol," which included a reference to his time on the treadmill:

> We banged the tins, and bawled the hymns
> And sweated on the mill,
> But in the heart of every man
> Terror was lying still.

Depending on the prison, inmates were required to walk the treadmill up to 10 hours per day, stepping for 10 to 30 minute intervals, then resting for 5 minutes. Despite cases of injury and even reports of death caused by the treadmills, wardens testified that the forced labor was beneficial, as it reduced recidivism and contributed to the prisoners' good health.[12]

In 1885 a *New York Times* reporter wrote of visiting the Coldbath Fields House of Correction in London's most murderous neighborhood, a place Charles Dickens researched before writing *Oliver Twist*:

> But now we come to the strangest of all the sights in this great prison — the gallery where the great treadwheel continually revolves with a dull, resounding clank. It is a fine, well-ventilated hall, lighted from above, and on either side

THE TREAD MILL.

Figure 1.7 Treadmill at Brixton Prison, London. Installed in 1821

are rows of gray-coated prisoners, the strangest collection of human scaramouches, as clinging to a wooden bar above them, they skip from step to step of the slowly turning wheel and are never an inch the further advanced for all their skipping. A sad, terrible sight of human degradation – as painful to witness, perhaps, as to endure – with a ludicrous touch about it, too, that seems to add to the degradation.[13]

The same reporter might have been surprised to learn that four prison treadmills had operated in the United States from 1822 to at least as late as 1841. Most remained in service only a few years, including one in New York, which was used to mill corn and averaged 50 bushels ground per day. Charleston, South Carolina's treadmill also ground grain, though it was used primarily for punishing slaves. In addition, local slave owners could hire out their slaves to the jail's treadmill. The owners would receive 18.75 cents per day for the captives' labor.[14] However, treadmills never caught on in the United States, not because of a greater sympathy for the incarcerated, but due to a shortage of labor. Prisoners were better put to use in light manufacturing, producing shoes, clothing, hardware, furniture, arms, and more, for which the institution could take profits. In Great Britain, treadmills continued to operate until as late as 1901, although their use was abolished by the Prison Act of 1898.

Walking on a prison treadmill would not feel like walking on a health club treadmill, but more similar to using a stairstepper machine. In case you want to test the comparison, you can hop on a prison treadmill in Wales at the restored Beaumaris Victorian Prison. In 2007 *TimeOut London* listed "Run on a prison treadmill" as No. 44 in their list of "50 best British summer holiday breaks."[15]

Recently, the controversy of forced human power has resurfaced. In a September 2007 commentary, Brendan O'Neill, editor of *spiked*, criticized prominent figures in the UK, including Prince Charles, for abetting what he termed "eco-enslavement." To make up for the carbon emissions of their flights, for example, they had participated in a carbon offsetting program managed by Climate Care. Climate Care's strategy includes funding a program in rural India that provides treadle pumps to poor farmers. "It seems that what was considered an unacceptable form of punishment for British criminals in the past is looked upon as a positive eco-alternative to machinery for Indian peasants today," O'Neill wrote. "What might once have been referred to as 'back-breaking labour' is now spun as 'human energy.'"[16] An article in the *Times* titled "To cancel out the CO_2 of a return flight to India, it will take one poor villager three years of pumping water by foot. So is carbon offsetting the best way to ease your conscience?" shared O'Neill's view.[17]

Climate Care responded to the criticisms, defending its distribution of treadle pumps. With the pumps, it claimed, farmers greatly improved their families' nutrition and increased income, thanks to on-demand crop irrigation. Where motorized agricultural machinery was too expensive or unavailable, this intermediate technology served a critical function. Further, the company stated, "It is very important to understand that no one is forced to have a…treadle pump…. It is up to an individual farming family to decide whether to buy and use a treadle pump, buy or hire a diesel pump, or just grow a single crop during the rainy season."[18]

It is not surprising that readers of the online article voiced strong opinions on the topic. Most agreed with the authors and railed against the class issues they perceived in British aristocracy relegating rural farmers to hard labor. One American reader sounded off, "The treadle pumps would be better placed in parks as devices where [overweight] kids of the first world could get some exercise…."[19]

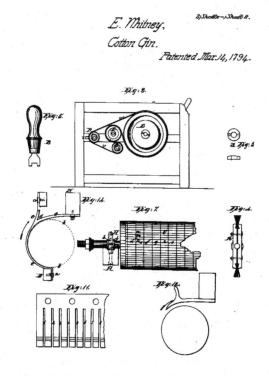

Figure 1.8 Eli Whitney's Cotton Gin

the seed drill had improved cotton yields, cotton was still harvested and cleaned mainly by hand. The latter task, removing the seeds from the cotton, was the next to benefit from a human-powered machine.

We've all been taught that Eli Whitney invented the cotton gin, but as with most inventions, the real story isn't that simple. Hand-cranked cotton gins (*gin* in this case stands for *engine*), used to remove seeds from cotton bolls, existed since at least the 14th century in China, India, Italy, and probably before that in the Middle East. These were simple roller gins, which contained two rollers wedged tightly together. The operator turned a hand crank that rotated the rollers. As cotton was fed between the rollers, the seeds were pinched off. Colonists in the Americas from as early as 1607 had roller gins, too.[20] But such machines couldn't clean seeds from the short-staple cotton grown in most of the southern United States.

Eli Whitney was a Yale graduate, skilled machinist and aspiring law student in 1792 when he traveled to Georgia to earn money as a private tutor on a plantation. The story goes that his employer and landlady, Catherine Greene, encouraged him to work on an invention that would separate the sticky seeds from the cotton grown in the area and thereby hasten cotton processing. Big profits were at stake for southern farmers. Whitney took on the challenge. He studied how cotton was cleaned by hand, then holed up in a workshop attempting to re-create those motions by machine. Months later he emerged with an improved cotton gin. His 1794 patent describes the device as follows: "The cotton gin cranked

Hargreaves's original machine consisted of eight spindles, but models grew in size until they included up to 120 spindles. He profited little from the machine, because he distributed the design and others copied it before he could patent it. Then in 1768, spinners, angered that the new labor-savings devices would put them out of jobs, broke into Hargreaves's home and vandalized several of his spinning jennies. In the coming years, several inventions, including the first mechanical stitching machines, would meet this same fate.

The spinning jenny became obsolete when engineers applied the steam engine to factory-sized versions. Then increased spinning capacity heightened the demand for cotton fiber in English textile mills. But although

cotton through rollers with teeth made of wire. The wire teeth tore the green seeds from the cotton. Iron slits let the cotton pass through, but not the seeds. A second rotating cylinder of bristles removed the seedless cotton from the wires. Through a simple arrangement of belts, the same crank turned both the cylinder with wires and another smaller one with bristles."

Controversy surrounded his claim to the invention. Some say Catherine Greene, Whitney's employer, conceived the design, but being female, wasn't eligible for a patent. Others say Whitney stole it from a neighboring plantation owner. He also made the mistakes of distributing the device before securing a patent and demanding exorbitant licensing fees for his machines, which encouraged others to copy and improve on his design. His sales schemes and his 1794 patent claim were contested for so long that when he finally left Georgia and returned to the north, he was nearly broke.

The hand-cranked cotton gin, Whitney claimed, could do the work of ten men. Later versions, which were powered by horses or water, could replace 50 men. Yet an unintended consequence of this machine was the significant increase in slave labor in the southern United States. Cotton was still harvested by hand. As the crop's profits and yields continued to grow, plantation owners wanted harvesting to keep pace. So although the cotton gin saved labor, it also created a demand for much more. Some say the invention was one factor leading up to the Civil War.[21]

In his time, Eli Whitney was better known as a firearms manufacturer. He's often credited with another pivotal invention of the Industrial Revolution, one which would transform the ways in which common men could apply their muscle power: interchangeable parts. Again, though, Whitney's legacy is subject to debate.

Interchangeable parts brought manufacturers one step closer to mass production. French gunsmith Honoré Blanc first demonstrated their use in the late 1770s. He made enough parts to construct 1,000 muskets, then sorted the parts into separate bins. As academics and politicians watched, he proved that he could reassemble a perfectly functional musket by picking parts from the bins at random. Thomas Jefferson, who had conferred with Blanc, brought the idea home to the United States. Interchangeable parts were first used by the US Ordnance Department in the production of small arms at the Springfield, Massachusetts, and Harper's Ferry, West Virginia, armories. Yet private contractors were also commissioned to make government weapons in this manner. In 1798 Jefferson granted Eli Whitney a government contract for 10,000 small arms. What was supposed to take Whitney two years took eight. In addition, scientists later determined that he had at least partially handcrafted the components and that they weren't truly interchangeable.

Uniform parts became the standard because machines could be fabricated (once the manufacturing infrastructure was in place) and repaired more swiftly. In the case of weapons, this proved a critical benefit on the battlefield. The US government funded progress in interchangeable parts. One historian wrote that "By specifying interchangeability in its contracts and by giving contractors access to techniques used in the national armories, the Ordnance Department contributed significantly to the growing sophistication of metalworking and woodworking (in the case of gunstock production) in the United States by the 1850s."[22] From Whitney's time until the Civil War, advances in precision measuring tools and templates, machine tools for milling, gear cutting, grinding and shaping, plus the division of labor according to task, contributed to a new style of manufacturing which was dubbed "The American System."

After weapons, interchangeable parts were next used in the manufacture of a human-powered device that transformed domestic life: the sewing machine. As one historian remarked, "Each sewing machine was made of dozens of little metal pieces. If those parts could be made by machine and could be interchangeable, sewing machines could be inexpensive enough for purchase by middle class families."[23]

The first mechanical stitching machine was put into commercial operation in France by its inventor, Bartholemy Thimonnier, who was a tailor. His device, patented after years of development in 1830, performed a chain stitch by using a barbed or hooked needle and was powered by treadle. By 1841, eighty of Thimonnier's machines stitched army uniforms in a Paris factory. But tailors concerned about losing their jobs mobbed the factory and destroyed his machines. Thimonnier fled Paris a pauper, and though he continued to work on stitching machines, he would never profit from his inventions. At the same time, American Walter Hunt was creating a sewing machine that made a lockstitch, the looping together of two threads, one from each side of the material being sewn. His was the first machine to perform an entirely new stitch, rather than mimic a hand stitch.[24] The lockstitch became the standard for sewing machines of that era and remains the standard today. Through the 1840s and 1850s, variations of the human-powered stitching machines proliferated in the United States and Europe. Perhaps the best known inventor is Isaac M. Singer.

Singer's company was renown, not because it made the first or best sewing machine; rather, it gained its reputation due to sales and advertising efforts. Isaac Singer was an actor as well as an inventor (many say a scoundrel too), and his sales techniques displayed theatrical flare. His company took women on tour to demonstrate and teach use of the machine. His advertisements featured gushing testimonials from supposedly real seamstresses and grateful customers. His business partner publicly entreated ministers to support machine sewing as a decent pursuit for respectable women. Singer also made purchasing the expensive devices more acceptable by offering installment plans, group sales and opportunities to lease, and by accepting older models as trade-ins for the latest machines.

Early on, manufacturers needed persuasive techniques because people didn't welcome sewing machines into their homes from the start. "The concept of domestic labor-saving machinery was an entirely new one, and neither the lack of it nor the necessity for it was readily perceived," one researcher wrote. "There were various reasons for this, the crudest one being that in most cases it was the man who earned the money and would have to pay for any such machine, while its sole beneficiary would be his wife. If a man's mother had run the home without a sewing machine, why could not his wife do the same?"[25] In addition, men questioned whether their wives were intelligent and strong enough to operate the sewing machines. Would operating the machines cause women nervous exhaustion? Or perhaps worse, enable them to live independently? Manufacturers had to convince men of the sewing machine's worth. A Singer booklet announced that

> The great importance of the sewing machine is in its influence upon the home; in the countless hours it has added to women's leisure for rest and refinement; in the increase of time and opportunity for that early training of children, for lack of which so many pitiful wrecks are strewn along the shores of life; in the numberless avenues it has opened for women's employment; and in the comforts it has brought within the reach of all, which could formerly be attained only by the wealthy few.[26]

The Singer Manufacturing Company sold 810 sewing machines in 1853, its first year of production. In 1880 it sold an estimated 500,000 machines. This was also the first year that Singer's products were truly made of interchangeable parts.[27] By 1890 the company boasted 80% worldwide market share, and in 1903 annual sales reached 1.35 million machines, nearly all of which were human-powered.[28] Forty years later, however, nearly all the machines sold were electric. To-

day, although they are the minority, treadle sewing machines are still sold by Janome in the United States and by other manufacturers overseas. Read more about them in Chapter 5.

Beginning in the mid-1800s, the increased mechanization and improved manufacturing techniques of the Industrial Revolution also brought the middle class affordable, human-powered shop tools. At this time most commercial metalworking or woodworking shops

Figure 1.9 Singer Sewing Machine Ad

wouldn't have used treadle or hand-cranked tools. Instead, an overhead shaft powered by steam or water drove the machines via a system of belts and pulleys. But the average farmer or factory worker had no electricity, water wheel or steam engine at home. Companies such as Millers Falls and W. F. & John Barnes recognized a market for smaller scale, human-powered tools that could help these folks fill their leisure time. Thus began the do-it-yourself movement.

Treadle and hand-cranked lathes had existed for centuries, and then the 19th century brought the addition of heavy flywheels, iron beds and precisely machined parts. Large scale production also became possible. In the late 1800s, human-powered lathes, saws, grinders, formers and other tools proliferated. Hundreds of manufacturers existed in

the US alone, concentrated in the east and upper midwest. The most revered lathe maker, however, was John Jacob Holtzapffel, a native of Germany who had set up shop in England in 1793. Holtzapffel lathes were finely crafted, expensive, and made for wealthy hobbyists, including aristocracy. John Jacob's son and other heirs carried on the craft after he died. His grandson, John Jacob II, also completed a five-volume encyclopedic take on ornamental turning, which his father had begun. The last two volumes were collected in a book titled *Hand or Simple Turning: Principles and Practice*, which remains in print today and is often referenced by traditional woodworkers.

In 1876 W. F. & John Barnes released the first foot-powered tools based on bicycle technology. Figure 1.11 shows one of their velocipede scroll saws. The company describes the benefits of this novel design in its 1880 catalog:

> [The] movement of the limbs in running this saw is easy and as natural as in walking, and the operator can work steadily without fatigue. All the muscles of the limbs are brought into healthful exercise, which should be a great consideration when selecting a machine. All old style foot-powers lack these advantages of ease of operation and healthful development of the muscles. An operator cannot run one of them steadily without tiring, and experiencing an unnatural cramping of the muscles of the feet, ankles and limbs.

Figure 1.10 Millers Falls Goodell Lathe with Saw Attachments

Figure 1.12 shows one of the W. F. & John Barnes company's pedal-powered grinding and polishing machines released in 1890. It's unique because it features a chain drive between the pedaled sprocket and the axle that holds the flywheel. Nearly all other foot-powered tools used belt drives exclusively. This machine sold for $18, which equals about $425 in today's dollars.

Unfortunately, of the hundreds of different models of treadle and pedal-powered tools made in the late 19th century relatively few specimens survive, although probably not because they fell into disrepair. These were heavy machines built to last for generations. Instead, most woodworkers and metalworkers abandoned them when more powerful, motorized shop tools became available just after the turn of the 20th century. Then, one writer surmises, due to their large volume of

metal, many old machines were donated for recycling during wartime scrap drives.[29]

The following pages list many hand- and foot-powered devices that were available during the late 19th century. In most cases, the hand-powered devices were hand-cranked, though some on this list were push-type machines. The foot-powered machines include both treadle and pedal-powered devices. Some, such as sewing machines and rip saws, were available in hand- or foot-powered models. For a fascinating reference from that time, see *Knight's American Mechanical Dictionary* (published 1876–1880) by Edward H. Knight. Images from the book can be found online, or you can order a reprinted set of volumes from Lee Valley Tools. Another book from the late 19th century that includes

Figure 1.11 W.F. & John Barnes's Amateur Saw #1

Figure 1.12 W.F. & John Barnes's Grinding and Polishing Machine

Human-Powered Devices

Hand-Powered

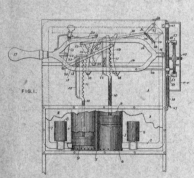

Cherry Pitter

**Hand-Cranked Dishwasher
(Top View)**

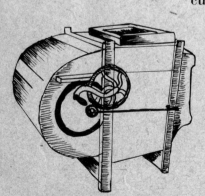

Fanning Mill

apple parer — fruit press
baler (or baling press) — glass-cutting lathe
bean sorter — grain huller
blower (for blacksmithing) — grain mill
bobbin winder — grain roller
bone cutter — grape crusher
book trimmer — hat printer
boring machine — ice-cream maker
box nailer — ice crusher
butter churn — jeweler's lathe
cement mixer — jeweler's polisher
centrifuge — juicer
chaff cutter — knitting machine
cheese press — laboratory shaker
cherry pitter (or stoner) — lard press
cider press — lawn mower (push-type)
coffee mill — marmalade cutter
copy machine — meat grinder
corn sheller — nut roaster
cream separators — oil press
crimping iron (for pleating skirts) — oilseed cake crusher
cultivator (push-type) — olive pitter
dishwasher — package bundler
drill press — paint grinder
edging machine — paper cutter (used in book binding)
(for hat making) — pea sheller
eggbeater — pencil sharpener
eggbeater drill — phonograph
fanning mill — picket maker
food chopper — planer (hand-cranked)
food mill — post drill
forage cutter — poultry delouser

of the Late 19th Century

Hand-Powered	Foot-Powered
printing press	blocking machine (for hat making)
radio transceiver	boring machine
raisin seeder	broom winder (broom making machine)
record player	cigar maker (or former)
rip saw (table saw)	circular saw
root grinder (or turnip pulper)	dentist drill
root washer (or potato washer)	dragsaw
rope maker (rope weaving machine)	drill press
rotary hoe (push-type)	former (shaper)
rotary sickle (push-type)	graphophone (dictating machine)
rotary tiller	harvester (treadmill-type)
sausage press (sausage stuffer)	hook and eye maker
seed broadcaster	knitting machine
seed cleaner	milking machine
seed potato cutter	miter saw
seed spreader	mortising machine
sewing machine	printing press
stamp mill (for beating rags	punch machine
to make paper)	rip saw (table saw)
steak crusher	riveting machine
sugar press	screw-cutting lathe
tenoning machine	scroll saw (jigsaw)
ticket printer (ticketing machine)	seed cleaner
tire shrinker	sewing machine
tobacco shredder	spinning wheel
tool sharpener	stave cutting machine
vacuum cleaner	thresher
washing machine	tip stretcher (for hat making)
water pump	tool sharpener
well driller	typewriter (with treadle return)
whale blubber mincing machine	vegetable bundler (or buncher,
wringer (mangle)	for asparagus or celery)
	weaving loom
	wood lathe

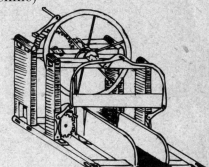

Poultry Delouser

Whale Blubber Mincing Machine

Dragsaw

illustrations and explanations of human- and steam-powered machinery is *Modern Mechanism: Exhibiting the Latest Progress in Machines, Motors, and the Transmission of Power* edited by Park Benjamin and published in 1892.

The Bicycle and Its Impact

With the Industrial Revolution, the middle class gained leisure time, and along followed ways to fill it. Bicycles of the late 1800s were designed mainly for pleasure, though as evidenced by the remarks of one commentator, not everyone embraced them.

> [W]hat queer crazes take possession of the public taste! Take cycling as an example. Walking, riding, skating and dancing we can understand as fit exercise for the fit and young; driving is precious to the indolent and delicate; but cycling seems to be such a doubtful kind of amusement — such a queer cross between the treadmill and the tightrope — demand-

Figure 1.13 Draisine

ing such a constant strain of attention to keep your balance, with such a monotonous and restricted action of the limbs as to render it a work of penance rather than of pleasure.[30]

Yet before the common man or woman even had the chance to try one, the bicycle had to evolve over decades of refinement. Centuries before bicycles came about inventors had dreamed of a human-powered carriage, a "mechanical horse." Attempts to build one in France, England and the United States during the late 1700s led nowhere. In fact, the public ridiculed those early, homemade human-powered vehicles. Then in 1818, after years of trying different models and styles, one determined German inventor, Baron Karl von Drais, patented a foot-powered vehicle. The Draisine, as it came to be called, consisted of two wheels, a padded seat on a frame, and perhaps most important, handlebars that allowed the rider to steer the front wheel. It was made almost entirely of wood and weighed about 50 pounds. The rider propelled himself by pushing his feet against the ground. Von Drais dubbed his invention the "velocipede," from the Latin words for *swift* and *foot*. (The term *bicycle* began to replace *velocipede* in the 1870s.)[31]

In an 1819 magazine article about the Draisine, one writer exclaimed, "The swiftness with which a person well practised can travel is almost beyond belief, 8, 9, and even 10 miles may, it is asserted, be passed over within the hour on good level ground."[32] One can imagine that it was especially swift downhill. It had no brakes. Figure 1.13 shows an illustration of a military courier astride a Draisine, from an 1817 booklet published by Karl von Drais.

Despite the impact his invention had on transportation history, von Drais's velocipede didn't catch on with the public in his native Germany, nor in France, where he also patented the design. In England, where the Draisine had not been patented, a London carriage maker named Denis Johnson copied and modified von Drais's design. For example, he replaced the parts of the bulky wooden frame with iron and lowered the seat in the center of the frame to allow for larger wheels and, therefore, faster running speeds. He simplified the steering mechanism, added footrests for times when riders coasted, and he also dropped the weight of the invention. Then Johnson opened a riding school to teach people how to ride his "hobby horse." Soon after, riding a velocipede became a craze among upscale Londoners.[33] The craze was shortlived, however. Public sentiment opposed the new invention, even passed laws outlawing it for safety's sake (unsteady riders whose velocipedes had poor handling and no brakes were harming pedestrians and themselves), and Johnson went back to making carriages.

The next most important development in the history of the bicycle, the addition of pedals and rotary cranks, didn't occur until the 1860s. Prior to that, Scottish tinkerers had purportedly devised a bicycle propelled by treadles attached to the rear wheel via crank rods. However, evidence of their existence is thin. In any case, it was the addition of true pedals that transformed the bicycle, making it faster, easier to maneuver, and more appealing to ride.

Credit for adding pedals to the front wheel of a bike has historically been given to Pierre Michaux, a Paris blacksmith. However, historian and author of the book *Bicycle: The History* David V. Herlihy points out that Michaux almost certainly copied his design from Pierre Lallement, a young Parisian mechanic who had worked with associates of Michaux's. Lallement emigrated to America in 1865 and filed a patent for his invention there in 1866. Details in Lallement's patent described Michaux's machine almost perfectly.[34]

Nevertheless, Michaux's invention was the one that changed history. Not only was his velocipede pedal-powered, but its wheels were closer together and its frame — made almost entirely of metal — was lighter than the Draisine's. Later versions came with brakes and a spring-suspension seat. Soon after Michaux began selling his velocipedes in 1867, Parisians went crazy for them, despite the relatively high cost and the safety concerns they raised. In 1868 one Paris newspaper claimed, "The velocipede is no longer a fashion, it's a rage. In six months' time, it will be an epidemic. One sees them by the hundreds on the public promenades, hurtling down the streets, and sailing through the parks."[35] Enthusiasm for bicycles spread quickly across Europe and the United States.

French leadership in bicycle design and manufacture withered when the Franco-Prussian War of 1870–1871 caused former bicycle factories to be converted into armament factories.[36] In the United States, a manufacturing and riding boom that began in 1868 and led some to claim that bicycling would make walking obsolete, faltered. The machine was still heavy and structurally unsound. American roads were fine for horses, but too rough for wheels. The front fork tended to jerk from side to side as one pedaled, and tires were still mostly made of wood or metal. The bicycle's nickname, "boneshaker," describes the result. Further discouraging sales, bicycle supply in the United States was cut when opportunistic businessman Calvin Witty bought out Lallement's patent and demanded steep licensing fees from every manufacturer.

Bicycles of this time still had no gearing, and so one revolution of the pedals equaled one revolution of the front wheel. Thus, the higher the front wheel, the faster a rider could go. In the drive for speed, front wheels began growing larger beginning around 1869. In 1870 British inventors James Starley and William Hillman patented the Ariel, a bicycle whose front wheel was about 48 inches in diameter. They were also the inventors of the spoked wheel and an automatic tensioning system. The Ariel featured these spoked wheels, plus ball bearings in its hubs, a hollow metal frame, and rubber tires. Although it was still a precarious ride, the Ariel was closer to the lightweight, maneuverable machines we recognize today. These high wheel, or "ordinary," bicycles proliferated and generated renewed interest in bicycles.

Starley and Hillman's Ariel bicycle was presented to Americans at the 1876 Centennial Exposition in Philadelphia, where it caught the attention of Albert Pope, a Civil War veteran and businessman. Pope commissioned one to be built for his personal use, and after riding it around his hometown, he became so enthusiastic about the high wheel

Figure 1.14 Velocipede, or Boneshaker

that he decided to both import and manufacture them. He turned a former sewing machine factory (which had previously been an arms factory) into a bicycle factory. Using the same precision manufacturing tools and following the American System, this and other former arms makers were soon fabricating bicycles.[37] Bicycle manufacturers in England, too, had converted former sewing machine factories to make their products.

Yet one more significant technological advance would be necessary before bikes appealed to everyone, including women, whose long skirts and corsets made riding a high wheel treacherous: the chain drive. In 1884

John Kemp Starley, nephew of James Starley, released a bike called the Rover. It had two wheels of equal size, a seat on the frame in between, and a chain connecting a pedaled sprocket to the rear wheel. This new design, which would look very familiar to contemporary cyclists, came to be known as the safety bicycle. With a chain drive and smaller front wheel, the effort required to operate a safety was less than that necessary for a high wheel. Yet the shorter spoke length characteristic of a safety didn't provide the same amount of shock absorption. It wasn't until James Dunlop introduced inflatable rubber tires in 1889 that this style gained preeminence over the

Figure 1.15 The High Wheel Bicycle

high wheel. By the 1890s, writes David Herlihy, "the Rover-style bicycle overtook all other cycles on the road." And in 1891 "Americans alone purchased a staggering 150,000 bicycles, effectively doubling the country's cycling population."[38]

The market for bicycles in the late 1800s also fostered the manufacturing techniques and infrastructure that allowed more sophisticated machines to follow. Technology designed for bicycles, such as bearings, seamless metal tubing and methods of joining it, stronger and lighter metal alloys, rubber-tubed tires, metal stamping techniques, variable speed gears, steering mechanisms, and brakes all contributed to future inventions, including most notably the automobile, the machine that replaced so many bicycles in the 20th century.[39] In addition, bicyclists and biking organizations were the first to lobby for a network of smooth roads that later benefited cars.

Bike technology also influenced aircraft design. Orville and Wilbur Wright were bike mechanics in Dayton, Ohio, before they designed airplanes. Their experience with bicycles surely deepened their understanding of steering, balance and momentum and informed their invention of a flying machine. They even tested wing designs by riding bicycles with models of these wings attached.

Figure 1.16 The Rover Safety Bicycle

Around the middle-class home, evidence of bike technology appeared in the foot-powered tools of the late 19th century, as described earlier. However, as electricity and gas-powered engines replaced pedal power, and bicycles were used more for play and sport than transportation, their development became irrelevant to housework and craftsmanship — at least in the Western world. In developing countries, pedal and treadle power serve as real alternatives to the more expensive and less available sources of power, such as fossil fuels or photovoltaic cells.

The next section describes how those of little means across the globe have used human-powered machines since the mid-20th century. Westerners faced with an impending shortage of cheap fossil fuel might find wisdom and inspiration in the ingenuity of these devices. In fact, history has shown the reliability of pedal power in times of crisis. The photo of a bicycle rigged to operate a gas pump in Figure 1.17 was taken the day after a devastating hurricane hit New England on September 21, 1938, and published in the New London, Connecticut newspaper *The Day*.

Human Power in Appropriate Technology

A human-powered household device, the spinning wheel, symbolized Gandhi's resistance to outsider-owned textile mills and his

Figure 1.17 Bike-Powered Gas Pump

vision for an independent India when it was ruled by Britain in the early 20th century. Where new technology arrived, it displaced and further impoverished traditional workers and craftspeople. Gandhi didn't oppose everything modern, but insisted on choosing technology that could help the poor work themselves out of poverty. This technology, he said, should depend on local materials and local skills. He called his philosophy of local self-reliance "swadeshi." He entreated his fellow Indians to spin and weave their own cloth as a protest against British industrialization. Gandhi himself made it a habit to spin daily and would sometimes open public speeches at his spinning wheel.

"The traditional old implements, the plough, the spinning wheel, have made our wisdom and our welfare."

MAHATMA GANDHI[40]

During the 1960s, E.F. "Fritz" Schumacher, a German-born British economist, studied Gandhi's teachings. He also witnessed firsthand India's extreme poverty, caused, he believed, by Western factories replacing formerly self-sufficient cottage industries. One problem with imposing mass production on developing countries was that it saved labor. These countries had labor resources in abundance, and conserving labor only put people out of work. In addition, advanced technologies required expensive upkeep and exploited

local resources, often harming a region's water, soil or forests.

"Ever bigger machines, entailing ever bigger concentrations of economic power and exerting ever greater violence against the environment, do not represent progress: they are a denial of wisdom," Schumacher wrote.[41] He imagined a better way of meeting peoples' basic needs, a type of technology more productive and effective than the primitive devices used in some remote areas, yet less capital-intensive and simpler than Western machinery. Something between a hoe and a tractor, for example. Something between hauling buckets from the river and a municipal water system. In the case of accessing water, the in-between, or intermediate, technology might consist of a well with a human-powered treadle pump, which was simple to use and maintain and could be fabricated from locally available materials.

Schumacher coined the term *intermediate technology*. He argued that at best such technology would be small, simple, inexpensive and nonviolent (though devices needn't conform to all four criteria). Later the term *appropriate technology* replaced *intermediate technology* as a more accurate reflection of what might be most beneficial on a local, case-by-case basis. Some technology, such as the use of penicillin to fight infectious disease or satellite communications to warn of impending floods, though not simple or intermediate, is very appropriate.

In 1966 Schumacher founded an organization for disseminating appropriate technology and information to help villages in the developing world become self-sufficient. His nonprofit, the Intermediate Technology Development Group (ITDG), continues operating today under the name Practical Action. Their work still draws on Schumacher's simple idea, "Find out what people are doing and help them do it better."[42]

Beyond ITDG, Schumacher's book *Small Is Beautiful: Economics as if People Mattered*, published in 1973, brought his ideas to a mass audience and inspired a movement. By 1980, 1,000 agencies with missions similar to ITDG's had materialized across the globe.[43] Some were nongovernmental organizations (NGOs), some formed at universities in both developed and developing countries, and others were established by Westerners disillusioned with the excessive consumerism in their home countries. Ian Smillie wrote that, during the 1970s and early 1980s, "Everywhere there were experiments with windmills, solar energy, latrines and energy-efficient stoves. Experimental pumps of every sort began to dot the yards behind workshops — pumps made of bamboo, wood, plastic; pumps powered by the sun, the wind, bicycles and oars."[44]

But critics found fault with the appropriate technology movement of this era. They claimed that developed nations did little to understand the conditions and needs of the communities they aimed to assist. Instead these organizations swooped in with arrogant attitudes and handed out technology that proved inadequate, unusable or unsustainable. Tinkering with technology took precedence over social, economic and political considerations. Further, many programs suffered from poor distribution as well as a lack of accountability. No one, it seemed, both-

ered to measure whether their efforts actually helped those it meant to serve. By the mid-1980s, many organizations that brought devices such as pedal-powered threshers, treadle pumps, windmills and low-power hydroelectric generators to communities in Africa and Asia had disappeared.[45]

Some, however, survived, and beginning in the 1990s those organizations, including ITDG, began to change their strategies. Significantly, they placed a new emphasis on process and participation. Engineers discussed designs with end users and local manufacturers and collaborated when making machine prototypes. The most successful appropriate technology transfer today follows this approach.

Amy Smith, who heads the D-Lab at Massachusetts Institute of Technology (MIT), a technology workshop for engineering students that devises solutions for specific challenges in developing countries, told me, "One of the things we try to do in our designs is make [them] understandable to the people who are using them so that they can also suggest improvements and do incremental changes and innovations to improve the technology.... We get great feedback from the people we work with, and it's actually embarrassing, the things we never thought about. Man, $40,000 of MIT education and I didn't think of that!"[46]

Amy also explained that simply giving away technology has failed, in the long run, to help struggling communities. Economically, it can wreak havoc on a village. She described the case of an NGO that handed out tens of thousands of treadle pumps. "[The treadle pumps] are very useful. Being able to irrigate during the dry season is very important. Farmers can double their output, and it's a technology that pays for itself in 6 months. But people won't buy them because they're waiting to see whether someone's going to come by and give them away again." She pointed out that by donating so many pumps, the NGO had forced local pump manufacturers out of business. Later, when villagers needed replacement parts for their free pumps, no one could help them. The pumps were eventually abandoned. Instead, Amy said, "You want to train the manufacturer how to make it, and then you identify the distributor who's going to sell it, and you make sure that everyone along the way is earning a profit. What you've done is you've given them the basic knowledge to get started, but you're not giving away the hardware, and it's worth it to the farmer because within a few months they'll have sold enough vegetables to pay for what they've invested in the pump."[47]

The most successful modern aid organizations have also improved their accountability. Ken Weimar, development director for KickStart, said that his organization measures sustainability in part by asking, "Do the people we've helped stay helped?"[48] KickStart, founded in Kenya in 1991 under the name ApproTEC by engineers Martin Fisher and Nick Moon, supplies human-powered appropriate technology to countries in east Africa. Fisher had been inspired by E. F. Schumacher's writings by the time he first visited Kenya in 1985. However, there he discovered that many of the small-scale technologies provided by aid organizations were poorly designed and

maintained. He set out to make something that wouldn't break in the field. One of his inventions is Kickstart's most popular device: a durable, portable treadle pump used for crop irrigation.

Kickstart's distribution follows an entrepreneurial model. "Every tool that we promote has to have a business model integral to that tool," Ken Weimar told me. "In this case irrigation is a very simple bridge for moving from subsistence farming into commercial agriculture. So that is the business model. If you irrigate in Africa during the dry season, you get three or four crop cycles a year, you have crops to sell in your local market when supplies are low, and the prices are high. Just that one simple little bridge allows people to significantly increase their farm income in a very short amount of time."[49]

KickStart measures whether their technology improves lives by finding out how many enterprises are built on the use of their pumps and how many users make money. "We actually go out and interview the farmers soon after they buy the pump and then again, 18 months later and take a look at the increase in income," Ken said. If a tool isn't changing its recipient's income — as was the case with an early hand-powered pump they made — KickStart discontinues it.[50]

Ken also said that KickStart's success depended on taking advantage of economies of scale. Instead of relying on local craftspeople to make the pumps, for example, they contract the manufacturing to a factory in an urban area near where the pumps will be used. "All of our tools are built to be mass manufactured in the largest and the most sophisticated facilities that we have available to us."[51] Centralized fabrication means lower prices for farmers who buy the pumps. It also results in greater consistency, quality and durability, which means less maintenance.

KickStart's manufacturing process has been refined to eliminate screws and bolts, which rust and require tools to replace. Instead, the pumps are welded together. As with any machine that has moving parts, wear is inevitable, however. When maintenance becomes necessary, Ken said, "[The] pumps can be taken apart. The piston cups would be the things that might wear out. In some cases they last for a very long time and in some cases, if [users are] pumping from a source that is particularly brackish or silty, they might wear out a little bit faster. But with nothing more than their hands, and maybe a rock, [users] can pull those piston cups off and replace them. And those replacement parts are also available through our supply chain. So they can go back to the store where they bought the pump and buy whatever replacement parts they need."[52]

A final key to successful technology transfer is honoring cultural differences. In most developing countries, women are the ones who collect water and wood, perform the household chores, and manage the family garden. Thus, they're frequent users of human-powered devices. When designing such machines, aid organizations need to determine what motions and positions women will accept. The founders of Maya Pedal, an organization that makes and sells bike-powered machines (bicimáquinas) to indigenous people in Guatemala, discovered this

quickly. The Mayan women still favor their traditional, tightly wrapped long skirts. Maya Pedal's first bicimáquinas were structured like upright bicycles, and while the women pedaled — which was already an unfamiliar activity — their skirts tended to ride up their calves. Reactions ranged from hilarity to horror. Richard Andrews, a bike mechanic from British Columbia and one of Maya Pedal's cofounders, told me, "We ended up changing it from sitting on a bike seat to sitting on something that looked like a normal kitchen chair with pedals in front of you and as low as you could get them without hitting the ground, so [the women] could maintain their modesty as much as is possible."[53]

Ken Weimar spoke of a similar experience when KickStart began designing a

Figure 1.18 KickStart's Moneymaker Pump

treadle pump for women in east Africa. With this machine, the longer the treadles, the more powerful the pump. Yet longer treadles require the user to be elevated higher above the ground. KickStart tested such a pump, but the women hated being in this position because it raised their posteriors to eye level. In addition, the long steps created a hip-swaying motion considered provocative in their culture. KickStart modified their design to create a pump with shorter treadles that were closer to the ground. Though less powerful, this design enabled women to work comfortably.[54]

Detailing all the human-powered devices that fall into the appropriate technology category is beyond the scope of this book. However, the following pages highlight some of the most dramatically useful and innovative ones. All are in use today.

Pumping Water

According to the United Nations, in 2006 at least one billion people — or 20% of the world's population — lacked access to clean drinking water. Unsafe water is now the single largest cause of illness worldwide and accounts for 6,000 deaths per day. Collectively, people spend 40 billion hours annually on finding and hauling clean water, and those people are usually women and children. Furthermore, the lack of access to water limits people's ability to grow food, build a business, and in general, advance beyond the cycle of poverty.[55]

However, effective pumps can be made with simple techniques and materials. They require modest amounts of power to draw water from wells even as deep as 200 feet. That means they're easily human-powered.

Hand pumps, which may be driven by a simple lever-like handle or a rotary crank, are still common around the globe and probably familiar even to readers in the Western world. However, hand pumps can raise only a limited volume of water and discharge it with less pressure than other types of human-powered pumps. Using the legs instead of the arms affords the user much greater power. In one aid worker's experience, the output of a rotary hand pump was improved by 300% when converted to leg power.[56] Thus, better yet still inexpensive and simple, technology exists in treadle or pedal-powered pumps.

Treadle pumps come in a few different styles, but nearly all rely on two pistons that are connected to the treadle pads and raised and lowered as the user steps. The pistons operate within tight-fitting cylinders, or sleeves. When a piston is raised, the volume in the cylinder increases, creating suction and drawing water up from the source. When the piston is lowered, the accumulated water rushes out of the cylinder on the outlet, or discharge, end. (In just the same way, the piston in a bicycle tire pump draws air into the cylinder when you raise its handle, then releases the air when you depress the handle.) The suction and discharge depend on one-way valves that close and open the inlets and outlets in concert with the pistons' movements. After water has been lifted from its source, it leaves through a spigot attached to the pump. On some pumps a pressurizer is added to the spigot so that water can be sprayed uphill or over a distance. The volume of water discharged varies with the height the water has to be raised — the greater the distance, the less volume the pump can emit, given the same force on the treadles.

Figure 1.19 illustrates the inner workings of a simple treadle pump. See Chapter 4 to learn how to make your own treadle pump.

The aid agency International Development Enterprises, India (IDEI) has sold more than 510,000 treadle pumps to small farmers through a wide distribution system that ends with local retailers. IDEI's pumps are simple and cost approximately $30. Bamboo is used for the treadles, because it's sturdy, widely available, and less costly than metal. The pistons are metal, however, and the pipe submerged in the water source is plastic. IDEI's treadle pumps are capable of drawing from a well no deeper than 25 feet, which limits their use to areas with a high water table (such as north and east India). Nevertheless, the treadle pumps allow farmers who cannot afford a diesel-powered pump to irrigate their fields, cropping through four seasons, increasing per-acre yield, and resulting in a 200–300% increase in profits compared to a nonirrigated farm.[57]

Treadle pumps are also the type sold by KickStart to help farmers in east Africa irrigate crops during the dry season. Their MoneyMaker and Super MoneyMaker treadle pumps are dual-piston pumps capable of drawing from a source as deep as 23 feet. The Super MoneyMaker pump is pressurized to allow irrigation of crops planted uphill from the water source. In 2007 KickStart began manufacturing and selling a new design which they call a hip pump. Instead of an up-

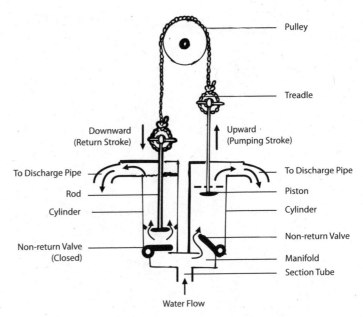

Figure 1.19 Treadle Pump

and-down Stairmaster-type motion, on this pump users make a motion more similar to rowing. It contains a single piston, as opposed to the dual-piston design of the organization's MoneyMaker pumps. It's also less than half the weight of KickStart's other pumps, so it's very portable, and less expensive. Figure 1.20 depicts a man in Africa using a hip pump.

At the time this was written, KickStart had sold more than 88,000 treadle pumps to customers in Africa, and the pumps had been used to create over 57,000 small businesses. Most customers used the pumps for farm irrigation, but some established distinctive businesses such as tree nurseries or car washes.[58]

Treadle pumps aren't necessarily single-operator machines, however. In an ingenious twist on an old technology, engineers in Gaviotas, Colombia, modified a child's seesaw to pump water for the small village. Gaviotas is

Figure 1.20 KickStart's Hip Pump

trees. "Gaviotas makes already stale phrases like 'sustainable development' and 'appropriate technology' seem not just believable, but fresh and surprising," said Alan Weisman, who wrote the book, *Gaviotas: A Village to Reinvent the World*, about the village.[59]

The Gaviotas seesaw pump has a piston under each seat. As the seat descends, it pushes down the sleeve around the piston. When the seat raises, it draws water up and toward the spigot. This type of design, in which the piston is fixed and the sleeve moves, can raise water from deeper sources than a traditional design in which the piston moves inside the sleeve. This is because lifting the sleeve, rather than the piston, takes approximately four times less energy.[60] Gaviotas has shared its seesaw pump design with thousands of other villages in Colombia. Figure 1.21 illustrates how the Gaviotas seesaw water pump works.

Seesaws are just one type of playground equipment used to pump water. In 1989 Trevor Field, founder of PlayPumps International, was visiting South Africa when he discovered a children's merry-go-round connected to a pump. A drilling engineer had invented the pump as entertainment for the children who often watched him at his work. Trevor saw the beginnings of a more sophisticated setup. With two business colleagues he licensed the engineer's invention and devised the PlayPump water system.

Each PlayPump is capable of drawing 1,400 liters of water per hour from a borehole as deep as 100 meters. Gears convert the merry-go-round's rotary motion into the up-and-down motion that drives the piston inside a cylinder below. As children spin, water

a unique community of about 200 people that was established by activist Paolo Lugari. In the late 1960s he and others envisioned an environmentally aware and self-sustaining village on the barren plains, or Llanos, of eastern Colombia. Today Gaviotas stands as a singular example of living harmoniously with nature and neighbors. Its residents rely on solar and wind power and have reforested land that was previously considered inhospitable to

is pumped from its source and up to a 2,500-liter water storage tank. Beneath the storage tank, a simple tap on a stand allows access to the gravity-fed water.

Because they are often the only playground equipment in a village, the merry-go-rounds rarely stand empty. In the unlikely event that the storage tank goes dry, it's easy for an adult to spin the PlayPump and quickly generate more water.[61] On the other hand, if the kids are spinning and the storage tank is full, water will simply return to its underground source. Figure 1.22 shows a PlayPump in use.

PlayPumps International receives requests for its water systems from across the globe, but currently focuses its efforts on sub-Saharan Africa. As of this writing 900 Play-Pumps were installed in villages from South Africa to Zambia. In 2006 the US government announced its support of $10 million, helping to launch a $60 million campaign to install 4,000 PlayPumps in ten countries by 2010.[62]

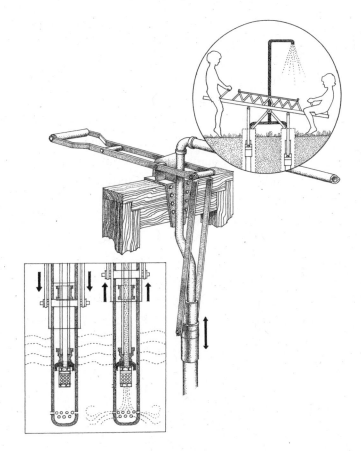

Figure 1.21 Gaviotas Seesaw Pump

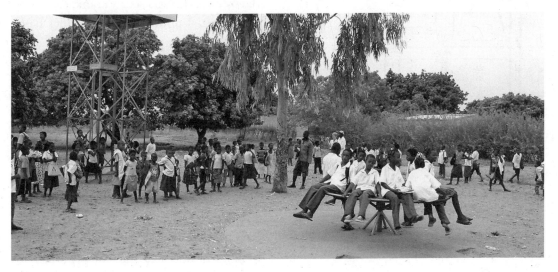

Figure 1.22 PlayPump

If you were to buy a PlayPump system, including hydrologic survey and installation, it would cost about $14,000. However, PlayPumps International donates the systems to needy communities. (It analyzes need carefully. For example, it will not donate a PlayPump to replace a functioning hand pump.) Four billboards on each storage tank fund maintenance of the system: two of these are commercial advertisements and two are public health messages.

So far all the pumps discussed in this section rely on pistons. However, a simpler type of human-powered pump is used to tap the deepest wells. The rope pump, also called a chain and washer pump, rope and washer pump or — because of its looks — a rosary

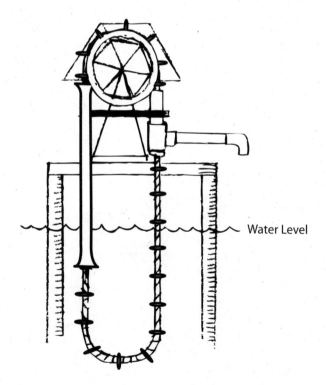

Figure 1.23 A Chain-and-Washer, or Rope, Pump

pump, originated over 2000 years ago in China. It uses baffles attached at regular intervals to a rope or chain to push water from an underground source up through a tube. It generates a constant flow of water once it gets going. At the top of the tube, above ground, the water is released into a spigot, as shown in Figure 1.23.

Because of its simplicity, the rope pump experienced a resurgence during the appropriate technology movement of the 1970s. In the 1980s it benefited from improved design, including the use of modern materials, such as PVC pipe and steel, nylon or rubber washers. (Ancient versions of this pump used leather, horsehair or rag balls as washers.) These additions made it more powerful and durable than its primitive predecessors.

Current versions of the pump can draw from a source as deep as 200 meters. At shallower depths they can discharge up to 35 liters per minute, given an input of approximately 50 watts (or .07 hp).[63] Rope pumps can be powered by hand, using a rotary crank, or by foot, using a pedal-powered drive. Besides being portable and inexpensive, rope pumps work effectively with less precisely engineered parts than piston pumps, which means they can often be manufactured locally. They also boast lower maintenance requirements. However, if they operate in an open system, these pumps threaten contamination of a water source, and also their outlets cannot be pressurized.

Rope pumps operate in many countries in Africa, Asia and Latin America today. In Nicaragua, for example, where they are called "bombas de mecate," they supply water for 50,000 Nicaraguan communities, or approximately 15% of the country's rural population.[64]

Figure 1.24 shows a bicycle-powered rope pump, or "bicibomba," made by Maya Pedal in Guatemala.

Processing Food

Jock Brandis studied to be an anthropologist, but spent most of his career in the moviemaking business. While accompanying a friend on a trip to Mali in 2002, however, his interest in anthropology resurfaced. There he saw women shelling rock-hard sun-dried peanuts by hand for hours until their fingers bled. He also noticed that land that could have been used for the life-sustaining and land-preserving legume crop was devoted instead to cotton. He reasoned that an easier means of peanut shelling would lead to growing more peanuts, which meant improving people's well-being. Jock returned to his Wilmington, North Carolina, workshop determined to design a simple, human-powered peanut sheller.

The result of his efforts was the Universal Nut Sheller, also known as the Malian Peanut Sheller. The shelling mechanism consists of two tapered cylinders made of concrete: a inner rotor and an outer stator. The rotor extends to within a peanut's width of the stator's interior. As the rotor turns, it scrapes and splits off the peanut shells against the wall of the stator. The peanuts drop out the bottom of the unit separated from the shells. Using Jock's sheller, a person can shell 125 pounds of peanuts per hour, about 40 times more than the women of Mali were capable of shelling by hand.[65] (In the 1970s, peanut shellers, or

Figure 1.24 Bicibomba (Bicycle-Powered Rope Pump) in Guatemala

decorticators, were designed and used in Africa and India, but records indicate that these cost at least twice as much as the Universal Nut Sheller and, in most cases, shelled peanuts at a much slower rate.[66])

Worldwide, approximately a half-billion people depend on peanuts as their primary protein source, so the Universal Nut Sheller has the potential to impact many lives beyond Mali. At the time this was written, it had been adopted in Uganda, Ghana, Liberia, Côte d'Ivoire, Zambia and the Philippines as well.

Jock's first design relied on a hand crank to turn its inner rotor, but later he and others made pedal-powered versions. Because the nut sheller uses simple materials and techniques, those with modest tools and skills can fabricate it virtually anywhere at a cost of between $50 and $75. Jock and some friends from the Peace Corps founded a nonprofit organization, Full Belly Project, to disseminate this

---

"You can quite easily avoid the grid just by using human legs…. If you can harness the human legs, then you've basically got the food processing problem solved. You don't need fossil fuels, you don't need solar panels, you don't need anything [except] two pedals and a couple flip-flops and a glass of water."

JOCK BRANDIS[67]

---

technology. The organization provides the fiberglass molds to make the concrete rotor and stator. They also furnish, at no cost, plans for making the Universal Nut Sheller; these can be found online at: instructables.com/id/Universal-Nut-Sheller/. Figure 1.25 shows a hand-cranked sheller in use.

Peanuts are not only a source of protein, but also an important source of dietary fat. In many sub-Saharan African countries, the consumption of dietary fats falls far below what's necessary to support healthy body functioning. Processing and selling oils from crushed seeds or nuts, including peanut, palm, soy, sunflower, rape and coconut make profitable

small businesses in the developing world. The challenge for obtaining the oil, however, is to extract it without using expensive machinery.

Until the 1980s most oil presses were too costly for rural farmers to purchase, operate and maintain. The machines crushed seeds under high pressure using a screw or plunger mechanism and required more power than any human being could generate. MIT researchers Amy Smith and Alyson Hynd wrote, "Although most of these countries did produce some type of oilseed, local production was insufficient for local needs, and both imported and domestic commercially produced oils were expensive and so unavailable to the rural poor."[68]

Making durable, inexpensive small-scale oil presses became a goal of the appropriate technology movement of the 1970s and 1980s. In 1985 Carl Bielenberg, an American engineer who had run a workshop in Cameroon, was asked to help improve a new sunflower seed press in Tanzania. Finding that press, at $1,000, still too costly and also too heavy, he conceived of an entirely new model. The ideal press, he believed, should be made of locally available materials and simple enough for local craftspeople to manufacture. It should also operate on nothing more than human power. His groundbreaking invention, the Bielenberg ram press, revolutionized small-scale oilseed processing and continues to be used in various forms today.

Bielenberg's press, illustrated in Figure 1.26, consists of a piston attached to a long handle. Lowering the handle causes the piston to crush a batch of oilseeds in a cage. As they're crushed, the seeds release their oil through the spaces in the cage, and the oil collects in a drip pan below. An adjustable pressure cone at one end of the press allows the oil-depleted seedcake to exit. After the seedcake has been expelled the user lifts the handle, and then a hopper mounted on top of the press empties more seeds into the cage.

In trials across Tanzania, Bielenberg's ram press proved capable of extracting 70 to 80% of the oil contained in sunflower seeds and even more if they'd been heated beforehand. Because of its small cage (which made human-powering it possible), its output was only 2 to 3 liters of oil per hour, significantly

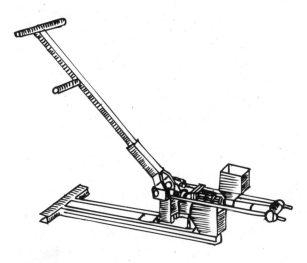

Figure 1.26 The Bielenberg Ram Press

Figure 1.25 Universal Nut Sheller

less than the older, more powerful technology. Yet this output proved satisfactory for most householders, who were able to increase their family's dietary fat intake and sell surplus oil. In fact, the Bielenberg ram press was responsible for a greater overall volume of oil production because of its usability and low cost. In addition, few press owners reported mechanical problems, and those who did were able to have their machines fixed locally.[69]

Twenty years after its invention, versions of the Bielenberg ram press continue to be locally manufactured and used in several countries. Martin Fisher, of KickStart, altered the press to make it easier to use and added oil filtering capabilities. Through the end of 2003,

Figure 1.27 VitaGoat Cycle Grinder

KickStart had sold over 1,050 of their oilseed presses in Kenya, where the machines are known as Mafuta Mali meaning "oil wealth" in Kiswahili.[70]

Generating business opportunities and improving nutrition are also the goals of Malnutrition Matters, a small nonprofit based in Canada that supplies its VitaGoat systems to villages in India, Bangladesh, North Korea and several African countries. The VitaGoat system consists of four components: a steam boiler, a pedal-powered grinder, a pressure cooker and a food press. Its original use, turning soybeans into soymilk, remains its most popular. And thanks to the pedal-powered cycle grinder, the system can be used where electricity is unavailable. (Malnutrition Matters makes another system, the VitaCow, which operates with electricity.) Users of the VitaGoat system can produce 8 to 10 gallons of soymilk per hour. A group or village typically shares one set of equipment.

VitaGoat's cycle grinder, pictured in use in North Korea in Figure 1.27, can also be used apart from the boiler, cooker and press to turn grain into flour or nuts into nut butter. In that case it replaces the labor of crushing seeds or nuts with a mortar and pestle, processing food ten times faster. Frank Daller, executive director of Malnutrition Matters, told me he and his partner devised the cycle grinder in 2002 after reading an article about pedal-powered machines that was published in the 1970s.[71]

As of this writing a complete VitaGoat system cost $3,500. Frank told me NGOs often purchase the systems on behalf of a community group or help groups secure financing. Experience has shown that groups can pay off their investment in about a year, given 3 to 4 hours per day of production. Currently, the VitaGoat systems are manufactured in India, but their design uses parts and techniques available in most developing-world villages. Malnutrition Matters aims to hire local manufacturers to build the systems closer to where they'll be used. Local fabrication will reduce the cost of their VitaGoat system by nearly one third.

In 1997 a Guatemalan organization sought help from two Canadian bike mechanics to transform cast-off bikes into pedal-powered mills that would allow the Mayan people to make their own chicken feed from corn and soy and avoid purchasing expensive commercial feed. Soon Maya Pedal was formed and the bicimolino (bike-powered mill), which remains the organization's most popular machine, was born. Thus began a decade of pedal-power invention. Bicimáquinas used in food processing include the bicidesgranadora (bike-powered corn sheller, which is sometimes combined with the corn flour mill), despulpadora (coffee depulper), bicilicuadora (blender), and bicimacadamia (macademia-nut sheller). A pedal-powered machine unique to Maya Pedal and Mayan culture is the bicinixtamal. *Nixtamal* is the Aztec word for hominy, which refers to corn kernels that have been soaked in lime to soften their hulls. It's used in making tortillas and other dishes. Maya Pedal's bicinixtamal, pictured in Figure 1.28, grinds the nixtamal into a paste, which is then formed into dough and cooked over a fire.

Read more about the Maya Pedal's operation and the bicimáquinas it makes in Chapter 2. In Chapter 3 you'll find information about ChocoSol, yet another organization using pedal power to process food — in this case, chocolate.

In the developing world human-powered machines are also used for accomplishing household chores outside the kitchen, manufacturing building materials, and generating electricity. Devices used for laundering clothes and making bricks, for example, are discussed

Figure 1.28 Maya Pedal's Bicinixtamal

elsewhere in this book. Devices that generate electricity, which have been used sporadically for decades in the developing world and are becoming increasingly popular even in developed nations, are described next.

Generating Electricity

During the Enlightenment, electrophysicists used hand cranks to turn a cushioned surface such as rubber or fur around a glass tube and generate static electricity. In 1744 Johann Winkler, a language professor in Leipzig, Germany, went further. Known in his time as the German Benjamin Franklin, Winkler adapted the principle of a spring pole lathe, used for turning wood, to the task of creating friction between a rubber pad and a glass cylinder. By mechanizing the process, he aimed to eliminate at least one of his lab assistants and produce as much electricity in the shortest time possible. One of his electrostatic generators, he claimed, could revolve 106 times per minute.[72] Figure 1.29 shows a technical drawing of Winkler's contraption as published in his book *Gedanken von den Eigenschaft, Wirkungen und Ursachen der Electricitaet….* In this book, Winkler, like Franklin, theorized that electricity could flow like water.

However, static electricity generated in such a way can't power motors. It would be another 90 years before Michael Faraday discovered electromagnetic induction, which led to a practical means of generating electric current. Shortly after Faraday's discovery, in 1832 French inventor Hippolyte Pixii invented the dynamo. To operate Pixii's dynamo, the user turned a hand crank that rotated a permanent magnet around a piece of iron wrapped with wire. Each time the spinning magnet passed the coil it generated a pulse of current. However, these pulses were intermittent. Later advances, including those patented by Thomas Edison and Nikola Tesla, enabled similar hand-turned generators to deliver direct current (DC) or regularly alternating current (AC). Modern dynamo technology still plays a role in electricity generation, from our smallest motors to our largest power plants.

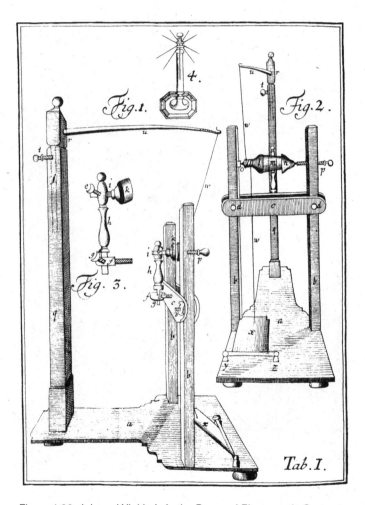

Figure 1.29 Johann Winkler's Lathe-Powered Electrostatic Generator

Hand- and Foot-Powered Electrical Generators

Technically, hand-cranked electrical current generators existed as early as 1832. However, by the time many consumers had access to electricity in the early 1900s, it was powered not by humans, but by steam, coal or hydro power. Exceptions existed, including hand-cranked telephone signaling and hand-cranked starters on Model Ts. But otherwise, human-powered electrical generators rarely left the laboratory — until they were needed by the military.

"Steady operation of the hand generator is desirable to prevent, on the one hand, too violent action of the interrupter and flaming, or, on the other hand, insufficient voltage to give a good spark." Such was the advice given to US signal corps personnel tasked with operating the hand-generators on a 1911 wireless "Pack Set" telegraph.[73] In World War I hand-cranked generators were used to power telegraph transmission, but they were so large and bulky they had to be transported by mules or wagons. Predictably, the giant hand-cranked generators soon met their demise with the development of more sophisticated, portable equipment.

Gifted Australian engineer Alfred Traeger made his first telephone transmitter at age 12 from materials found on his family's farm: pitchfork tines, tobacco tin lids and charcoal he stole from the kitchen wood stove. Twenty years later he constructed a pedal-powered wireless transceiver. The sets were needed by doctors who flew around the country serving rural outback communities. Therefore, the transceiver had to be inexpensive, portable,

rugged and simple to operate. Traeger used bicycle pedals to turn a flywheel attached to a generator. The inner workings were housed in a cylindrical casing and made part of a complete transmitter-receiver set. Using a pedal generator, rather than a hand-cranked one, left an operator's hands free to tap out Morse code. A biographer wrote, "Once the first pedal sets had been introduced in Queensland in 1929, the invention created a communications revolution by diminishing the loneliness of the inland world."[74]

Figure 1.30 Alfred Traeger's Pedal-Powered Wireless Transceiver

Although Traeger's invention, pictured in Figure 1.30, was supplanted by more modern technology in Australia, similar pedal-powered transceivers continued to be used in developing countries such as Tanzania and also by Great Britain's military until as late as the 1980s. Some designs included a battery, while others required the operator to keep pedaling for the duration of signal transmission or reception.

By World War II, hand-cranked field generators had become smaller and more powerful and commonly supported radio transmission, not just telegraph or telephone signals. They were used in the field routinely by Axis and Allied armies. They were also supplied (in waterproof housing) to pilots to be used as rescue transmitters.

In fact, today's military continues to use hand-cranked generators. They're valued for recharging batteries for devices such as cell

Figure 1.31 High Tide Associates' Palm-Power HTE-425 Generator

phones, Global Positioning Systems (GPSs) and night vision goggles in remote locations. At the time this was written the US Army relied on a model that was designed before 1980 and weighed 10 pounds. However, in 1999 the government began partnering with technology firm High Tide Associates to develop a newer, lighter hand-cranked generator. I spoke with Albert Hartman, founder of High Tide Associates, about his firm's Palm-Power HTE-425, which is pictured in Figure 1.31. He said it's unique in that it incorporates advanced electronics and magnetics, concepts he understood from his previous career in the computer hard disk industry. Digital circuitry in the Palm-Power HTE-425, for example, regulates voltage to match the needs of various devices. Previous hand-cranked generators, he said, "essentially had no electronics in their devices. So if you wanted more volts, crank faster, if you wanted less volts, crank slower. That was it." High Tide's generator also allows the user to select his effort level, which results in optimum energy harvesting. Just as a single bicycle gear isn't appropriate for every type of terrain, a single degree of resistance isn't appropriate for every user. This generator, which is rated for an output of 25 watts, includes a power monitoring display. Efforts to add more features — and lower its cost — are in the works. Currently it's available only as a prototype to the US Department of Defense.[75]

You don't have to be a soldier to have a human-powered electrical generator, however. Engineers have designed hand- and foot-powered generators for consumers as well. These lack advanced voltage regulation and variable resistance capabilities. However, they're practical and simple to use. Two companies sell pedal-powered electrical generators in North America: Windstream Power Systems, LLC, and Convergence Tech, Inc. Read more about these companies and their products in Chapter 6's discussion of commercially available devices. In the same chapter you can also learn how to make your own pedal-powered electrical generator.

Nothing makes the reality of energy use more tangible than having to generate it ourselves. Converting human power to electrical power can be a memorable hands-on (or legs-on) lesson for kids. Educators have built curricula around pedal-powered generators that include physics, math, physiology, the environment and, in the case of homemade generators, shop skills. A few organizations make these generators for the classroom. Like most commercial pedal-powered generators, educational generators consist of a bicycle training stand, a permanent magnet DC motor and a circuit. Kids can bring their own bikes to mount in the stand and then pedal to generate DC electricity. The pedal generators differ from commercial models in that their output is sent to an educational display board and can only power the devices on that board. Children use their muscles to illuminate incandescent light bulbs, compact fluorescent bulbs, a fan, a radio, a beverage warmer or a hair dryer. In fact, they can *try* to power all the appliances at once.

One educational pedal-powered generator is the Energy Bike, from the National Energy Education Development Project (NEED) in Manassas, Virginia. A description of their technology and a comprehensive curriculum for using the generator in a classroom can be found online at: need.org/needpdf/Energy Bike2005.pdf. The Pedal Power, pictured in Figure 1.32, is an educational human-powered generator that's been used in schools throughout Wisconsin. It, too, comes with lesson plans that were "developed with the assistance of teachers, engineers and energy professionals with the goal of providing a fresh perspective on energy topics."[76] As it's designed to be used in schools, the manufacturer, A1 Cable Solutions, has made the Pedal Power virtually indestructible.

Academics have studied the effectiveness of pedal-powered generators as teaching tools. In a 2006 longitudinal study, Susan Stein and Jennie Lane followed up with educators and students at seven Wisconsin schools where pedal-powered generators had been used. Not surprisingly, they discovered

Figure 1.32 The Pedal Power Educational Generator

that demonstrating the pedal-powered generator before mass audiences resulted in greater exposure, but that those exposures lacked the breadth of technical insights the unit could offer. A richer educational experience resulted when a single teacher spent more time with fewer students. Success also depended on a teacher's willingness to fully delve into scientific details. The researchers praised the improved durability of today's models over older models distributed in the 1990s. Interviews with students showed that the pedal-powered

generators increased awareness and knowledge of environmental and scientific topics. However, researchers did not find a statistically significant change in the students' "behavioral intention;"[77] for example, they were no more likely to turn off lights when they left a room.

The precise number of people living without electricity across the globe is unknown, but an oft-quoted estimate is 2 billion. Many inventors have aspired to bring more portable, efficient, and reliable human-powered

David Sowerwine's Village-Scale Human Power Plants

Establishing village-scale human power plants was not part of David Sowerwine's plan when he and his wife Haydi moved to Nepal in 1991. The California-based engineer and businessman thought they'd concentrate on fostering relationships between peasant farmers and local businesses. But soon he and Haydi found themselves involved with other development projects, including forestry, small business incubation, waste management and the construction of wire bridges for crossing monsoon-swollen rivers. The bridge design won an economic development award and attracted skilled volunteers to help build them.

When these volunteers found themselves with extra time, David suggested they tackle the problem of bringing electricity to Nepalis' homes. Like many of the world's poor, 80% of Nepalis have no electricity. Children do homework by the light of kerosene lamps or wood fires, whose fumes pose health hazards. Conventional alternative energy technologies like solar, wind or hydro power just don't make sense for many parts of Nepal, because they're too expensive or because the right conditions – like a nearby river

or reliable sunshine – don't exist. David told me, "People need two things: they need a source of power that's not dependent upon these conventional renewables, and if that's a large, lumpy source of power and more expensive than an individual household can afford, then they need a way of distributing whatever power they have so that the people on the margin or up on the hillside can have access to it." He envisioned a way to generate electricity inexpensively in a central location, then make it as portable as a bottle of milk.

With the help of volunteers and local fabricators, David's company, EcoSystems, designed and built its pedal generator in 5 months. In this design, an operator sitting in a recumbent-style frame pedals a chain drive connected to a DC motor, which charges a 12-volt deep cycle battery. On average, pedalers generate about 70 watts. They can gauge their output, as well as the amount of charge left on the battery, because David's team incorporated digital circuitry to calculate and display this data. Villagers visit the generator and charge their portable 6-volt batteries off the 12-volt battery. Then they return home

generators to these people. Perhaps the most famous is British entrepreneur Trevor Baylis. In 1991 Baylis learned from a TV program that many people in Africa risked getting AIDS simply because they lacked access to information. Radios were the primary means of communication, but people couldn't afford the batteries or electricity from the mains, or grid. Baylis set out to make an educational tool that needed no plug.

His first radio contained a spring wound by a hand crank and connected to a clockwork mechanism. (Thus its nickname, "The Clockwork Radio.") As the spring relaxed it drove an electrical generator, and the radio would play — about 14 minutes, given a fully wound spring. Baylis recruited investors who believed in the radio's worth and with them founded the Freeplay Energy Group. His radio won a prestigious British product design award in 1996. Since that time the radio has evolved. It's lighter and can run for an hour after only 20 seconds of cranking. Although Baylis is no longer involved with the organization,

with these smaller batteries, which weigh less than 2 pounds, where they power LEDs for general and task lighting, water sterilizers, telecommunications devices and more. EcoSystems also supplies affordable LED-based lighting packages. David estimated that with these packages a fully charged battery can supply a household with light for 2 or 3 weeks.

Figure 1.33 shows a woman in Nepal pedaling one of EcoSystems' electrical generators.

In 2006 the pedal generator and lighting system design won a World Bank grant. That allowed EcoSystems to continue developing and distributing the systems. When this was written, generators had been placed in 14 Nepali villages, and engineers were collecting user feedback to improve the durability and usability of the machines.

David referred to the generators as a new kind of power company, and he emphasized their positive impact on more than just those who purchase the generators. "We're going to work out a way here to microfinance helping [small groups] to get the cash to buy it. Then they become a little power company and they can supply power to the local school, where the school can run a TV and DVD player to augment their education program. They can also bottle electricity in these little batteries and light up peoples' homes and so forth. It's a lot of fun, it's a very new approach. It's enabling for dozens of other programs that are trying desperately to find some way to have enough reliable power that they can get off the ground."[78]

Figure 1.33 Pedal-Powered Electrical Generator in Nepal

Freeplay Energy continues to make and sell hand-cranked radios and flashlights. According to the company's Web site, it has sold over 3 million units since its inception.[79] Newer models also allow for solar-powering.

In 1998 the company established a non-profit group, the Freeplay Foundation, which distributes products for humanitarian purposes in sub-Saharan Africa. One, the Lifeline hand-cranked radio, is shown in Figure 1.34. Freeplay Foundation describes it as "a robust radio that [can] be operated easily by adults and children alike, heard by groups of up to 40 and powered by either wind-up or solar-powered energy."[80] In addition, the organiza-

tion provides groups with the Weza Portable Energy Source, a foot-powered generator, pictured in Figure 1.35. (*Weza* is a Swahili word for power.) It's charged by repeatedly stepping on the treadle bar. To store energy, the Weza contains a rechargeable 12-volt lead-acid battery. It can be used to power any DC device. At the time this was written, it was also available to consumers in the West for about $300.

Meanwhile, Trevor Baylis continues to release new human-powered devices and now also heads a firm that advises inventors. Read about his latest human-powered creation, a hand-cranked media player, in Chapter 6. That chapter also compares hand-cranked ra-

Figure 1.34 Freeplay's Lifeline Radio

dios, flashlights and small electronics chargers made for consumers in developed nations.

Another renowned human-power endeavor is the One Laptop Per Child (OLPC) program. Established by MIT Media Lab founder Nicholas Negroponte in January 2005, the aim of this not-for-profit organization was to bring inexpensive, lightweight, durable and power-independent laptops to children in developing countries. Many years and obstacles later, OLPC's computer, the XO, has finally arrived in the hands of school children.

The laptop draws only 2 watts, which is approximately ten times less than what typical laptops use. It's capable of being powered by muscles, by the grid, or by solar cells. The country that orders the laptops determines what type of power supplies come with it. But the original hand-crank design and now the pull-cord generator (PCG) designed by Po-

tenco have attracted much attention. I spoke with Colin Bulthaup, Potenco's CEO, about the generator. He said he and his colleagues "considered all the different energy sources out there, did the numbers, and decided on human power."[81] Once they came up with a prototype, they spent countless hours testing its design to make sure kids could operate it comfortably and successfully.

The PCG winds a bobbin when you pull its cord, converting linear motion into rotary motion. One minute of pulling, Colin said, could power 20 minutes of cell phone talk time or between 10 and 20 minutes of laptop use. Potenco has developed two versions, in fact: one with a single cord, and another that has two cords and allows alternating pulls with two hands. The former, which is pictured in Figure 1.36, can deliver 25 watts, whereas the other delivers up to 40 watts. The advantage of the pull-cord generator over a

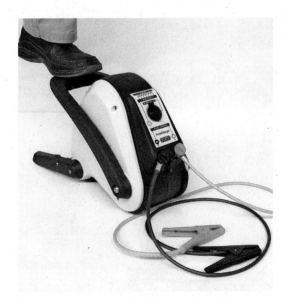

Figure 1.35 Freeplay's Weza Foot-Powered Generator

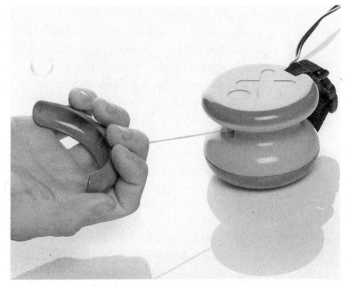

Figure 1.36 Potenco's Pull-Cord Generator

hand crank is that it can engage more muscle groups and generate more energy. For example, you could attach the PCG to a table leg and operate it by foot in a treadling motion or attach it to the ceiling and pull down.

Colin told me he uses the PCG routinely to charge his own cell phone. And although the generator isn't available to consumers in the US yet, he foresees a future in which everyone human-powers their gadgets. No wonder he's optimistic. When I spoke to him he'd recently attended a consumer electronics show where he said 40,000 people tried the generator and wanted to buy it. His prediction for the coming decade: "We will all get used to being power-autonomous."[82]

Raj Pandian's Electricity-Generating Seesaw

Raj Pandian makes power from child's play, turning seesaws, swings, merry-go-rounds and video game stations into small electrical generators.

With a background that combines electrical engineering and economic development, Raj has long sought to design technology that's useful to ordinary people. Years ago he worked on pneumatic devices for the elderly that harnessed energy from walking, stored it, then later returned it to assist users in rising from a seated position. Raj figured that similar principles could be applied to the motion of children on seesaws. He fixed a simple bicycle pump beneath each seat. As children bounced up and down, they pumped air into a pressure tank. Then the compressed air was released to power a generator, which charged a battery. In this way the children could output an average of 20 watts. Raj applied similar pneumatics to his designs for power-generating swings and merry-go-rounds.

Raj Pandian's seesaw ranked among *The New York Times Magazine's* Outstanding Ideas of 2003. Even better, the equipment was popular with kids. "One advantage of using the cylinders, the compressed air systems, was that when children were playing on the seesaw they found kind of a cushioning action, therefore they liked it better [than a traditional seesaw]," he told me.

Unfortunately for the children, however, the compressed-air design was not as efficient as a power generation system in which human work is transferred directly to a motor's shaft. More recently, Raj has been developing these types of devices.

He admitted that the idea of hooking up an electrical generator to a bike isn't new. In fact, it was part of his upbringing. "When I was a child in the middle school in India, we often used to have blackouts, and then if our mother was do-

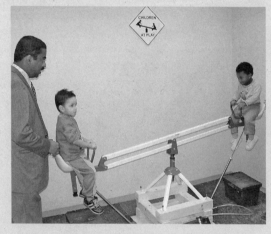

Figure 1.37 Raj Pandian's Electricity Generating Seesaw

So far all the methods of generating electricity discussed in this chapter have required someone to deliberately apply her body to that task. But what if we could generate electricity unintentionally while going about our daily business? The remainder of this chapter describes inventions that allow us to do just that.

Passive Energy Harvesting

Passive energy harvesting refers to the collection of human energy, whether mechanical, thermal or chemical, to generate power, given a person's minimal or unconscious effort. It's also known as parasitic energy harvesting or energy scavenging. The last term is probably the most accurate. As any physicist will point

ing something in the kitchen, she would be in the dark. So we used to take our bicycle inside — in India in those days, like in some places in Europe, we still had the dynamos attached to the rear tires — and put it up on a stand and then get on the bike and pedal away." The bicycle's headlight provided enough light for the women to finish cooking.

In college Raj aspired to invent power generation technology for developing countries because, as he put it, "electricity or energy in the US or in the western countries is so inexpensive that usually people don't bother to turn off lights when they leave a room." But then he realized that although Americans don't suffer as many power outages as those in less privileged nations, they had a different reason to consider human power: poor health due to inactivity. Thus, he aimed to make power generation a motivating way for kids to stay in shape. Public health studies reveal that colorful playgrounds prompt children to be more active than plain ones. Building on this idea, Raj envisioned human-powered play equipment with lights and music, audio and visual stimulation. In 2005 he designed a human-powered video game that consisted of a console connected to a pedaling station. "When you move the pedal to turn on the video game you're

going forward, when you slow down, you're going slow, and you can turn the handlebar left and right [to turn left or right] on the video game." He suggested that the game could be educational, and if multiple stations were interconnected, students could compete and compare their outcomes. His invention attracted the attention of not only kids, but also schools, utility companies, the US National Institutes of Health, and corporations looking to license his technology.

In 2005 Hurricane Katrina prevented the first pilot test of his play equipment, which was slated for a school in New Orleans' Lower 9th Ward. Since then, however, other implementation possibilities have arisen. When I spoke with him, he was seeking funding for a new project that would combine learning and exercise. A school wanted to connect his power generators to their playground equipment, add up the total energy generated, and then exhibit the results in LED displays. This setup could motivate children to improve their health, but equally as important, Raj pointed out, to recognize that they have accomplished work, that they have produced something "which is a precious item — that is, energy." [83]

out, we never get something for nothing. No matter how passive this type of energy collection seems to be, it nevertheless exerts a load on the body. For example, even a burly athlete would feel more fatigued after a day walking in energy-harvesting boots compared to walking in his regular hiking boots.

Still, bearing in mind that it does exact some physical toll on the body, passive energy harvesting offers a uniquely modern opportunity for generating power. Two paths of scientific progress have converged to make it practical: (1) the development of electronic devices with ever-decreasing wattage requirements and (2) advances in materials and fabrication techniques that can convert small vibrations, tiny amounts of heat, and biological processes to electricity.

An old example of an object powered inadvertently by human motion is the self-winding watch. In the case of the wristwatch, a wearer's shaking, stretching and scratching all kept the timepiece ticking. Self-winding pocket watches capture the vibration of a walker's gait. In fact, such "pedometer watches" date to at least 1770 and might have existed as early as the 1600s. However, self-winding watches didn't become popular until after the 1930s, when their cases could be hermetically sealed and kept safe from dust.[84]

Inside such watches a small weight mounted off-center on a spindle causes the spindle to rotate as the wearer jiggles it. This rotation then winds the timing mechanism. Only a tiny amount of energy is necessary to keep the watches functional, and the weighted spindle is so small that the added energy toll doesn't even register with the wearer. Also,

minimal energy is lost in converting human motion to watch winding in this way, as it's a direct mechanical-to-mechanical transfer of energy.

Converting human motion into electrical energy in unnoticeable ways proves more challenging. One approach is to use piezoelectric material. Piezoelectrics, including natural crystals such as quartz and synthetic polymers such as lead zirconate titanate (PZT) or polyvinylidene fluoride (PVDF), experience a change in electrical potential when they're stressed. This change induces voltage across the material, which can then be directed to a circuit. For example, walking on a floor underlined with piezoelectrics could generate a small amount of electrical power. The key word, however, is *small*.

The most notable research into piezoelectric human power has been funded by the US military. It aimed to make a passive energy harvesting device to supply portable, renewable power to soldiers in the field. The outcome was an energy-harvesting boot whose heel contained a piezoelectric generator. However, the boot's power output was, at best, little more than 1 watt, and its mechanical-to-electrical conversion efficiency was, depending on the implementation, between 1 and 10%.[85] In addition, testing revealed that walking in the boots all day was taxing, similar to walking through sand, and the military abandoned the project.

Another example of piezoelectric energy harvesting comes from engineering professor Henry Sodano, who, along with his fellow graduate school students, invented a backpack that one day might power mobile electronics for military personnel. The backpack's straps contain piezoelectric material. "Your normal gait causes the backpack to move up and down during each step, resulting in a force in the pack's straps," Sodano said.[86]

Walking isn't the only human activity that can be used to excite piezoelectrics. Researchers have proposed harnessing energy from typing, sitting, limb swinging, blood pressure and even breathing. For example, the pressure from inhalation and exhalation could cause stress on a band worn around the chest. If this band contains piezoelectric film, it will generate power. The advantage to breathing is that unlike walking, it's continuous. The disadvantage, of course, is that it doesn't require much effort, and therefore, can't generate much wattage. According to researcher Thad Starner, at a rate of ten breaths per minute and an "ambitious" force applied, the utmost potential output would be .83 watts.[87] (Other methods of capturing power from respiration have been tested or proposed. One consists of a turbine housed in a breathing mask, which was described as "causing significant stress to the user." Another idea was to attach a ratchet and flywheel to a chest band. However, the inefficiencies of this technique, its potentially cumbersome nature, and the low potential output make it an unlikely choice.[88])

Critics argue that in a piezoelectric system the amount of energy returned compared to the amount of energy input is too small to make the technology practical. Also, piezoelectrics create very high voltages, which then have to be stepped down before they can be used to power low-voltage devices such as cell phones. Power conditioning adds inefficiency

to the system. Further inefficiency comes with necessary battery storage. Nonetheless, designers persist in experimenting with piezoelectric-based human energy harvesting. Examples that have received recent media attention include a proposed energy-harvesting dance floor in Rotterdam, a Tokyo subway where commuters walking through turnstiles power the lights, and an energy-harvesting floor for London's Victoria Station. The collective energy of crowds might make piezoelectrics practical. However, my research revealed that most of these proposed or pilot projects are more hype than reality. The small amount of energy generated probably doesn't justify the expense of installing such floors. In any case, layers of piezoelectric film under your kitchen linoleum aren't going to power your microwave — or even your small clock radio — anytime soon.

Materials that hold more promise than piezoelectrics are dielectric elastomers, or rubbery films sandwiched between electrodes. When stretched, they cause voltage to pass between the electrodes, and this can be harnessed in a circuit. The research arm of the US Department of Defense has also funded scientists investigating these materials. A resulting product was the heel-strike generator, developed by SRI International and shown in Figure 1.38. Smaller and lighter than the piezoelectric generator boot, it was capable of producing between 1 and 10 watts. At the time of this writing, the government had cut funding for further research into energy-harvesting dielectric elastomers. However, a scientist at SRI International told me that his company had continued to pursue the technology with a commercial footwear manufacturer. Now they're following other possibilities (which, out of respect for his client, he couldn't disclose). In particular, he said, SRI International has improved the lifetime of such dielectric elastomers to 1,000,000 cycles, which approaches the average number of steps a shoe takes in its life.[89]

Another, perhaps more promising, way of passively converting human motion to electricity is to use gears that move when we move to power small electrical generators. Scientist Larry Rome and his colleagues developed a backpack that does just that. As the wearer walks, the backpack bounces and rolls gears along its frame. His backpack is capable of producing up to 7.4 watts and with little metabolic cost to the wearer.[90]

More recently, in February 2008 researchers unveiled a knee brace, dubbed the "Biomechanical Energy Harvester," that generates energy from the wearer's stride. What's unique about this device is that it only attempts to generate power when the wearer decelerates, or stops her leg before bringing

Figure 1.38 Heel-Strike Generator

it forward again. In this way, the inventors claim, the device requires much less energy from the wearer than other types of passive harvesting devices. The knee brace can generate up to 5 watts, and the article announcing the invention claimed that because of its relatively high output-to-input ratio, the device was "well-suited for charging powered prosthetic limbs and other portable medical devices."[91]

In Chapter 2 you'll read about the body's processes that naturally transform food into energy, generate power and exude heat. Scientists have also tried to capitalize on these processes to power small devices. For example, they've investigated transforming the body's thermal energy to electricity, which might be accomplished via a tight body suit made of heat-absorbing material. The returns are limited, however. In a perfect, closed system, the most power your body's heat could generate is estimated to be under 5 watts. And a tight body suit that robbed you of heat might be uncomfortable. As an alternative, scientists have proposed wrapping only parts of the body's core, such as the neck, in such material.

Thermal human power technology has, in fact, made it to the consumer market. In 1998 Seiko came out with the Thermic wristwatch, which contained ten thermal conversion modules and generated only microwatts, just enough to power the clock mechanism. Heat was absorbed from the back of the case, which touched the wearer's skin, and dissipated through the watch's face. The larger the temperature differential between skin and air, the better these thermal-electric generators worked. Because sufficiently high temperature differentials can't be counted on, the watches contained a small battery to store the energy. In fact, Seiko's Thermic was short-lived. Besides being expensive, the watch had to be worn tight against the skin, and ambient temperatures had to remain below 75°F for effective thermal-to-electrical energy conversion. The Eco Thermo, a similar watch released from Citizen a year after Seiko's product, was also taken off the market.

Another harvesting method converts chemical energy to electrical energy. Scientists at Panasonic's Nanotechnology Research Laboratory have experimented with enzymes that can strip blood glucose of its electrons to create a charge. They suggested that their "bio-nano generators" circulating in the bloodstream could be used to power an implanted medical device.[92] Meanwhile, the US Department of Defense is researching what they call "biomolecular motors." These virus-sized devices can capture the energy of blood glucose reactions and turn it into mechanical work — without your ever having to move a muscle. In 2000 researchers at Cornell University announced that they had created a biomolecular motor made of an enzyme with an attached propeller made of nickel. The propeller was about 750 nanometers in length and 150 nanometers in diameter."[93] (For comparison, a human hair is about 1,000 nanometers in diameter.) It spun 8 revolutions per second. Potential applications include medical sensing and drug delivery devices. For example, a biomolecular motor could travel throughout the body and dispense drugs in appropriate dosages based on chemical signals it received from cells. One researcher predicted

that human trials of the biomolecular motors are still 8 years away.[94]

For those who prefer noninvasive passive harvesting devices, scientists in Singapore have created a fuel cell that's run by urine. In fact, it was developed as a tiny battery on a "biochip" used to test for diseases such as diabetes. (Any number of ion-rich substances, including fruit juice or tears, could be used in place of the urine to carry charge between the electrodes. But because the urine was needed for the medical test, it served a dual purpose.) One drop of urine on the biochip can issue about 1.5 volts with a maximum power output of 1.5 milliwatts. The batteries are limited to one use. However, Daniel Kammen, director of the Renewable and Appropriate Energy Laboratory at the University of California, Berkeley, welcomed the technology and emphasized its wider potential. "For example, we can integrate a small cell phone and our battery on a plastic card. This can be activated by body fluids, such as saliva, during an emergency," he said.[95] The challenge lies in scaling up the battery to produce much more power.

Energy-harvesting boots, heat-absorbing body suits, and bloodstream motors aren't likely to be leeching off your body soon. Materials and fabrication advances will continue, and these technologies will mature, yet they'll be used in medical, research and military applications long before they're available to consumers. Meanwhile, however, much can be harvested from the old-fashioned kind of human power. The following chapter explains how muscles use energy and deliver power and how best to put that power to work.

CHAPTER 2

PUTTING HUMAN POWER TO WORK

"Great ideas originate in the muscles"

THOMAS EDISON

*"There's so many goofy machines out there,
and I've been involved in building a few silly ones."*

RICHARD ANDREWS[1]

How do you know what kind of machine you can power with muscles and how best to go about making it? Richard Andrews, cofounder of Maya Pedal, told me the story of a German engineer who visited the organization intent on building a pedal-powered band saw. "He proceeded to take over the workshop for nearly a month and we were all sort of enthralled because it seemed like a brilliant project, but…it was so silly. We spent all this time making this fabulous, beautifully machined, big, bloody saw that was just so painfully impossible to operate. As soon as the wood touched the blade, it just stopped."[2] Before you head to the workshop to work on your pedal-powered dream machine, it's helpful to understand how muscles generate power, how much they can generate, and how best to harness it.

This chapter begins by describing what scientists mean by work, energy and power and how each is measured. Then it explains how humans store energy and deliver power. You'll learn how muscles compare to motors and other power sources and how we can each improve our personal power output. Next, the chapter details and illustrates the elements common to most human-powered machines. Finally, it provides suggestions for designing and constructing custom, human-powered devices. By the end of this chapter, you'll possess sufficient knowledge and, I hope, inspiration to retreat to your shop and piece together your own human-powered machine.

Terms and Measures

We say we have energy for ideas, expend energy running to catch the bus, guzzle energy drinks, conserve energy by lowering the thermostat in winter, and tell friends about a band that displays boundless energy on stage. But only some uses of the word would satisfy a physicist. And just as we use the term *energy* loosely and metaphorically, we similarly toss out the words force, work and power, all of which have specific meanings in physics. Does it matter? Probably not when talking with friends. But when analyzing and devising alternative power sources, it could.

To get to energy and power, you first need to understand force. Force is the intensity with which we act upon an object, the measure of our punch, pull, kick, slap or shove. Say you're in line at a crowded airport, and as the line shortens, you nudge your rolling luggage ahead of you with your leg. Your leg is exerting a force on the luggage. This force can be measured in newtons (N, named after Sir Isaac Newton). If your luggage moves forward in response to that force, you have accomplished work. However, if your luggage is so heavy with souvenirs that it doesn't budge when you push against it, then you have not accomplished work. By scientific definition, work only occurs when something is displaced by force. (This displacement isn't limited to forward motion. It can also involve pulling, lifting or rotating, for example, as when pedaling a bike.) The distance an object is displaced is measured in meters. Therefore, work, which is force times distance, can be measured in newton-meters. More often, however, work is described in joules (J), named after James Prescott Joule, a 19th century English physicist. One joule equals one newton-meter.

To determine whether our muscles can operate a machine, we're most interested in the concept of power. Power is the rate at which work is accomplished. In the example above, power would represent how far you could move your luggage in a certain amount of time. *Power = Work/Time*, and it's measured in joules per second. One joule per second equals one watt (W), named after James Watt, the Scottish engineer who designed steam engines. Ironically, James Watt established a different measure for power, horsepower (hp), and today, either distinction is acceptable. One horsepower equals 746 watts.

As for energy, even physicists debate how best to define it. It's the capacity of something or someone to do work. It's an inherent characteristic, a potential. Without energy, no force can be exerted and thus, no work can be accomplished, nor any power produced. Energy gives us the ability to perform work while power indicates how quickly (or slowly) we perform. Energy, like work, is also measured in joules.

One joule is a very small amount of energy. "About thirty micrograms of coal — or two seconds' worth of a vole's metabolism account for one joule."[3] By contrast, a barrel of crude oil represents 6,000,000,000 joules, or 6 gigajoules (GJ), of energy. One watt is also a small unit. The tealight candle burning on your nightstand, the hummingbird's flight from bush to feeder, and the LED illuminating your computer's on-off switch, all use one watt or less of power. The 200-mph winds of a tornado, on the other hand, can generate one billion watts, as much power as two nuclear reactors.

You're probably familiar with the watt — or kilowatt (kW), which equals 1,000 watts — from looking at your electric bill or reading the labels on appliances. A toaster, for example, might be rated for 1,000 watts. A laptop computer might use 20 watts. Table 2.1 lists some common appliances and the amount of power each is rated to use. However, these power ratings are only approximate. Actual power consumption depends on many factors, as described next.

When assessing or predicting an appliance's power usage, consider the following:

- A motorized appliance, such as a blender, will require a brief, initial burst of power upon startup that's higher than the amount of power required to maintain a certain operating speed.

- The number of watts listed on an appliance's label is the *maximum* amount of power it will use while operating. An inkjet printer, for example, might be rated for 20 watts, but use that amount of power only when it's printing. When it's sitting idle (sleeping, or in standby mode), it might use only 3 watts.

- Some appliances, such as TVs, stereos, plus other devices that require AC-to-DC converters, and even gas stoves with clocks, use a small amount of power when they are not operating. This is sometimes called a phantom load. To curb phantom load, plug these appliances into outlet strips and turn off the outlet strips when you're not using the devices.

- The wattage listed on some appliances' labels reflects the amount of power they output, but not the input wattage they require. For example, you might purchase "100 watt" stereo speakers, but the speakers might require 120 watts from the amplifier to generate the speaker's full potential of 100 watts. (The lost 20 watts

Table 2.1 Power Ratings for Household Appliances

APPLIANCE	POWER USED WHILE OPERATING (IN WATTS)
Alarm clock	2–5
Night light (incandescent)	4–5
Electric toothbrush	1–10
Laptop computer	10–20
Inkjet printer	50–75
Ceiling fan	20–100
Stereo	30–100
Sewing machine	75–100
Color TV (CRT-type, 19" to 34" screen)	100–300
Color TV (plasma, 50" screen)	300–400
Food processor	350–450
Blender	300–400
Refrigerator (electric, running off AC)	500–600 (newer model; up to 1,200 for older model)
Washing machine	500–900
Microwave oven	750–2,000
Electric coffeemaker	800–1,500
Window air conditioner	850–1,000
Toaster	1,000–1,500
Portable space heater	1,000–1,500
Vacuum cleaner (upright)	1,000–2,000
Table saw	1,200–2,000
Electric clothes dryer	4,000–5,000

NOTE: 1 watt = 1 joule/second

reflects the inefficiencies of the device.) The louder you turn up the volume, the more watts you'll use.

The best way to determine how much power an appliance uses is with a wattmeter. Plug the wattmeter into an outlet, plug your appliance into the meter, then turn on the appliance, and the wattmeter will display the amount of power the appliance draws at that moment. Wattmeters such as the Kill-A-Watt and the Watts-Up meter sell for between $30 and $80. In some places local energy cooperatives or libraries make them available on loan to customers or patrons.

Knowing how much power a device requires will help you determine whether your muscles can operate it. The following section describes how your body obtains and applies energy.

Human Power Generation

Energy can be expressed in many forms: kinetic (or mechanical), thermal, chemical, electrical, electromagnetic, nuclear and gravitational. Any biomass, be it a fern, a barrel of oil, or your body, stores chemical energy. Chemical energy alone fuels your muscles. This chemical energy comes from food, and we measure its potential — as you know, if you have ever watched your diet — more often in calories rather than joules. (In fact, what consumers recognize as a calorie scientists know as a kilocalorie, which can also be denoted by the capitalized Calorie.) Joules represent mechanical energy while calories represent thermal energy, or the amount of heat created while burning. But despite being expressed in different forms, their energy potentials can be compared.

One Calorie equals 4,186 joules. Therefore, if you follow the US Department of Agriculture (USDA) recommended diet, for example, which suggests that moderately active adults consume 2,200 Calories a day, you would ingest $4,186 \times 2,200$, or 9,209,200 joules of potential energy. Sounds like a lot, doesn't it? Recall that 1 watt equals 1 joule/second. Dividing 9,209,200 joules per day by 86,400 seconds in a day equals 106.6 watts. Compare this to the power requirements of appliances listed in Table 2.1 and you might reason that you could connect a human-powered generator to a small color TV and run it all day on nothing more than your normal caloric intake. Alas, it's not that simple. When it comes to performing work, the human body is an inefficient machine.

First, consider that your body continuously devotes some of its energy to maintaining basic functions — breathing, digesting, pumping blood, heating and cooling, regenerating cells, and yes, even thinking. (Reading this page will cost you a few extra watts.) This maintenance-level energy burn is known as your basal metabolism. Basal metabolism varies from person to person depending on size, age, body composition and environment, but as long as you live, it will always consume energy. An average 132-pound (60-kg) woman's basal metabolism requires about 68 watts of power. An athletic, 176-pound (80-kg) man's basal metabolism might require 90 watts. Of our total basal metabolism, the heart uses approximately 2% to keep beating, while the brain, a relative power hog, consumes 20% —

even when fast asleep. But remember, basal metabolism accounts only for fundamental body functions. If you do anything besides lie in bed all day, you need more energy. Daily activities typically increase your power usage by 30% of your basal metabolism. Thus, the 132-pound woman would use about 88 watts and the 176-pound male athlete, 117 watts.

In addition to basal metabolism, your body has a work metabolism, which kicks in when you exert yourself, when you call on your muscles and cardiovascular system to transform chemical energy into mechanical output. Work metabolism is tallied as actual joules or Calories of work divided by an estimated efficiency factor that ranges from .2 and .3. In other words, your body can convert only ⅕ to ⅓ of its available chemical energy into work. As a result, operating a 100-watt color TV with your human-powered generator for one hour would place a demand equivalent to 333 and 500 watts of power on your body. (And this calculation ignores the inefficiencies of the mechanical and electrical apparatuses involved.) That translates to 287 to 480 Calories per hour *above* your basal metabolism's requirement.[4] Curiously, the peak efficiency of a human body is about the same as a modern combustion engine's peak efficiency. (Neither, however, usually functions at peak efficiency.) And as with an automobile engine, the energy lost in conversion is released as heat.

Since the muscles' transformation of chemical energy to mechanical work relates directly to human power potential, it bears a closer look. What follows is a simplified overview of how muscles work. (To read a thorough and fascinating account, check out Steven Vogel's book, *Prime Mover: A Natural History of Muscle.*)

Muscles are bundles of many thin, cylindrical fibers that perform work by shortening in opposition to a load. A lattice of connective tissue surrounds and weaves through a muscle. In some types of muscles this connective tissue leads to tendons at either end to form a muscle group that links one joint to another. Such muscles are called skeletal muscles. They're the ones that accomplish work in response to our brain's commands, allowing us to pedal a bike or wind a top, for example. Each skeletal muscle pulls in only one direction, and thus, must work as part of a team. For example, to lift a dumbbell your bicep muscle shortens as it raises your arm at the elbow and lifts the weight. However, the bicep cannot release the weight simply by relaxing. Instead, the triceps muscle on the back of your arm contracts to extend your arm and let the dumbbell down.

Muscle cells rely on one source of fuel, adenosine triphosphate, or ATP. A tiny amount of ATP resides in the muscles, but only enough to power a mere 2 to 4 seconds of activity — say, jumping out of the path of a knife you've dropped. As soon as a muscle's store of ATP is depleted, the fuel must be replenished for the muscle to continue working. ATP can be synthesized or delivered to a muscle in three different ways: using creatine phosphate, glycolysis, or aerobic respiration.

Even before its small reserve of ATP is depleted, the muscle begins splitting apart a readily available substance called creatine phosphate. This reaction releases phosphate, which is combined with another substance in the muscle, adenosine diphosphate (ADP), to create ATP. Now the muscle has more quick energy, but only enough to last 10 to 20 seconds — enough time to dash away from a menacing cougar (perhaps!). For more sustained output, muscles break down glycogen, the product of the carbohydrates and sugars we eat, in a process called glycolysis. Glycolysis uses only the glycogen already present in the muscles. It can fuel one or two minutes worth of work — time enough to run to the corner store, but not to run a marathon. As no oxygen is required for glycolysis, the process is called anaerobic.

For sustained physical activity, muscles rely on aerobic — or oxidative — respiration. At this stage fats and sugars stored elsewhere in your body are called upon to fuel your motion. As its name implies, aerobic respiration requires oxygen, which assists in breaking down any glycogen that remains in the muscles plus glycogen passed on from the liver and intestines (derived from your last meal). It can also transform fatty acids from your body's fat reserves into ATP. And unlike the conversion of creatine phosphate or glycolysis, aerobic respiration can power your muscles for a very long time.

It seems intuitively true that a muscle's size must influence its potential power output, and it does. The amount of work a muscle can do is directly related to its volume. Theoretically, our muscles are strong enough to put out 90 watts per pound (or 200 watts per kilogram) of mass. That means that a 150-pound (60 kg) person with an average muscle mass of 40% could generate 5,600 watts, or 7.5 horse-

power![5] Yet humans are rarely more than 25% efficient at converting energy to power output. How is this possible, if muscles are so powerful? It turns out that muscles don't limit how long and at what intensity we can exercise. The heart and lungs do.

Remember that a muscle's long-term fueling process, aerobic respiration, requires oxygen (in addition to fats or sugars) to work. The heart pumps blood through the lungs, where the blood becomes oxygenated, and then to the muscles, where it delivers the oxygen. Therefore, muscle power depends on the efficiency and capacity of the heart and lungs. In fact, the rate at which the body can consume oxygen while exercising, called VO_2max, is a decent measure of how much power it can generate during sustained efforts.

To some extent, your VO_2max is genetically determined. Also, women's VO_2max levels are typically 15 to 20% lower than men's. Further impacting a person's VO_2max is her breathing capacity, which is partly a genetic characteristic, but also age-related. Beginning at age 40, a person's breathing capacity starts dropping precipitously, and by age 80, it is half of what it was at 20.[6] Figure 2.1, which is excerpted from David Gordon Wilson's book *Bicycling Science*, 3rd ed., illustrates how oxygen consumption, and consequently, a person's potential power output, decreases as one grows older.

However, with fitness training — in particular, aerobic exercise — you can improve your VO_2max. According to Ray Browning, a research instructor at the University of Colorado Health Sciences Center, fitness consultant, and winner of seven Ironman triathlons, the extent to which we can improve our personal power output through training is dramatic. As an example, he explained that a 70-kg. man who basically lived a sedentary lifestyle could generate maybe 100 watts for an hour on a cycling ergometer, a machine that measures an individual's power output as he exercises. By contrast a highly trained Tour de France cyclist of the same size could sustain close to 400 watts for an hour. And although genetic variation accounts for a small degree of difference, most is due to how the body adapts to dedicated physical work. "Your heart grows larger, you deliver more oxygen to muscles, you get increases in muscle fiber size, the muscles get more vascular, the mitochondria (the energy producing units in the muscle fibers) increase in number. There are all these mechanisms that take place that allow you to produce higher levels of power."[7]

One additional component figures into determining a person's power potential: the mind. Not surprisingly, when one is inspired, motivated, cheered on, or going for a record, one can generate more power and for longer periods.

Human Power Potential

Now that you know how many variables affect a person's ability to convert chemical energy to mechanical work, you might be thinking it's impossible to try to predict how many watts *your* muscles can deliver. But without setting up a research lab with an ergometer, you can still make an educated guess. Several scientific studies provide a glimpse of what's possible and what's practical. For example, the graph in Figure 2.2 is reprinted from David

Gordon Wilson's book *Bicycling Science*, 3rd ed. It summarizes data from multiple studies, most of which tested subjects on cycling ergometers.

Notice in Figure 2.2 that at least one athlete has achieved power output in excess of 3 hp — but maintained it for only 3 seconds. Human power output decreases over time. It drops quickly in the first few minutes of effort, and after that, tapers off more slowly. NASA rates the average long-term power output for a male adult exercising at a comfortable pace as 75 watts, or about 1/10 hp. But fit individuals

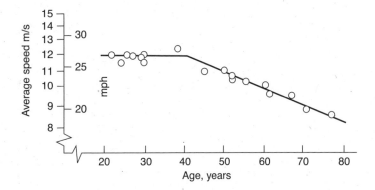

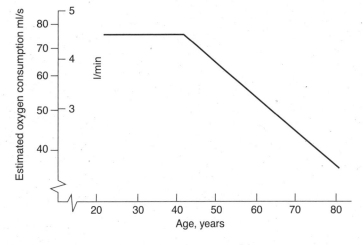

Figure 2.1 Average Speeds and Breathing Capacities of 50-Mile Time Trialists Versus Age

might easily sustain more than 100 watts for several hours and more than 300 watts for at least 10 minutes. Lance Armstrong is said to have averaged between 475 and 500 watts for 38 minutes during an uphill climb in the 2001 Tour de France.[8]

Many people reason that if an athlete were to use his legs and arms — for example, row, or combine pedaling with hand-cranking in some way — he could generate much more power than pedaling alone. Scientists have investigated this possibility, too. One study found that for periods up to one minute, hand cranking and pedaling together produced 11 to 18% more power than pedaling alone.[9] Another study placed the power advantage as

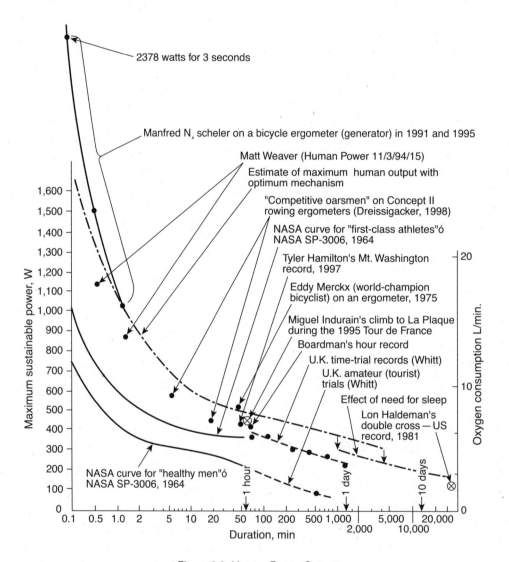

Figure 2.2 Human Power Output

high as 30%.[10] A third study, which compared various types of rowing to pedaling, showed that after approximately 5 minutes of exertion, a 15% advantage of using both arms and legs wanes into statistical insignificance.[11] The question of what happens after 5 minutes requires more research. Physiologists argue that, because of the cardiovascular limits on long-term output, the power gained by involving the arms will vanish once aerobic respiration kicks in. In other words, after a short while leg muscles alone can absorb all the oxygen the heart and lungs can deliver.

In any case, for practical reasons it's wise to rely on the legs to operate devices that require significant power. Humans descended from long-distance hunters, and we're built to run. Our legs excel at generating power. They're up to four times more powerful than our arms, mainly because they have more muscle mass. Meanwhile, arms and hands are better suited to controlling a device. Imagine how continuously turning a crank would hamper your ability to steer and dodge obstacles while bicycling.

Still, hand cranking is sometimes more convenient than pedaling — when charging your cell phone as you ride the subway or powering an LED flashlight in your tent, for example — and provides sufficient, if small, output for many items. Consumer electronics like cell phones, LED flashlights, radios and MP3 players can be easily powered by hand. One study concluded that under optimal conditions, a healthy adult can generate approximately 28 watts over long periods of hand cranking.[12] As with pedaling, more power can be generated in shorter periods. For ex-

ample, participants in another study were able to generate 54 watts for 30 minutes, enough to power a windup cell phone to last 19 hours.[13] Cranking a windup radio such as the Freeplay radio requires approximately 20 watts. Incidentally, cranking away from you — for example, if you are right-handed, rotating a handle clockwise — generates up to 30% more power than cranking toward yourself.[14]

So far, this discussion has focused on active human power generation. But as you learned in Chapter 1, human power can also be captured when we don't exert ourselves. Vibrations from breathing, pressure from walking, and even the chemical reactions in our blood can generate low wattage. This passive energy harvesting yields much less power than intentional effort such as hand-cranking or pedaling.

Table 2.2 summarizes the results of many studies on how much power humans can generate during various activities. Note that these are measures of potential *output*, not required input. Also, accept these figures as rough estimates for a fit person (not an elite athlete) — and know that in nearly all studies the subjects were adult, though not elderly, males. Your experience will vary.

Earlier you learned that you can improve your potential power output by as much as 400% through fitness training. Following are tips for making the most of your human power potential:

- Keep moving. Muscles can generate more power over longer periods of time when used dynamically than when used statically. Imagine extending your arm and suspending a bucket of water from it. This is a static use of muscle power. Your arm will fatigue and fail much more quickly than if you lifted that bucket up and down many times, a dynamic use of muscles. Partly this is because, like a pump, a muscle in motion allows oxygen to flow in and byproducts of exertion to flow out much better than a fixed muscle can. It follows that moving your muscles so slowly as to approximate a static condition will exhaust you faster than moving at a comfortably brisk pace.

- Optimize your pace. If your machine is pedal-powered, in general a rate of 50 to 70 revolutions per minute (rpm) delivers the most power over long periods of time.[22] Pedaling at 60 rpm, in the middle of this optimal range, you'd complete one turn of the crank every second. Ideal cadence depends on the rider's condition and body type, however. Also, for shorter periods of exertion, a higher cadence might be preferable. Experiment to find out what works best for you.

- Use your legs. For devices like pedal-powered cement mixers or washing machines, which require a significant amount of power, rely on leg muscles as your primary power source and leave hands and arms free for control.

- Train. If you're serious about powering devices with human power, think and act like an athlete. Use aerobic endurance and interval training to increase VO_2max. Use

Table 2.2 Human Power Output Potential for Various Activities

ACTIVITY	DURATION AT MEASUREMENT	POTENTIAL OUTPUT (WATTS)[15, 16, 17, 18, 19, 20, 21]
Respiration (passively harvested)	Unlimited	.1–1
Pushing a button	Unlimited	.3–.6
Heel strike and shoe flexure (passively harvested)	Unlimited	2–20
Squeezing a lever	> 1 hour	4–12
Pulling a 1-meter long cord	Unlimited (repeated pulls)	10–25
Hand-cranking (one-armed)	1 minute	110–140
Hand-cranking (one-armed)	30 minutes	40–45
Hand-cranking (one-armed)	> 1 hour	10–30
Pedaling	1 minute	400–500
Pedaling	10 minutes	300–400
Pedaling	1 hour	225–300
Pedaling	Unlimited	75
Rowing	1 minute	600–750
Rowing	5 minutes	350–380

resistance training to increase your muscle mass and strength.

- Stay cool and hydrated. When pedaling a bicycle, wind helps to cool you as you exercise. But when operating a stationary human-powered device, no such cooling advantage exists. By some estimates, a person working at just half his maximum power output on a hot or humid day risks collapsing from excessive heat. To avoid this, remain in the shade, cool yourself with a fan if necessary, and drink plenty of water.
- Find your fit. Improve your efficiency by designing your human-powered device to fit your body properly. You might be surprised to learn that the leg- or arm-crank length that allows you to exert your maximum strength is not necessarily the same length that allows you to sustain a reasonable power output for an hour. The same goes for seat height and position relative to the device you're powering.
- Don't work upside-down. If, like Michelangelo, you've been tasked with adopting this inelegant position, be advised that it places your muscles at a great disadvantage.

Caution! Before attempting any form of exercise, consult with a medical professional to ensure that your planned activity will not cause you harm.

If you're interested in measuring your power output, you have a few options, besides finding an exercise research center with a cycling ergometer. One is to use exercise machines at a gym that include power output in watts as part of their display, though the accuracy of these readouts varies widely. Alternatively, if you're a cyclist, you can purchase products to attach to your bike that will calculate your power output instantaneously and over time as you ride. They do so by measuring the torque on your bike's crank arm or rear hub plus your velocity and multiplying the two to get power. Products include the Power Tap by Saris, the Power Meter by iBike, SRM's Powermeter, and Quarq's CinQo, among others. The cost of such devices ranges from several hundred to one thousand dollars. However, with increasing popularity among athletes and increasing competition among manufacturers, their prices are expected to drop.

"Always remember that humanpower is more sacred than motorpower."

— David B. Perry[23]

How Do Humans Compare?

Energy sources can be compared based on many characteristics: power output, energy or power density, portability, duration of power generation, cost, ease of use, efficiency and environmental impact. An exhaustive analysis of all these factors is beyond the scope of this book. Instead, this section explores a few important variables that help justify or rule out using human power depending on the situation. The characteristic that usually attracts the most attention is an energy source's raw power potential.

Measured against gasoline engines, power plants, windmills, solar panels or draft animals, human power is micropower. Our ancestors realized this several thousand years ago as they devised ways of harnessing the animals they'd already domesticated for meat, milk and fur to take over their previously human-powered chores. They used primarily oxen, horses, donkeys and mules, though dogs, camels, yaks and elephants were called into service as well. The amount of work an animal can deliver is related to muscle volume, so it makes sense that an ox can pull a greater load than a person. Larger animals possess advantages beyond greater muscle volume, however. As a mammal's mass increases, its basal metabolism does not increase proportionally. In other words, an elephant maintains its basic functions by using a lower percentage of energy relative to its weight than a dog does. Furthermore, while exerting themselves larger animals can boost their metabolisms at a greater rate than smaller animals.[24]

Even today in many developing countries draft animals continue to be a significant power source, particularly in agriculture. They are comparatively inexpensive and self-sustaining. Unlike tractors, they don't need imported replacement parts, costly fuel, or a technically trained operator to remain functional. And at best they can outperform humans by a factor of ten. Table 2.3 compares the average weights and power potentials of draft animals and humans.

Notice that Table 2.3, which is based on data from the Food and Agricultural Organization of the United Nations (FAO), assigns horses a power output of 1 horsepower. However, most scientists agree that when James Watt invented the horsepower unit of measure he probably overestimated a horse's potential. On average, a horse's true output is closer to .75 hp.

Watt settled on horsepower while touting the benefits of his new invention, the steam engine. He needed a way to compare the engine's power to something his customers already understood. In fact, the first engine he patented was capable of producing about 1 hp. Historians consider Watt the father of the Industrial Revolution, and in the 230-some years since he installed his first steam engine, inventors have designed ever beefier power sources that cost less to operate. Ford's 1926 Model T was capable of about 22 hp, while a 2008 Ford Taurus is rated at 263 hp. The tractors that have replaced most draft animals range from 5 hp for a light-duty lawn tractor to 600 hp for the largest agricultural behemoth.

The obvious advantage to using fossil fuels such as coal, natural gas and oil along with greener technologies such as wind, solar and hydro power is their ability to generate much greater output than animate beings can. Offering a simple view of how humans com-

Table 2.3 Weights and Power Potentials of Various Draft Animals[25]

ANIMAL	WEIGHT (LBS)	HORSEPOWER
Bull (Ox)	1,100–1,985	.75
Cow	880–1,320	.45
Water buffalo	880–1,985	.75
Horse	880–1,540	1.00
Mule	770–1,100	.70
Donkey	440–660	.35
Camel	990–1,100	.67
Man	130–200	.10

pare, Table 2.4 lists the power potentials of commonly used energy sources. It also lists the operating efficiency of harnessing this power. Efficiency is measured as the energy output divided by the energy input converted to a percentage. Efficiency of some sources varies widely and depends on many factors. In the case of solar arrays, for example, efficiency depends on the site location, temperature, quality of light, and the material used to make the panels. In most cases, the figures in Table 2.4 represent average or estimated ranges for these variables, culled from a variety of sources.

Despite our relatively minuscule power potential, humans do compare favorably to other energy sources when it comes to dexterity, portability and environmental considerations. In the agricultural realm, for example, people still outperform machines in transplanting delicate seedlings. A person can quickly judge the quality of a seedling and determine its correct planting depth, spacing and angle, whereas a mechanized planter can merely repeat one programmed motion, neglecting to reject inferior plants or verify the soil conditions. Humans excel at handling fragile items, too. Lifting an egg from the carton, we can sense and balance the amount of pressure necessary to support the egg without breaking it. And when it comes to ease of use, human effort bests most other methods

Table 2.4 Comparison of Power Potentials and Efficiencies

ENERGY SOURCE OR STORAGE DEVICE	POWER POTENTIAL (WATTS)	OPERATING EFFICIENCY[26,27,28,29]
One AA battery	3 per hour	85–95%
Human, pedaling continuously	75–150	15–25%
Electric golf cart engine	150–600	90–97% the charging process is much less efficient, however)
Household-sized windmill	300–5,000	30–50%
Household-sized hydroelectric turbine	500–10,000	50–60%
Photovoltaic cells	70–150 per square meter	10–30%
Natural-gas-powered furnace	5,000–25,000 per hour	90–97%
Automobile gasoline engine	40,000–200,000	15–25%
Diesel pickup truck engine	120,000–275,000	30–35%
Large tidal power plant	100,000,000–250,000,000	80–85%
Coal-fired power plant	500,000,000–1,000,000,000	35–45 %
Nuclear reactor	1,000,000,000–1,300,000,000	32–50%
Hoover Dam	2,074,000,000	90%

of generating power. Any child can operate a pull-cord electrical generator, and in fact, this is one of the reasons this interface was chosen for One Laptop Per Child's XO laptop.

Portability makes human power popular in remote areas. No matter where you are, you have a source of energy. The US Department of Defense has long worked to capitalize on this so that soldiers can power small communication and detection devices in the field where a windmill or power plant can't follow. The heel-strike generator described in Chapter 1 is one example. Other projects include hand-cranked battery rechargers and tiny implants that use vibrations from the body's motion to run sensors or biomedical devices. Meanwhile, scientists in Japan are experimenting with human-powered robots to assist in potentially dangerous search-and-rescue operations at disaster sites, such as buildings ruined by earthquakes, where power from the grid might be temporarily unavailable. Portability and availability also make human power well-suited to charging consumer electronics, like cell phones and MP3 players, on the go.

Finally, the benefit no fossil fuel nor any "green" technology can claim is that human power, as a form of exercise, contributes to our good health. Some human-power enthusiasts go so far as to suggest that human power is a cost savings for society, as it counters health conditions caused or worsened by inactivity.

Could human-powering your appliances save you money? Let's look at some of the fac-

Ray Browning: Improving Health Through Human Power

When it comes to designing human-powered machines, Ray Browning strives for *less* efficiency, not more. As a researcher in obesity and movement at the University of Colorado's Health Sciences Center, Ray wants to make walking, cycling and even lifting weights just a little bit harder.

Humans have designed their environment to minimize personal energy expenditure. Even when we do put our muscles to work — walking, rather than driving the few blocks to the post office, for example — we have incorporated energy conservation. For example, sidewalks, hard and flat, take the least amount of effort for us to walk on. A grassy, undulating surface, by contrast, would require roughly 30% more energy.

Similarly, walking on a somewhat pliable energy-harvesting floor would require more energy than walking on a hard surface. Such a floor is one idea Ray considers as he aims to help clients improve their fitness levels along with their environmental awareness. That means encouraging them to work a little harder to convert their energy to electricity. Citing research from the mid-20th century, Ray told me that when people choose a comfortable walking pace they typically expend 25 to 35% of their maximal output capacity. At 50% of our maximal capacity, we begin to get uncomfortable. But before that, how much energy would people willingly add to their normal expenditure, and for how long? Ray hopes to answer these questions through a human-powered gym project with an area middle school.

He pointed out that adult behavior is difficult to change, so he's especially interested in working with kids who are overweight or obese. He

tors to be considered in forming and answering this question.

The equipment needed to pedal-power a TV — for example, a bike, trainer stand, generator, battery and inverter — costs a fraction of the price of a coal generator, nuclear reactor, solar array or hydroelectric dam. Human-powering your TV also doesn't require expensive distribution systems. However, once power-generating infrastructures are established, the costs of making electricity from muscles don't compare favorably.

Recall the example of operating a small color TV with a pedal-powered electrical generator. Suppose your body is 25% efficient at converting its chemical energy to work (an optimal, and probably high, estimate), and

assume that the generator is a magical, perfectly efficient machine. You would need approximately 380 Calories to power the TV for an hour. That's the same number of Calories you'd get from one Starbucks apple fritter, which costs $1.60. (Ignore, for now, the energy needed to make and transport the food or the equipment that allows you generate power.) It sounds like a pretty cheap way to power your TV, doesn't it? Yet compared to household electricity, it's not.

At the time this was written, consumers in the continental US paid an average of about $.10 per kilowatt-hour (kWh) for electricity delivered by the grid, whether generated from coal, natural gas, nuclear fission or water flow. (Note: You can find the current average cost of

envisions school gyms full of energy-harvesting equipment, including not only treadmills and stationary bikes, but also resistance machines, like bench presses and leg presses. "A lot of our at-risk kids in particular have no relationship with movement because what they've been told is that 'Well, you need to do more exercise, that's why you're overweight.' And by that, they hear, 'Oh, I need to walk or run or ride a bike,' three things they don't like to do, because they're not really very good at them." But these same kids do enjoy lifting weights, because they excel at that. Ray wants to give them the opportunity to participate and succeed.

When we spoke, Ray had partnered with the engineers at Potenco (producers of a pull-cord electrical generator) to design special, energy-harvesting gym equipment. He'd also found a

middle school willing to install the equipment, and he'd applied for grants to fund the project.

Ray admitted that the amount of energy harvested would not go far toward reducing the school's monthly utility expenses. Still, he believes kids like to be involved in helping solve a big problem, like global warming, for which the first step is to realize how much energy we use — and could avoid using. "It's not necessarily that everyone's going to use a lot less energy," he said, "but we're going to raise the level of consciousness so at least kids will recognize that 'Oh, that gas mower versus that push mower, I understand the differences between those two. One's a little bit easier to use, but it pollutes a lot. The other is a little harder to use, but it doesn't.'" [30]

electricity by going to the US Department of Energy's Energy Administration Information Web site at: eia.doe.gov/fuelelectric.html.) A kilowatt-hour represents the amount of power used over the course of one hour. Therefore, running your small, 100-watt TV for 1 hour would use 100 watt-hours of electricity, or ¹⁄₁₀ of a kilowatt-hour. That means it would cost you $.01 — one penny! — to plug in your TV and watch it for one hour. Compared with eating an apple fritter and pedaling, running your TV off household electricity costs 160 times less. (On the other hand, some might argue that because many of us in the Western world operate on a calorie surplus, pedal-powering a TV for an hour needn't require the added input of an apple fritter.)

Yet the relatively low prices of fossil fuels mask expenses beyond what it costs to produce or purchase them. While utilities have factored extracting, refining and transporting these resources into the prices we pay, they ignore other costs. The Union of Concerned Scientists puts it best:

Pedal-Powered Concerts

One of the first questions people ask about human power is "Can I run my stereo (or TV, or lights) by pedaling my bike?" The answer, of course, is yes. But experienced human-powered-machine designers agree that generating electricity isn't the best use of human power. Instead, it's more efficient to power a machine mechanically — that is, to convert your muscles' output directly into mechanical work, as in spinning the shaft of a blender with a bicycle wheel. Doing so, you avoid the intermediate step of creating electricity and the energy loss that inevitably results.

Still, generating electricity with your muscles is a good way to learn about power. Pedaling and sweating, we feel what we take for granted when we plug in an appliance. "There's nothing like a pedal-power sound system to totally blow peoples' minds," bike mechanic Richard Andrews told me. "I've never seen a stronger impact on people than having them sitting on a bike, riding it, and then running a DJ setup and having somebody feed them cherries. It's such a neat experience, to know that the food you're eating is fueling the music you're listening to."[32]

Some inventors embrace pedal-generated electricity as a serious alternative, however, and not just for demonstrations. With technical assistance from Nate Byerley, founder of Byerley Bicycle Blenders, the rock band Shake Your Peace used a pedal-powered amplification system for their concerts while on tour in Utah. Not only that, but they traveled the 600 miles between destinations on bikes, so the system had to be lightweight and portable. Nate views their concert

Figure 2.3 Pedal-Powered Amplifier

Some energy costs are not included in consumer utility or gas bills, nor are they paid for by the companies that produce or sell the energy. These include human health problems caused by air pollution from the burning of coal and oil; damage to land from coal mining and to miners from black lung disease; environmental degradation caused by global warming, acid rain and water pollution; and national security costs, such as protecting foreign sources of oil.

Since such costs are indirect and difficult to determine, they have traditionally remained external to the energy pricing system, and are thus often referred to as externalities. And since the producers and the users of energy do not pay for these costs, society as a whole must pay for them. But this pricing system masks the true costs of fossil fuels and results in damage to human health, the environment and the economy.[31]

tour as a new incarnation of the old American dream. "One of the components of our American dream is doing the road trip, getting into your Mustang, cruising across the country and having your wild experiences. Clearly that model is no longer appropriate to what our world can sustain, and it doesn't really feed us like it used to, because you don't have that many personal experiences when you're cruising in a car anymore. Bikes are the next thing. There's going to be this pedal power revolution and there's going to be a lot of people going out and really experiencing the world on a bike in the ways we used to try and experience the world in a car."[33]

If individual human power is micropower, collectively humans can generate macropower. Bart Orlando of Arcata, California, built what he calls the "human energy converter" (HEC). The HEC, a trailer that holds 14 pedaling stations connected to a battery bank, is capable of generating just over 1 kilowatt. It has powered sound stages at rallies and music festivals across northern California. Without a doubt, the whole pedaling crew feels the power. Bart said, "If it was

powering an a cappella blessing…it would be running at maybe 300 watts. But if it was…rock and roll, you could see that the output would jump up to 900 to 1,100 watts. Depending on if there was a bass solo that night and if the bass player was using a tube amplifier, people pedaling said they could feel every note in a bass solo [as they had to pedal harder]."[34] At one event, the HEC became child care. Children would line up to use it, then stay and pedal-power music until the early morning hours, after which they would fall into bed exhausted. Parents loved it.

The HEC also became a vehicle for community-building. Bart said, "A lot of times people feel alienated and lonely and if there's a place where people can feel empowered, literally and figuratively empowered, and where they can both literally and figuratively plug in, they'll gravitate toward it so they don't have to stand alone or feel uncomfortable. So there was always a line at the concerts. In fact, people would line up to pedal-power the concert and ask 'how much does it cost?'"[35]

In other words, burning fossil fuels levies environmental and health tolls that can't be easily quantified. True, human power also comes with environmental costs, as humans expel carbon dioxide and other wastes, and equipment requires energy to build. Further, if your human-power fuel includes meat or foods shipped from far away, your contribution to greenhouse gases increases. In fact, assuming your caloric intake matches the North American ideal, the amount of energy you'd save by eating food grown in your own yard rather than typical grocery-store fare could power your TV for 256 hours! But no matter what your diet, the overall environmental consequences of human power are less detrimental than those of burning fossil fuels.

In summary, human power is best suited to applications that require small amounts of power, that benefit from portability or exist in remote locations, and that need to be available on demand and that are relatively inexpensive. It's also well-suited to those who want a healthy body and a healthy environment.

Elements and Principles of Human-Powered Devices

If you're a cycling enthusiast, you have probably heard that the world's most efficient form of transportation is a bicycle. Variables abound, so the equations that lead to this claim differ, as do their results. Nevertheless, it's true that using the same amount of power, you'll go farther bicycling than you would walking, running, swimming, riding a horse or driving any motorized vehicle. For example, a 154-lb (70-kg) man can ride at 15.5 miles per hour (or 25 km/h) on a flat stretch using 100 watts. The same man would burn 100 watts walking at 3.1 miles per hour (or 5 km/h).[36] Thus, bicycles are five times more power-efficient than walking. Meanwhile, in a car, 100 watts wouldn't even get you out of the driveway. By some calculations bicycles are 25 times more energy-efficient than gasoline-fueled automobiles (if the bicyclist's fuel is locally grown and vegetarian).[37] Figure 2.4, which is from David Gordon Wilson's *Bicycling Science*, 3rd ed., illustrates the results from one study analyzing the efficiency of various modes of transportation.

The bottom line is that bicycles are uniquely well-suited to harnessing human power. That's one reason so many human-powered machines begin with bicycles or stationary bikes. Also, they're widely available and relatively inexpensive. Many good intentions begin with an exercise bike in the basement and end with it abandoned on the front lawn or at the thrift store. Cast-off conventional bicycles are even more plentiful. Later in this chapter you'll find tips on where and how to look for the best bicycle parts for making human-powered machines.

Though not all human-powered machines are based on bikes, the following explanations use them as a familiar context for introducing fundamentals. If you shy away from technical topics, the good news is you don't need to know anything about braking, steering or fixing flats — and the rest is pretty simple.

Human-Machine Interfaces

Industrial designers scrutinize the points where human and machine connect, and research what helps them to work in concert. On human-powered devices, these connection points include handles, pedals, cranks and seats. Not surprisingly, experts disagree on the precise optimal specifications for these elements. However, they do offer some guidelines.

With pedals and handles attached to their ends, cranks, also known as crank arms, accept power from the user and deliver it to the drive. For maximum output while hand cranking, cranks ought to be situated at heart level. In this position they make the best use of a body's cardiopulmonary functioning and give the user the best mechanical advantage.

Cranks also ought to conform to certain dimensions — though the optimal length depends on the user's physiology. Researchers have determined that hand cranks that are straight and range in length from 6.5 to 7.5 inches (165–190 mm) allow one to generate the most power during sustained efforts.[38]

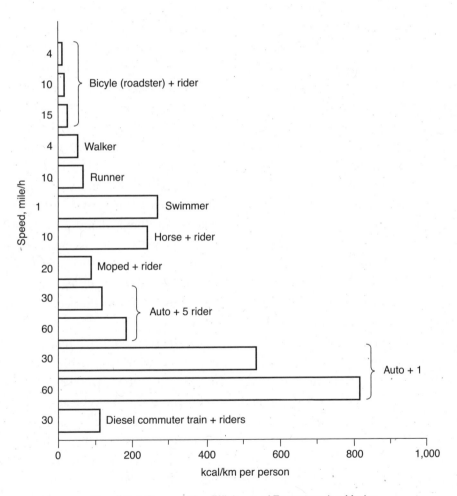

Figure 2.4 Comparative Efficiency of Transportation Modes

Using shorter or longer cranks is more taxing, and using curved cranks does not convey as much power. Bear in mind, however, that nearly all of these studies were conducted with male subjects, whose arms are on average longer than females'. Therefore, expect the optimal crank length for women to be at the low end of this range or possibly shorter.

Optimal handle sizes have also been studied. According to researchers at the Delft University of Technology, handles should be between 1 inch (25 mm) and 3.75 inches (95 mm) long.[39] In addition, scientists have shown that cranking on a horizontal axis delivers more power than cranking along a vertical axis. And, as mentioned earlier, cranking away from oneself also delivers more power. Combining these requirements, you can envision the optimally proportioned hand-cranked device, perhaps a grain grinder affixed to a waist-high table with a straight, 7-inch crank arm whose handle is 2.5 inches long and whose grinding burrs operate on a horizontal axis.

Bike racers and trainers have long sought the magically sized crank arms that will allow them to generate the most power. However, unless you special-order or make your own parts, choices are limited. Walk into your local bike shop and measure the crank arms of the bikes on display, and you'll find they deviate little from the standard 170 mm (roughly 6.7 inches). That's considered good enough for most of the population. However, people taller than 6 feet will enjoy more power and better endurance over time with a slightly longer crank arm. People who stand under 5 feet 6 inches will probably feel more comfortable using a shorter crank arm. Pedaling a bike whose crank arms are too long can cause knee or hip pain due to the awkward position of your legs at the top of your rotation, just before you bear down with the most force to push the crank forward. Many cycling references suggest a formula for gauging crank arm length: multiply your inseam in inches by 5.4 to get your ideal crank-arm length in millimeters. For example, a man with a 33-inch inseam should use a 178-mm crank arm.

Another measure of comfort and efficiency in pedal-powered machines is the seat height, which determines how far your legs will have to extend to move the pedals. Too high and you'll have to roll your hips after fully extending your legs to make the pedals turn; too low, and you'll lose power, because your leg muscles can't complete their extension. In general, you want to gain maximum advantage from your legs by allowing them to fully extend, but not strain beyond that. To find your proper seat height on an upright bike, sit on the bike and press your foot on one of the pedals until its crank arm is parallel with the seat tube. Then adjust your seat to the position where your leg is fully extended with your foot flat on the pedal and parallel to the floor.

As for seat comfort, human-powered machines vary widely. Some, like a treadle sewing machine or Alfred Traeger's pedal-powered radio transceiver, accept any type of chair. Many others rely on a bicycle seat, and a few use custom seats, usually made of wood. One human-powered machine designer told me that he started with a fixed plywood seat, but it quickly became uncomfortable. The latest version of his machine features an adjustable, wide, cushioned version of a bike seat.

Engineers continue to investigate the optimal proportions for generating the most power over time on upright bikes, recumbents and hand-cranked devices. However, if you're seeking to maximize output, the advantage gained by manipulating crank-arm length or seat height is small. Instead, your creativity might be better applied to designing the most appropriate drive for your needs.

Drive Types

The heart of any machine is its mechanical drive, or the means it uses to capture power and deliver that power to the machine. The drive may also be called a drive train or transmission.

Earlier in this chapter, an example of work was given as pushing luggage along an airport's floor. Work isn't limited to flat surfaces, however. In pedaling or hand-cranking, work results as your hands or feet apply force in a rotational motion. This force is known as torque. When turning a crank, power equals torque times rotational speed. (Rotational speed is a function of the distance cranked in a certain amount of time.) Translated into common sense, you generate more power as you push harder and turn faster, whether using your legs or arms. Each drive discussed in this chapter is equipped to transform your human-generated torque into power.

When engineers design a drive, they seek to make it as efficient as possible, which means capturing the greatest amount of torque and applying as much of it as possible to the work a machine produces. To calculate a machine's efficiency, divide its energy output by its energy input. In the context of a person pedaling a bicycle, for example, you could divide the number of joules your bike produces by the number of calories you expend. No drive is 100% efficient — machines inevitably lose energy through friction or slippage, for example — but some come very close.

Human-powered machines can be built to run on one of a handful of different drive types. The most common are the chain drive, belt drive, gear drive and friction drive. The simplest, however, is a direct drive.

Direct Drives

In a direct drive, the power applied to the machine is converted directly into work. No gears, chains, springs or belts intervene. Unicycles and children's tricycles are examples of direct drives, as are simple hand-cranked devices such as tabletop corn shellers, cherry pitters and grain grinders. On a unicycle, for example, pedals are connected to crank arms, which are connected to the wheel's axle. One revolution of the pedals rotates the wheel once. Similarly, turning the crank on a grain grinder makes the auger and burr inside rotate once.

While a direct drive is efficient, it doesn't allow for much flexibility or precision. A child on a simple tricycle can't vary her power output from one pedal revolution to another. She can only go faster by pedaling faster. Riding up hills is problematic, because it requires more power. The same amount of effort a girl uses to make one pedal revolution on a flat sidewalk might get her only $\frac{1}{10}$ of a revolution on a steep hill. At that pace, she risks stalling

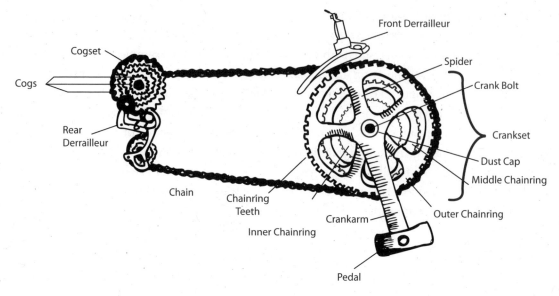

Figure 2.5 Chain Drive

out or even losing ground and rolling down-hill. With a different type of drive, however, she could modify her pace and power output, thereby striking a balance between effort and speed.

Chain Drives

You're undoubtedly familiar with the kind of drive that traditional bicycles and stationary bicycles use: a chain drive. In a chain drive, a chain connects one toothed wheel attached to the pedals — which can be considered the driving gear — to a second toothed wheel on the tire it's rotating — the driven gear. It transfers power from the driving gear to the driven gear, and when you pedal, the wheel turns. In the case of a traditional bicycle, the chain drive rotates the rear wheel. On a stationary bike, it usually rotates a front wheel. Figure 2.5 depicts a typical chain drive separated from the bicycle frame, with its parts labeled. A de-

scription of these parts and how they interact follows.

Generally speaking, toothed wheels are also called sprockets. In the context of cycling, the toothed wheels attached to the pedals are called chainrings (or chainwheels), while the toothed wheels attached to the rotating rear tire are called cogs (or rear sprockets). Many bikes have multiple chainrings and multiple cogs. The group of cogs attached to the hub of a bike's rear tire is called a cogset or cassette. Notice how teeth on the cog and chainring fit into the chain's links to transfer power from one sprocket to another. The collection of parts that includes the chainring, pedals and crank arms is known as the crankset. (Sometimes it's also called a chainset.)

On a mountain bike or road bike a crankset typically contains two or three chainrings. On most stationary bicycles, it contains only one. The advantage of having multiple chainrings and multiple cogs on the rotating wheel relates to varying gear ratios (discussed in the next section). For example, a ten-speed bike might have two chainrings and five cogs, giving you ten possible gear combinations. To shift from one chainring to another, you press a lever or turn a knob on the handlebar which activates the front derailleur, which moves the chain between chainrings. To shift from one cog to another, you engage the rear derailleur, which moves the chain between cogs.

Except for the direct drive, the chain drive delivers more power to your machine and results in more output than other drives described in this chapter. A recent study by engineers at Johns Hopkins University revealed that bicycle chain drives are as much as 98.6% efficient. That means that in the best case only 1.4% of your muscles' energy is lost to the bike's operation. (Even the lowest data point in the study showed an impressive 81% efficiency.) James Spicer, the faculty member who supervised the study remarked of the results, "This was amazing to me, especially when you realize the essential construction of this chain drive hasn't changed in more than 100 years."[40] The study also showed that larger sprockets led to better efficiency, as did greater tension in the chain. This makes sense, because keeping a chain or pulley belt tight helps transfer more power from your muscles to the machine you're operating.

Following are some additional tips for making the most of your chain drive:

- Ensure that neither the bushings inside each link of the chain, nor the teeth on the sprockets, are worn. Chain drives work most efficiently when the fit between the links and sprocket teeth is tight. If a chain or sprocket is worn, consider replacing it.
- Clean and lubricate the chain regularly to avoid the inefficiencies caused by grime trapped in the chain. Cleaning can be as simple as wiping off the chain with a rag after each use. Lubricating involves applying a wet or dry lubricant (your preference) to the chain when it's clean.
- Avoid operating the chain drive in dirty or wet conditions, as both increase the likelihood of slippage, and dirt will contribute to wear.
- Ensure that the sprockets (for example, the chainrings and cogs) around which the chain is wrapped, are properly aligned. Chains subjected to transverse stress will wear out faster.

If you decide to create your own chain drive or modify one that came with a bicycle or exercise bike, make sure to use compatible sprockets and chains. Compatibility is a matter of matching sprocket tooth size with chain width and pitch. Bicycle chains come in widths of $\frac{3}{32}$" (the most common type, found on road bikes and ten-speeds) or $\frac{1}{8}$" (found on fixed-gear or track bikes). Chain width represents the *inside* width of each link, that is, the distance between the inner plates. A bicycle chain's pitch, which is the distance between the centers of the two rollers that make up a link, is always $\frac{1}{2}$". Consequently, the pitch on a bicycle sprocket, or the distance between the centers of two teeth, is also $\frac{1}{2}$". The width of the sprocket must be slightly less than the chain's width, so that the teeth can fit inside the links. The sprocket that corresponds to a

Maya Pedal's Bicimáquinas

The bicycle you left on the curb the last time you moved might be grinding corn or depulping coffee beans in Guatemala right now. Maya Pedal, a nongovernmental organization based in San Andrés Itzapa near the highlands of Guatemala's Mayan country, accepts crates of cast-off bikes from organizations in North America and transforms them into household appliances.

Maya Pedal's bicidesgranadora/molino, a combination corn sheller and corn flour mill, is the most popular bicimáquina, or bike-powered machine, to come out of their shop. Others include the bicilicuadora (bike blender), bicibomba (pedal-powered water pump), bicivibradora (a bike-powered machine that vibrates the bubbles out of concrete as it forms roofing tiles), a despulpadora (coffee depulper), bicimacadamia (macadamia nut sheller), biciesmeril (metal tool sharpener), and a cargo bike. A bicilavadora (pedal-powered washing machine) designed by students at the Massachusetts Institute of Technology (MIT) is still in the prototype phase, as is a pedal-powered electrical generator.

Volunteers from around the world visit Maya Pedal and offer their time and skills, but the organization is sustained by just a few locals, including its chief inventor and mechanic Carlos Marroquin Machàn. Carlos, 38, was for a long time a rural farmer, like most of Guatemala's indigenous population. Then in 1997 he hooked up with the newly formed Maya Pedal and added "mechanic" to his resume. After 11 years of building bicimáquinas, Carlos excels at combining gears, custom flywheels, bike frames, angle iron, rebar and traditionally hand-cranked or electrically powered devices to make the best use of human power. For example, in the popular bicidesgranadora, Carlos mounted a formerly hand-cranked corn sheller on an angle-iron frame and connected it to a pedal-driven chain drive, as shown in Figure 2.6. Using pedal power, customers can shell corn three to four times faster than they could by hand.

Though it currently relies on donations for a portion of its budget, Maya Pedal aims to be entirely self-sufficient, funding its work through sales of refurbished bicycles. Bicimáquinas, of which an estimated two thousand have been distributed during its 11-year existence, are sold at cost. A bicilicuadora costs around US$40, a bicimolino about US$185, and a bicivibradora goes for about US$250.[41]

Because the machines can cost as much as 2 months' pay, they are usually purchased by

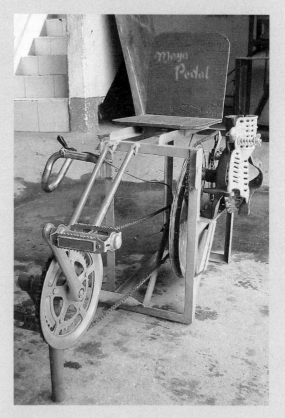

Figure 2.6 Maya Pedal's Bicidesgranadora (Corn Sheller)

groups or collectives. In a land where approximately 80% of the population lives in poverty, bicimáquinas can empower people to make a better life. Doña Ana speaks on behalf of fifteen women who purchased a bicilicuadora to establish a small business: "We decided to cut leaves of the local aloe and herbs, put some money into soaps, tags and plastic bottles, and make shampoo. The blender creates a good liquid consistency and we didn't need electricity, only our legs. Although it's not easy to sell anything in the local market, at least we have a product which the fifteen women can produce and support our larger families."[42] Figure 2.7 shows one of Maya Pedal's bicilicuadoras, which, with its ingenious gearing, can spin the blender shaft at over 6,000 rpm.

Don Santiago, a young man whose family founded a business on making concrete roofing tiles with a bicivibradora, said, "These machines are a positive symbol that empowers one to make his own livelihood. The advance of technology is the hope that can make us self-sufficient."[43]

In addition, Maya Pedal customers and staff appreciate the fact that the bicimáquinas rely on recycled parts and renewable energy. Carlos told one MIT volunteer, "We're burdened with the question of the natural environment, air pollution, water contamination.... I want to be a model for not just Central America, but I want North Americans to see that we can really live a rich life with less resources."[44]

Figure 2.7 Maya Pedal's Bicilicuadora (Blender)

³⁄₃₂" chain, for example, has a width of .084" (though they are called ³⁄₃₂" sprockets).

When rigging your own chain drive, you might have to resize a chain. To do this, you'll need a special chain link tool that can remove and reset link pins, available at bicycle stores. You'll also need to know how to measure and fit your chain to ensure the correct length. A tutorial for chain customization and a common source for the necessary tools is Park Tools, online at parktool.com/repair. To learn more about chain drives, their components, types and operation in general, refer to a comprehensive bike repair manual or *The Complete Guide to Chain*, edited by Makoto Kanehira, which is available in print and online at: chain-guide.com.

Many examples of chain-driven human-powered machines exist, and most are based on bicycle gearing and modified bike frames. On some machines (for example, Maya Pedal's bicimolino (grain mill) and bicidesgranadora (corn sheller), the chain drive operates in the same direction and as it would on a regular bike, powering a wheel behind the crankset. On other machines, such as the bicilicuadora (bicycle blender) and bicimacadamia (macadamia nut husker), the direction of a normal bicycle's chain drive is reversed. The bicilicuadora pictured in Figure 2.7, for example, has the cogset attached to the front wheel's hub, and thus, pedaling turns the front wheel, which drives the blender shaft. Practicality often dictates which direction the drive faces. In the case of a pedal-powered tool grinder, for example, it's necessary for the grinder to be mounted in front of the operator.

Gear Drives and Gear Ratios

Even in this age of computers and nanotechnology, crack open any machine, poke around, and you're apt to find a gear inside. Gears drive the rollers and cartridges in printers and the door that opens and closes when you insert a DVD in your player. And when it comes to manually operated machines, gears figure prominently.

In a gear drive, power is transferred from one gear to another gear via interlocking teeth. Many types of gears exist, and they can be arranged in various numbers and positions for different results. The simplest type of gear, known as a spur gear, is shown in Figure 2.8.

Gears are used in combination to change the speed, direction, axis of rotation, or force of an action. Changing the speed or force relies on a size difference between those gears. This difference is called the gear ratio.

Gear ratio is a comparison of the sizes of gears used in a drive. Sizes can be measured in diameter, circumference or number of teeth per gear. Usually, gear ratio is expressed as the size of the the driven (output) gear compared to the size of the driver (input) gear. For

Figure 2.8 Spur Gear

example, if you drive a gear 4 inches in diameter by rotating a gear 8 inches in diameter, the gear ratio is 1:2. Each time you rotate the driving gear once, the driven gear will make two revolutions. By pairing these gears, you're able to spin the shaft of the second gear at twice the rate as you could if you paired two gears of equal size. However, to accomplish the same amount of work, driving the gear combination will require more effort. Varying gear ratios is always a tradeoff between force and the rate at which work can be accomplished.

Pairing the same 8-inch-diameter driver gear with a 16-inch-diameter driven gear would give you a 2:1 gear ratio. In this case, turning the first gear would require less effort, yet the driven gear would accomplish work more slowly. Compared to the 1:2 gear combination, in fact, the 2:1 combination would require ¼ the force and accomplish work at ¼ the rate. This might be desirable in cases where the driven gear must turn a heavy load or when the motor (or operator) that runs the driving gear requires a faster cadence (that is, more revolutions per minute) for the sake of efficiency or stamina. Figure 2.9 illustrates 1:1, 1:2, and 2:1 gear ratios between spur gears.

Gear ratios, and the advantages of varying speed and force, also apply when operating chain drives and belt drives. Imagine a bike that has only one chainring 8 inches in diameter and only one cog, also 8 inches in diameter. A chain drive using this combination of gears gives a fixed, 1:1 gear ratio. Riding such a bike, every time you made one revolution with the pedals, the cog would also make one revolution, and your rear wheel would rotate once. You couldn't shift down to a lower gear when the pedaling got tough, nor shift up to a higher gear on an easy stretch of road. Of course, this isn't how most modern bikes work. Instead, they offer you a choice of different gears for variable gear ratios.

As described in Chapter 1, early bicycles, including ordinary bicycles and boneshakers, featured no chain drive and no variable gears.

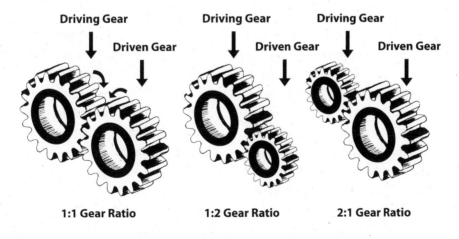

Figure 2.9 Varying Gear Ratios

Thanks to these advances, by applying the same amount of power, we can go twice as fast on modern-day bicycles as we could have on their 19th-century forerunners.[45]

When it comes to bicycles, gear ratios are calculated not by comparing gear diameters, but by comparing the number of teeth on the chainring to the number of teeth on the cog. For example, suppose you have a mountain bike with three chainrings and the largest chainring has 44 teeth. While in this gear you shift to a cog that has 18 teeth. In other words, your gear ratio is 44:18, or 2.44:1. For every one revolution of the chainring you pedal, the cog and rear wheel will rotate 2.44 times. If your wheels are 26 inches in diameter (which equals 82 inches in circumference), you'll advance 82 inches × 2.44, or 200 inches, with each revolution of the pedals. That means that while maintaining a comfortable cadence of 60 rpm, you'll travel 60 × 200 inches, 1,000 feet in a minute — in other words, just over 11 mph (18 km/h).

This seems like a comfortable gear combination for biking flat terrain. But suppose you encounter a slight incline, which causes you to shift down to the lowest gear on your chainring, one that has 22 teeth. Now you've changed your gear ratio to 22:18, or 1.22:1. Each time you complete one revolution of the pedals, the rear wheel rotates 1.22 times, which means you move forward just 100 inches. If you maintain your 60-rpm cadence, you'll go 500 feet in a minute, or 5.5 mph (9 km/h). You'll advance half as fast, but turning the pedals will be easier than before.

When building a human-powered device, you can optimize its efficiency and ease of op-

eration by first calculating the most appropriate gear ratio, then building that ratio into the device. For example, suppose you're converting an old water pump to be pedal-powered. You've decided to replace the pump's worn-out electric motor with a variable-gear chain drive. Now suppose the pump requires at least 300 rpm to function. Even if you could pedal as fast as 300 rpm, you could not sustain it for long. Instead, you decide you can spin at 100 rpm. Therefore, you need to modify the rotational speed of the drive with gears and achieve a 300:100, or 3:1 gear ratio. Assume the largest chainring on the bike you've chosen to operate the pump has 44 teeth. Therefore you want a cog with 44/3, or about 14.6 teeth to achieve the gear reduction. You could mount a 14-tooth or 15-tooth cog on the shaft of the pump's motor and connect the chain between it and your bicycle's chainring. (Of course, this implies transforming the profile of the machine from a bicycle to a pedal-powered pump. Customizing frames and chassis is covered later in this chapter.)

Bicycle cogs with fewer than 11 teeth are rare, so if, in the previous example, your pump required significantly higher rpm, you could not achieve the necessary gear reduction with just one pair of sprockets. That doesn't mean giving up on the idea of pedal power, however! Instead, you could combine several sprockets to achieve more drastic gear ratios. Multiple gears arranged in series this way make up what engineers call a "compound drive train."

Suppose the water pump you chose to pedal-power required 1,200 rpm to work. If you pedal at 100 rpm, that means you'd need a 12:1 gear reduction to spin the motor's shaft at

1,200 rpm. Given that your largest chainring has 44 teeth, you'd need a cog with 3 or 4 teeth on the shaft if you tried to use only two sprockets in your drive. No such cog exists, however, nor would it be very functional if it did. Instead, you could achieve the 12:1 gear reduction by creating a compound gear train. In this example you could connect your 44-tooth chainring to a 14-tooth cog which shares its shaft with another 44-tooth chainring that's, in turn, connected to a 11-tooth cog. The gear ratio between the first chainring and cog is 44:14, or about 3:1. The gear ratio between the second chainring and cog is 44:11, or 4:1. Altogether, then, this combination of gears results in a 12:1 gear reduction, as illustrated in Figure 2.10. For every single revolution you pedal, the pump's shaft will revolve 12 times.

Even if you never calculate a gear ratio, it's helpful to remember the basic principle that varying gear ratios is always a tradeoff between speed and force. As you decrease the size of the driving gear relative to the driven gear, pedaling or hand-cranking becomes easier, but the power applied to the machine will also decrease. Therefore, you'll take longer to accomplish your task. (In the case of a bicycle, you'll go a shorter distance for each revolution of the pedals.) The reverse is true as you increase the size of the driving gear relative to the driven gear. Pedaling will feel harder, but you'll send more power to the machine. This tradeoff applies whether you're using gears connected by chains or pulleys connected by belts.

Variable gear ratios offer the most advantages in human-powered machines that: require a significant amount of power, like a cement mixer; require high rpm, like an electrical generator; or require differing amounts of power at different points in their operation, like a washing machine. Varying gears is not especially useful when a device requires relatively little power and operates well at low rpm, as in the case of a hand-cranked coffee grinder, ice-cream maker or flashlight.

In addition to varying force and speed, gear drives can also change the direction of motion, as in the case of a hand-cranked eggbeater: the handle rotates a gear on a horizontal axis, but that gear drives another gear whose axis is vertical. Consequently, the beaters spin on a vertical axis.

Several types of gears can accomplish a perpendicular transfer of motion, including bevel gears and worm gears, pictured in

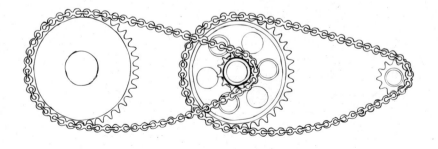

Figure 2.10 Compound Gear Reduction

Figure 2.11 Worm Gear and Bevel Gear

Figure 2.11. Figure 2.12 shows an antique, gear-driven apple peeler manufactured by Reading Hardware around 1870. In this machine, the bevel gear combination (near the center of the photo) connects the hand-cranked axis to a turntable that holds a paring arm. Thus, rotating the hand crank causes the turntable to spin. It also causes the apple to spin, because

Figure 2.12 Gear-Driven Apple Peeler

of the spur gear combination above the hand crank that's attached to the fork that pierces the apple.

The efficiency of gear drives varies widely depending on the number and type of gear combinations. The more precisely gears are manufactured and the closer the fit between interlocking teeth, the more efficient the drive. Manufacturing advances in the 20th century improved gear precision, so the apple peeler or ice-cream maker you picked up at an antique store might not be as efficient as its modern counterpart (then again, it might, depending on the quality of the 21st-century device). Gear efficiency also varies widely depending on the type of gear, from as low as 40% for certain worm gears to as high as 98% for precise spur gears.

Whereas many hand-cranked machines use gear drives, pedal-powered machines more often use chain or belt drives.

Belt Drives

In a belt drive a belt connects one or more pulleys, also called wheels or sheaves. Like gear and chain drives, a belt drive can transfer power from one drive shaft to another, change the direction of motion, or, by varying the size of the connected pulleys, trade off speed and torque.

Pulleys are made of steel, cast iron or aluminum. Belts are usually made of rubber, polyurethane or leather, but canvas, ropes, cords and cables can also be used. (And at least one inventor has recommended using a loop of pantyhose in a pinch.) Pulleys or wheels with flat rims use flat belts. Pulleys with grooved rims use V-belts, which are V-

or U-shaped in cross-section and fit snugly into grooves. Because of the way they fit together, V-belts and grooved pulleys transfer power more efficiently than flat belts and smooth-rimmed wheels. Therefore, engineers prefer V-belts over flat belts. Figure 2.13 illustrates the placement of flat belts and V-belts on wheels and pulleys.

Compared to gear drives and chain drives, belt drives are the simplest and most economical to build. Examine a stationary bike with the idea of using it to power a machine, and a belt drive transmission seems like the obvious choice. After removing the tire, if one exists, you can use the front wheel as a pulley. Then all you need to do is wrap a belt around the stationary bike's front wheel and a pulley or wheel on the shaft of the device you want to power. On some exercise bikes, such as spinning machines, the front wheels are even grooved pulleys, and you can use the more efficient V-belt.

To design and optimize a belt-driven device, you need to take some fundamental measurements. First is the diameter of your drive's pulleys. For the purpose of making human-powered machines from scrounged parts, measuring a pulley's diameter from edge to

edge across the face is sufficiently accurate, if slightly generous. (Engineers measure pulley diameters in a more complex way.) Knowing the pulleys' sizes allows you to optimize your device. Pairing a large-diameter driver pulley with a small-diameter driven pulley, for example, you can increase the speed of the machine's revolution. Even with belt drives, the ratio of the diameter of the driving pulley to the driven pulley can be called the gear ratio — or more generally, the drive ratio.

To design a belt drive you also need to know the length of the belt you'll use to connect your pulleys. Scientists use a formula for calculating the precise length. However, an easier way to estimate it is to find a long piece of string, wind it snugly around your two pulleys as if it were the belt, and measure how much string you need to return to the starting point.

Finally, you need to fit the width of the belt to the pulley. In the case of a smooth rim and flat belt, you can choose a width slightly narrower than the rim. In the case of a grooved pulley, you need to match the width at the top of the belt to the width at the top of the groove and the height of the belt (in cross-section) to the height of the groove. Standard

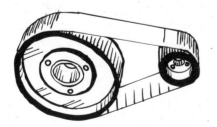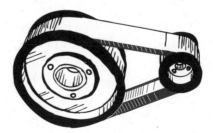

Figure 2.13 Flat Belt and V-Belt Placement

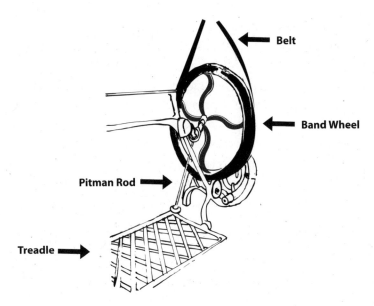

Figure 2.14 Treadle Belt Drive

V-belts are all similarly shaped, with each side slanting at a 40-degree angle from top to bottom. V-belts are sized based on the thickness and height of the belt. The standard sizes are assigned to series labels, from A to E, plus a few others. For example, suppose you want to connect your hand-cranked grain grinder's pulley to a stationary bicycle. The pulley's groove is ½-inch wide at the top and 5/16-inch high. This matches standard "A" series V-belt dimensions. In fact, A-series belts are the most common. Don't worry about memorizing the specifications of each series. These can be determined at the hardware or auto parts store, where V-belts are sold, by you or a helpful employee.

Belt drives also form the basis of many treadle-powered machines, like treadle sewing machines, spinning wheels and treadle woodworking tools. In a treadle belt drive, typically the treadle you press is connected via

a rod, known as a Pitman rod, to a crank on a wheel, as shown in Figure 2.14. (The wheel is also known as a band wheel.) As you treadle, the rod moves up and down (or back and forth) and causes the wheel to rotate. In the case of sewing and woodworking machines, that wheel is connected via belt to another wheel which drives the device.

Treadle sewing machine bases — the part that contains the stand and the belt drive — are relatively easy to find in North America's junkyards, flea markets and classified ads. They can be used not only for sewing, but also for running devices like low-power grinders, jigsaws (or scroll saws) and even electricity generators. In many developing countries treadle sewing machine bases are coveted drive trains, and therefore, even where they may be plentiful, they're hard to obtain.

Some engineers combine one or more drive types in the same human-powered machine. Job Ebenezer, who heads Technology for the Poor, designed a dual-purpose bicycle that can power a peanut sheller, woodworking lathe, grain thresher, circular saw and other devices. His machine includes both a chain drive and a pulley drive. This combination offers the efficiency of a chain drive when harnessing human power plus the flexibility of a belt drive for a simple, forgiving connection to an array of devices.

Job's invention is similar to a design from David Weightman called the Pedal Power Unit (PPU), developed in the late 1970s.[46] Both stand out because they can be attached to any bicycle without ruining the bike as a means of transportation. As Figure 2.15 illustrates, the dual-purpose bicycle transforms a bike to a pedal-powered engine by first resting it on a stability stand. The bike's regular chain is then removed from the chainring. A different chain is positioned around the chainring and connected to a sprocket on a shaft that's affixed to the bike's top tube. On the other side of this shaft sits a pulley, which is used to operate a device via a belt drive. The shaft with its sprocket and pulley may remain affixed to the bike without interfering with the bike's use as transportation. (Though to lighten the load, it can be detached easily.) Even the stand may remain attached to the bike, after being flipped up and out of the way. In this position, it functions as a luggage rack. Job's pedal-power drive is currently used in Zambia, Mexico, India and other countries.[47]

The VitaGoat cycle grinder from Malnutrition Matters also combines a chain and belt drive. As pictured in Figure 2.16, another unique feature of this machine is its use of step pulleys on both shafts. A step pulley combines graduated pulleys to allow for variable drive ratios. In the case of the VitaGoat cycle grinder, for example, a user could move the belt to a smaller pulley on the chain-driven shaft and a larger pulley on the belt-driven shaft in case she felt pedaling was too difficult, or vice-versa if pedaling felt too easy and grinding too slow.

The efficiency of a belt drive depends largely on the amount of tension the belt maintains. Over time, with wear and use and subject to heat and friction, belts elongate. A new, properly designed and installed V-belt drive can be 95 to 98% efficient. But when belts stretch or pulley grooves wear down, efficiency drops considerably. If you're starting with a well-used belt drive — for example, a treadle sewing machine base from a neighbor's garage sale — and the belt is worn thin or stretched, it's best to replace it. (Such belts cost less than $10.00.) The same applies to worn grooves in pulleys. According to one belt drive manufacturer, a new belt, used properly and never overheated (above 140°F), should last you from 20,000 to 25,000 hours of use. Still, even before that much use belts can stretch, so check the tension on your belt drive periodically and ensure that it's taut.

Following is a list of tips for improving belt drive efficiency and life:

- Use a V-belt rather than a flat belt, when possible.
- Keep sufficient, but not excessive, tension in the belt.
- Make sure pulleys in a drive are properly aligned to avoid transverse stress on the

Figure 2.15 Job Ebenezer's Dual-Purpose Bicycle

belt (though belts, because they're flexible, can withstand more skew than can chains).

- As long as the belt is not made of leather, if you're having troubles with slippage, try dusting rosin on the belt to help it grip.
- Bear in mind that larger pulleys prove more efficient than smaller pulleys, because of the larger pulley's greater area of contact; also, flexing belts around small pulleys puts more strain on the drive.
- Wherever possible, avoid dirty, dusty working conditions, as particles can adhere to belts and reduce their effectiveness.
- Also avoid operating in wet or oily conditions, as these will encourage slippage.

The transmission of power over a belt actually depends on friction between the belt and pulleys. Consequently, belt drives can slip when the force demanded by the powered device exceeds the friction forces between the belt and pulley. For machines in which high torque is a necessity, it might make sense to choose a chain drive or gear drive instead.

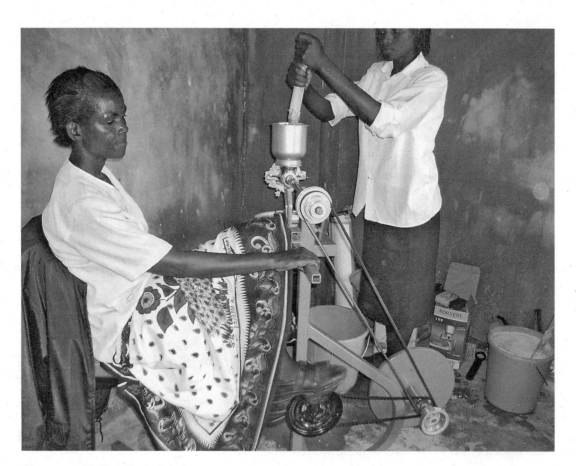

Figure 2.16 VitaGoat Cycle Grinder

On the other hand, in cases where the possibility exists of a shaft sticking and causing tremendous and potentially damaging force on the drive, a belt drive's slipping can be considered a safety feature. Another advantage to using belt drives is that they tolerate greater side-to-side movement than chain drives. For this reason, Alex Gadsden's bike-powered washing machine, the Cyclean (featured in Chapter 5), for example, relies on a belt drive. He told me his first design used a chain drive, but during the spin cycle, as the machine jostled around quite a bit, the chain drive would jump off its sprocket. A belt drive allowed greater flexibility.[48]

Though belt drives technically depend on friction between the belt and wheel to transfer force, when engineers speak of "friction drives," they usually mean something else.

Friction Drives

In a friction drive a wheel on one shaft presses against a wheel on a second shaft to transfer torque to the second wheel, thereby causing the second shaft to spin. In this configuration, the second, smaller wheel is often called a spindle. A friction drive is so-named because it depends on friction between the driving wheel and the spindle. If there were no friction — for example, if both the driving wheel and the spindle were smooth and coated in lubricant — the driving wheel would spin right over the surface of the spindle.

In many human-powered friction drives, a bicycle wheel acts as the driver while a small spindle is positioned against it. Figure 2.17 illustrates a friction drive in which the rear wheel of a conventional bicycle suspended on an indoor training stand powers a small electrical generator. This type of drive forms the basis for some commercial pedal electric generators, including Windstream Power's Human Power Trainer. It's also the basis for Woody Roy Parker's Juicycle (featured in Chapter 3) and David Butcher's Pedal Powered Prime Mover (featured in Chapter 6). Friction drives are commonly used to create bicycle blenders. In this device, an extended blender shaft ends in a small wheel (for example, a discarded rollerblade wheel) which is positioned to rub against a bike's wheel. It's easy to make one of these from a stationary bike, in which case the front wheel turns the

Figure 2.17 Friction Drive in an Electrical Generator

blender's spindle, or from a conventional bike on a trainer stand, where the rear wheel turns the blender's spindle. (You'll find plans for making a bicycle blender in Chapter 3.)

Friction drives are simple to make and simple to use. In the example of the pedal-powered electrical generator shown in Figure 2.17, you don't even need to modify the bike you ride every day to turn it into a power source. After you've generated electricity, all you have to do is remove your bike from the training stand to use it on the streets again. Making a bicycle blender is nearly as simple.

Besides being simple, friction drives are also quieter than chain drives or gear drives. And, like pulley drives, friction drives can accommodate, in one pairing, the large gear reduction necessary for applications that require high rpm. Consider the pedal-powered electrical generator in Figure 2.17. If the bicycle wheel is 27 inches in diameter, and the spindle's diameter is 1 inch, the device uses a 1:27 gear ratio. The motor needs high rpm to generate electricity. A chain drive would need more than one gear pairing to accomplish the same reduction, because very small sprockets are not practical. Using a pulley drive would be problematic, because the radius of the belt around the motor's shaft would be so small as to greatly reduce its efficiency.

However, generally speaking, friction drives are the least efficient of all drives discussed in this chapter. Engineers rate their peak efficiency from 80 to 90%. Dust or grime on either the driving wheel or the spindle will further compromise their effectiveness. So will moisture. Perhaps you've seen or heard of the small gas or electric motors that can be attached to your bike to boost your human power, helpful when climbing hills or riding against strong winds. Some of these rely on a friction drive to transfer power from the motor to the rear wheel. People who test these kits often lament that they're useless in the rain, because water so dramatically reduces friction between the motor's spindle and the bicycle's wheel.

For best operation, the driving wheel and spindle must be pressed tightly together, though not so tightly as to cause pressure on the shafts. Also, greater surface area of contact between the two wheels improves friction drive efficiency. You can predict then that in a human-powered friction drive the ideal tire would be wide and mostly smooth. Knobby tires (such as those found on mountain bikes) transfer less power because less of the tire's surface area makes contact with the spindle. In the case of the friction-drive electrical generator built by Windstream Power, which has a drive similar to the one pictured in Figure 2.17, physicist and inventor Colin Kerr told me he and his team experimented with knurling the spindle to provide additional friction. However, they discovered that the knurled spindle caused more noise and, because the pressure of the tires never exceeded the friction present with a smooth spindle, didn't add greater efficiency.[49]

Besides their lower average efficiency, friction drives present some additional disadvantages compared to other drive types. Foremost among them is wear. Maybe you won't use your pedal-powered blender or electrical generator long enough to find out, but the very friction that the drive depends upon to transfer torque will also, in time, deteriorate the wheel. One manufacturer of friction-drive motors for bicycles predicts that users will have to replace their bicycle tire after 500 to 1,000 hours of contact with the motor's spindle. Such a lifespan is much shorter than the life of a chain drive, gear drive or pulley drive.

Flywheels

So far, most examples of pedal-powered drives in this chapter have assumed that your design will use a bicycle wheel — that is, a spoked wheel. However, for sustained efforts that require a steady amount of power, and especially when significant power is needed, it's better to use a heavy flywheel. A flywheel is a disc that relies on its mass and rotational speed to continue generating power after it's been brought up to speed. Flywheels operate on the principle of Newton's 1st law, which explains that a body at rest tends to stay at rest and a body in motion tends to stay in motion. Once you get a flywheel spinning, it wants to keep spinning. Furthermore, as a flywheel spins faster it accumulates more energy. As it slows down, it releases that energy. Flywheels store kinetic (in this case, rotational) energy and then return it to the system. Some people call them mechanical batteries. The heavier and larger the flywheel, the more energy it can store — but also, the more energy it requires to get it spinning.

The advantage to using a flywheel is that it evens out normally jerky torque inputs. Pedaling, treadling and hand-cranking, especially one-armed cranking, issue force periodically, mainly on the downstroke. The graph in Figure 2.18 depicts how power output varies while pedaling a bicycle, as measured by crank-arm angle. When one leg is partially extended and the crank arm is at about 90 degrees past an upright position (in other words, pointing forward and parallel to the ground), the power output for that leg peaks. The other leg's power output peaks in the same relative position, when the crank arm angle is at 270 degrees. Adding a flywheel to a pedal-powered drive would smooth out the periodic curve in Figure 2.18 to a nearly straight line, representing a nearly constant application of power.

Force applied to a treadle sewing machine varies in a similar manner. Without a flywheel connected to the treadle, the machine would make a few stitches each time your foot pressed the treadle and then pause until you pressed the treadle again. The flywheel evens out your foot pressure, storing it, then releasing it when you aren't pushing on the treadle, so that stitching continues uninterrupted. It

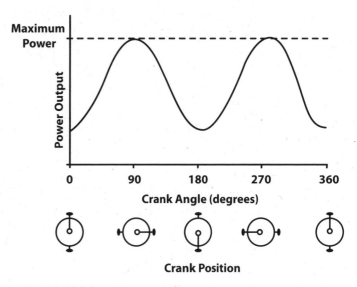

Figure 2.18 Pedal-Power Output at Varying Crank Angles[50]

Figure 2.19 Potter's Kick Wheel With Concrete Flywheel

will spin until it spends all of its stored energy or until you apply pressure to stop it.

(Technically speaking, a spoked wheel, like a bicycle wheel, is a flywheel, because it does have mass and velocity when spinning, and therefore it stores and releases energy you put into it. But because it's so lightweight it isn't considered a powerful flywheel.)

Some human-powered potter's wheels, like the one shown in Figure 2.19, use heavy flywheels in direct drives to spin the wheel-head on which a pot is shaped. In this instance, a potter kicks the wheel to start it and continues to rotate it with her foot. This type of wheel is called a kick wheel. Another type of human-powered pottery wheel uses treadles to keep the flywheel spinning.

The 2-inch-thick flywheel shown in Figure 2.19 is made of cast concrete and weighs 140 pounds. Potter Scott Cooper, who prefers a human-powered pottery wheel says, "I've never used an electric wheel for any extended period of time. I find them to be loud, abrupt, too fast, and prone to being out of control. I enjoy the quiet hum of the concrete flywheel as it spins by beneath my feet; the direct physical connection between the energy I expend into the wheel and the speed of the wheel-head (and thus the available energy for making pots)."[51]

What if flywheels, as mechanical batteries, could effectively enable one human to triple or quadruple his output by storing human power for some period of time, then releasing it suddenly? This question led J. P. Modak, professor and mechanical engineer, to design what he calls the Human-Powered Flywheel Motor (HPFM). The machine, refined over the last 30 years, combines a bicycle's chain drive with a gear drive to deliver power to an 80-cm-diameter flywheel. The flywheel, with the aid of another gear drive, delivers power to a device that would otherwise require fossil fuels or electricity. It has successfully powered brickmaking machines, water pumps, algae processing machines, wood laminate cutters, drop forge hammers and winnowers. In the case of the brickmaking machine, Modak and his students determined that the motor works best when the operator pedals for 60 to 90 seconds at approximately 40 rpm, after which the flywheel spins at about 240 rpm with an accumulated force of approximately 1,490 newtons. Then a clutch is engaged to release the gearing from the bicycle drive and rapidly redirect the flywheel's stored power to an auger, which compresses a lime-flyash-sand mixture

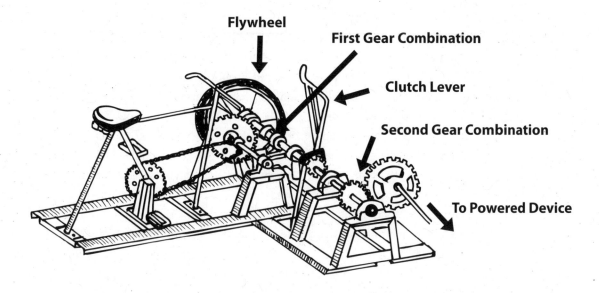

Figure 2.20 J. P. Modak's Human-Powered Flywheel Motor

into a long brick. Modak estimates the Human Powered Flywheel Motor could generate up to 6 hp from the efforts of one person![52]

The diagram in Figure 2.20 offers a simplified schematic of Dr. Modak's invention. The chain drive between the bike's chainring and the first shaft has a gear ratio of 3:1. The gears between the first shaft connected to the chain drive and the shaft connected to the flywheel also have a gear ratio of 3:1. Thus, the total increase in rotational speed between the pedals and the flywheel is 6:1. The gears on the other side of the clutch, which transfer the flywheel's rotation to the device it's powering, have a ratio of 1:4, thereby multiplying the force delivered to the device.[53]

While considering whether to incorporate a flywheel in your design, you might wonder about its optimal characteristics. The desired mass of a machine's flywheel depends on the device and its purpose. One designer whose machines power tool grinders and electrical generators says he aims for flywheels that weigh from 25 to 35 pounds. By contrast, as mentioned above, the flywheel for a commercially made potter's kick wheel weighs 140 pounds.

Some stationary bikes and spinning machines (found mostly at fitness centers) have heavy, cast metal flywheels as their front wheel. If you don't have this type of exercise bike, or if you're making a machine from a used bicycle, you can replace the spoked wheel with a homemade flywheel. Figure 2.21 shows a pedal-powered macadamia nut sheller (bici-macadamia) built by Maya Pedal, which uses a large, custom flywheel.

Custom flywheels can be crafted from wood, concrete, or metal or adapted from parts found at junkyards or flea markets. The flywheels pictured in Figures 2.19 and 2.21 are made from concrete, a common substance for flywheels because it's weighty, widely available, and can be molded. In addition, if extra friction is desirable along the faces or edges of the flywheel, as in the case of a kick wheel, one can use a broom to lightly score the cement before it's dried. To make a cement flywheel, you need a form that's perfectly symmetrical, so that the wheel will be true, and you also need reinforcing material to embed in the cement. The reinforcing material could be wire mesh, rebar (steel reinforcing bar), or even an old cast-iron gear. Carlos Marroquin Machàn, chief mechanic for Maya Pedal, made the flywheel pictured in Figure 2.21. He began with a bicycle wheel as the frame, then used disk wheels — the lens-shaped plastic wheel covers that bike racers attach to their rims to reduce

Figure 2.21 Maya Pedal's Bicimacadamia (Macadamia Nut Sheller)

drag — to create the mold around the frame before pouring in the concrete.

A flywheel could also be made from rebar wound around a tire rim four or five times, then cinched or welded in place. Others have built flywheels from plywood, for example, by simply cutting the wood in a circle. For a heavier flywheel, glue or bolt several of these circles together. If you're a metalworker or know one, you could also cast a flywheel from iron or aluminum. A simple solution is one recommended by human-powered machine inventor David Butcher: use a round table top for a flywheel.

When constructing a flywheel, no matter what the material, it's vital to make the wheel as true, or balanced, as possible. Ideally, it should be symmetrical in thickness and width from the center hole to the edge.

Also note that the weight of the flywheel is more effective when it's located toward the outer edges of the circle. In other words, a tire rim wound with rebar is actually more advantageous than the flying-saucer shaped flywheel pictured in Figure 2.21. (However, Maya Pedal's customers preferred the looks of this flywheel to others.) On ChocoSol's pedal-powered cacao bean grinder, featured in Chapter 3, the flywheel is made out of a thin inner tube filled with sand and fixed onto a bicycle wheel rim. Potters who make their own kick wheels sometimes make them from two disks of plywood with bricks sandwiched in between, evenly distributed near the edges and bolted in place.

I hope this section's discussion of drives and other design elements has prompted you to think about what will best suit your human-powered machine. The following section offers ideas on how to best collect and support your assemblage of parts with the appropriate frame.

Frames and Supports

There's no single, ideal frame for a human-powered device. Depending on what the device operates, whether you begin with a bike, stationary bike or treadle base, and what type of drive you choose, your frame might be as simple as a bicycle trainer stand or as complex as the ceiling-high rig designed for Just Soap's bicycle blender (featured in Chapter 3). This section offers principles to guide your frame choices, plus an overview of materials and ideas for piecing together found parts.

When designing and constructing a frame, consider the following:

- Function and Durability: Obviously, the frame has to be suited to its purpose. A blender, for example, can be attached to a stationary bicycle with minimal modification, but it would be more challenging to adapt a treadle sewing machine base to run this appliance. Also consider whether a frame is sufficiently strong to power the device you intend to run. Many stationary bikes, for example, are constructed for moderate home use and not for powering a load like that imposed by a cement mixer or washing machine. Pushing the manufactured frame beyond its capacities can result in failure.

- Stability: Many human-powered machines work by rotating something — the burrs of a grinder or sheller, the paddles and cylinder of an ice-cream maker, the

drum of a washing machine. The less balanced the rotating mass and the greater the torque, the more the frame will want to wobble or tilt as you operate the machine. Therefore, it's necessary to construct a solid, evenly weighted frame. Where the potential for movement or tipping is great, as in the case of a pedal-powered cement mixer or washing machine, bolt the device to the floor or at least a large base (for example, one made of wood) for greater safety and efficacy.

- Ease of Construction: Decide how much effort and technical expertise you're willing to put into your design. Using a training stand or a stationary bike requires little of both, while welding a custom frame — though it might last longer and handle greater loads — calls for special skills. Ease of construction, like cost, also depends on the availability of parts. It may be simpler to use what's in your garage or basement than to seek out unique parts from different sources.

- Size and Portability: Most of the machines featured in this book are meant to be operated in one place, like a backyard or garage, and not to be transported. As such, their weight, size and stability take priority over portability. To make a portable machine, consider adding small wheels to the front feet of your frame, which can be engaged when you tilt the frame forward. Or, you could design a collapsible frame such as the one used by EcoSystems's pedal-powered electrical generator, used in Nepal and pictured in Figure 2.22. This frame can be disassembled into three parts. And though at about 77 pounds (35 kg), including its shipping container, it's not necessarily lightweight, it is definitely portable. Inventor David Sowerwine remarked that its weight matches that of a Nepali porter's typical load.[54]

- Comfort: If you're pedal-powering a machine, figure out how long you might spend grinding grain or blending smoothies and make sure you can tolerate your seat and frame dimensions for that amount of time. Besides following the fitting instructions offered earlier in this chapter to determine the appropriate seat height, find a frame with a seat tube appropriate for your inseam. Also make sure the handlebars, if you'll rely on them, are fixed at a comfortable height and distance from your seat. Furthermore, determine whether the demands of operating the device warrant variable gearing, and if so, how you'll integrate the gears. For example, on a pedal-powered machine where will you attach the chainring and cogset, where will you position and affix the flywheel, if you're using one, how many gear combinations will you allow, and in what direction does the chain need to be driven in order for the device to operate? (In some machines, the chain drive must be reversed compared to its normal orientation on a bicycle.)

Figure 2-22. EcoSystems's Foldable Pedal-Powered Electrical Generator Frame

- Cost: Machines featured in this book have cost between $10 and several thousand dollars to make. They have depended on teams of MIT engineering students, military contractors, overseas manufacturing facilities, bike mechanics hired to make custom parts, or simply ingenious individuals wielding wrenches in their workshops. If you can find cheap cast-off bikes in good condition, and if you have the knowledge to reassemble their parts in new ways, I encourage you to follow the least expensive route. At the same time, aim for excellent power transmission and don't skimp on the safety of the device that's holding you up.

In case you choose to recycle an exercise bike or traditional bike for your design, it's helpful to familiarize yourself with their structures. Figure 2.23 identifies parts of a basic bike frame. Stationary bikes have similar frames, though usually they lack a top tube and variable gearing and substitute a stand for the rear wheel. Of course, the structures of bikes and stationary bikes vary from model to model.

If you begin with a traditional bike, bear in mind that you might be modifying the frame by cutting, rearranging or adding pieces from other bike frames or parts from the hardware store. In the case of a stationary bike, you probably won't have to tear apart the

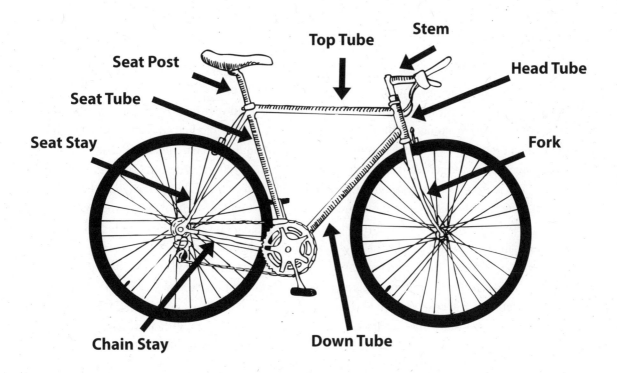

Figure 2.23 A Basic Bike Frame

frame, or at least not for the sake of function. But you can always modify it for greater comfort, for example, by changing out the saddle, pedals and handlebars. You might also want to change the chainring or cog on the front wheel to better suit your device's power requirements.

Bike frames are typically made of steel alloys, aluminum, carbon fiber composite or titanium. Each material possesses varying properties that make it desirable in different situations. For example, steel, though heaviest of the four, is the strongest and most durable frame material. In almost all cases, stationary bike frames are made of steel tubing. Traditional bicycles built before 1980 were all made of steel, as are many bikes today. Some elite bicyclists shun steel frames because of their weight. However, for a stationary human-powered machine, the weight isn't a disadvantage and, in fact, could enhance the device's stability.

When making your own human-powered device, steel makes an excellent choice. It's an easy material for an amateur to work with. You can cut it apart with a hacksaw and then weld or braze pieces together to create a strong joint. If you're not a welder, you can drill holes and bolt steel parts together without risking cracks or weakening the surrounding material. You can bend, twist and reshape steel to a greater extent before failure than you can aluminum. Also, steel frames are widely available at relatively low cost. Nearly all frames depicted in this book are made of steel.

Since you're making your own device, however, you aren't limited to the materials professionals use to make bike frames. Indeed, many independent bike builders experiment with nontraditional materials such as bamboo and wood (even 2 × 4s). And you'll undoubtedly be adding structural members that didn't come from a bike, such as angle iron, slotted angle iron, square steel tube, round steel tube, round bar stock, or square bar stock. Other materials, such as conduit, plywood and flat bar stock can be used for supporting an appliance — for example, to attach a blender to a stationary bike — though these materials wouldn't be strong enough to make up the frame itself.

Consider recycled materials, too. Lee Ravenscroft of the Working Bikes Cooperative in Chicago buys old bed frames from the recyclers who canvas the city's alleys, then uses the bed frames to make bicycle stands for his pedal-powered electrical generators. Human-powered device inventor David Butcher recommends using steel shelving supports. Both of these materials make sense, because they're predrilled with holes for bolts.

To study a creative frame, take another look at the bicimacadamia built by Carlos Marroquin Machàn of Maya Pedal pictured in Figure 2.21. In this design Carlos has dismantled a steel-framed bike, switched the gearing to the opposite side of the frame, traded the handlebars for a seat, and welded a fork onto the previous seat tube to connect the drive to the nut sheller frame. The sheller's flywheel is supported by a box made of angle iron in the horizontal planes and recycled bike tubes for the vertical posts. Other creative bike-based frames pictured in this chapter include Maya Pedal's bicidesgranadora shown in Figure 2.6 and the bicilicuadora in 2.7. The VitaGoat cycle grinder in Figure 2.16 is an example of a sophisticated, custom fabricated frame.

When considering what type of frame to build, you might wonder whether a person pedaling in a recumbent — or leaning-back — position can deliver more power than pedaling on a traditional, upright bike frame. Several studies, summarized in David Gordon Wilson's book *Bicycling Science,* 3rd ed., have shown that the two positions differ little in the amount of power one can deliver.[55] (Recumbent bikes have, however, proven faster than upright bikes in road tests, mainly because of their lower wind resistance.) Despite the fact that it doesn't typically deliver more power, some individuals find the recumbent position more comfortable for extended periods of pedaling. It relieves pressure from the operator's hands, wrists and shoulders.

Bikes are not necessarily the starting point for all pedal-powered machines. In the 1970s British-born engineer Alex Weir worked in Uganda, Zimbabwe and Tanzania making pedal-powered winnowers, threshers, water pumps, corn shellers, grain grinders and other devices from first wood, and then steel. He was inspired by the late Stuart Wilson, who in 1968 conceived of a central pedal-power drive that could be connected to various appliances, which he dubbed a "dynapod," from the Greek words *dyna*, meaning power, and *pod*, meaning foot. Weir's early designs relied on wood frames, because that's what was available and inexpensive where he was at the time. In later designs, Weir used mostly square or tubular steel frames. Also, like Maya Pedal's bicimacadamia, some of Weir's designs incorporate a flywheel that's made by casting concrete over

a bicycle wheel. Figure 2.24 depicts a wood-framed, two-person dynapod with a grain mill connected to it. This one was designed by Alex Weir and used in Tanzania. He has also invented pedal-powered machines that can be operated by as many as four people at once.[56]

Another custom-framed dynapod was developed by Dick Ott and featured in Rodale's 1977 book *Pedal Power In Work, Leisure and Transportation.* Called the Energy Cycle, its drive could accept several types of tools, including food grinders, shredders, dough mixers, grain mills, knife sharpeners, meat slicers and more. Engineers made the prototype ver-

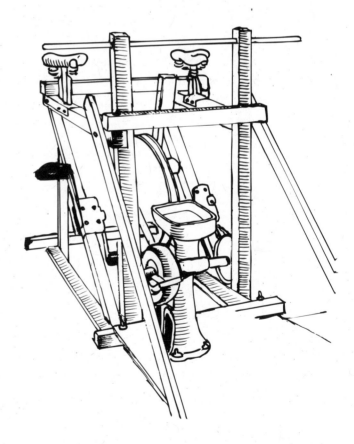

Figure 2.24 Alex Weir's Two-Person Dynapod

sion's frame of angle iron, but used 1.25-inch diameter steel pipe in later versions for added stability. The Energy Cycle also featured adjustable seats and an adjustable working table. Testers appreciated how it eased or hastened household chores, though author Diana Branch wrote, "One of the biggest problems encountered by the researchers was to find a universal means of attaching each implement."[57] Researchers tried different ways of replacing or extending a tool's shaft to be integrated with the Energy Cycle's drive, but according to the book the problem was never satisfactorily resolved.

Other pedal-powered inventions featured in this chapter share the dynapod concept of adapting one power train to many uses — for example, J. P. Modak's human-powered flywheel motor and Job Ebenezer's dual-purpose bicycle, based on David Weightman's Pedal Power Unit design.

Figure 2.25 Bicycle Trainer Stand

Not commonly available when Wilson, Weir, Ott and Weightman were devising multi-use pedal-powered drives in the late 1970s was the indoor bicycle trainer stand. Trainers would still be rare in developing countries today, but in North America they're plentiful. Available for as little as $20 used and from $90 new, a trainer like the one shown in Figure 2.25 offers a simple foundation for a pedal-powered device. One merely sets a bicycle in the stand and tightens the handle on the large bolt that presses against the rear wheel's axle. The bike is fixed in place with the rear wheel suspended and available for power generation. Most trainers include means for modulating the amount of resistance applied to the wheel so that cyclists can vary their workouts. However, these resistance devices can be disabled or disengaged so that all of your pedal power goes to the device you're operating.

Using a trainer stand still relies on the traditional bike drive to deliver power to a device. Some inventors believe we should let go of this notion altogether when conceiving new human-powered machines. Eric Hollenbeck, founder of Blue Ox Millworks in Eureka, California, told me, "It seems to me that in order to be efficient at human power we've got to really begin thinking about manufacturing human-powered machines, not just converting a bicycle to do something, because I don't think a bicycle was ever [meant for that]. I don't think that the sprockets are big enough, the chains are big enough, the drive force is big enough. You know, it had a whole different intention when it was manufactured, and to try and convert that to do something else, in a lot of cases I've seen, seems to have done an injustice to the idea itself."[58] In addition to having extraordinary mechanical prowess, Eric enjoys the advantage of owning a mill as well as blacksmithing and casting facilities.

Scrounging For Parts

Some of the most creative inventions have been born not only out of necessity, but also out of whatever materials were cheap and within easy reach at the time. This section offers ideas for looking beyond our basements and garages for the parts to make a human-powered machine. Potential scavenging grounds include:

- Antique stores: Good sources for old, hand-cranked devices such as cherry pitters, apple peelers and corn shellers; old woodworking, farm and garden tools; treadle sewing machines; and other belt- or gear-driven machinery. Some antique stores specialize in certain periods or objects. Avoid the precious china or fine furniture boutiques and head for places like "The Old Tool Shed" and "Grandpa's Attic." Even if a store doesn't have what you need, knowledgeable shopkeepers can often suggest additional places to visit. Antique stores are typically more expensive than other sources listed here, but prices are always negotiable. If you're an educator, mention that the desired item is for a class experiment to help wheedle a better discount.
- Flea markets, resale shops, auctions and rummage sales: Inventory is less predictable, in general, than an antique store's, proprietors less knowledgeable, and qual-

ity varies significantly. Flea markets and auctions can be a good source of older mechanical devices, but perusing tables of mixed junk or waiting for a particular lot to be auctioned requires an investment of time. On the other hand, the inventory costs less than it would at an antique store. If you're looking for bicycles to part out, police auctions, which in most cities occur at least annually, are an excellent source. Contact your local police department to find out when your city's auction is held.

"This is what we need: somebody…to convince people to trust and understand that they are capable of doing anything with what they've already got on hand. It's not necessary that they keep searching for something from outside, no,…we, ourselves, can do anything once we've got great ideas."

CARLOS MARROQUIN MACHÀN[59]

- Junkyards: Always an adventure. Leave several hours for hiking through acres of detritus, then sitting under a shade tree and listening to the owner talk about beer, the neighbors and bargains of the past as you intermittently feign interest in a few rusty pumps or washing machines until you finally negotiate a price in a way that makes both of you appear as if you've tragically and foolishly conceded the steal you hoped would crown the visit.

- Dumps and dumpsters: Follow the Freegans: *Freegan* which derives from *free* and *vegan* is a term for one who lives outside of the consumerist conventions of many first-world countries and sustains her needs by gleaning basic resources from, among other places, dumpsters and curbside castoffs. The US alone discarded ap-

Bart Orlando

Among all the people I interviewed for this book perhaps the most enthusiastic and experienced human-powered machine inventor is former pre-med student, bike activist and self-described agitator, Bart Orlando. Bart has built pedal-powered blenders, tool grinders, drill presses, sewing machines, washing machines and electrical generators. His inventions don't stop with human-powered machines, either. He's also passionate about solar-powered cookers. Locals in his hometown of Arcata, California, had told me that on any sunny morning I could find Bart in front of the food co-op demonstrating the heating power of these big, silver parabolas, and indeed, that's where he was the day of our scheduled interview. Even without the solar-cooker backdrop, Bart was unmistakable with his long, orange hair, wide-brimmed straw hat, and the electric-hybrid pedicab (with attached chaise lounge for tourists like myself) that serves as his only transportation. After he shook my hand he urged me to hold that same hand close — but not too close — to the apex of focused sunlight and feel its heat. We added more vegetables to the frying pan and left the solar cooker to prepare brunch while we talked.

After 15 years of working with human-powered machines, Bart has many opinions on how best to design them. He's used exercise bikes as the foundation of most machines because "they're available and they're cheap." He advised starting with the sturdiest bike possible, and in particular he recommended the classic bronze-colored Schwinn exercise bikes released in the 1970s. (Another advantage to these models is their large chainring.) One can often find the old Schwinn exercise bikes in thrift stores, sometimes free, or through online classifieds. Also durable are the spinner bikes now popular in health clubs. Bart suggested searching for a bike with a heavy, cast-iron flywheel, rather than a spoked wheel. The flywheel helps to even your output, which is especially important when generating electricity.

It's also best to find a front wheel whose rim has edges or a center groove to help hold a belt in place. (If the wheel has a tire on it, you have to remove the tire to find out whether a groove exists.) If the rim doesn't have a groove or edges,

Figure 2.26 Bart Orlando

proximately 245 million tons of garbage in 2005, according to the US Environmental Protection Agency (EPA). Much of the trash was paper and yard waste, but 7.6% consisted of metals.[60] It's impossible to know what quantity might be useful for human-powered machines, but one gauge is the number of abandoned bikes that recycling organizations such as Boston's Bike Not Bombs and Chicago's Working

---

Bart advised welding on a grooved rim or applying gritty, friction tape, like the kind that's used on pool steps, to the wheel. What's most important when using any belt drive, he emphasized, is to keep the belt steady and taut.

For generating electricity, Bart proposed connecting a pedaled shaft to the shaft of a permanent magnet DC motor in a direct-drive arrangement as the most efficient way to harvest muscle power. This, he admitted, was not always possible or simple, so the next best thing would be connecting a pedal-powered flywheel to a permanent magnet DC motor via a belt. Further, he said, "I recommend not having a battery in the system. When the battery runs down it's harder to run the system because you're charging the battery, so it actually makes the system three or four times harder to pedal." Many more of Bart's tips and design ideas are incorporated in instructions throughout this book.

Bart has taught and inspired other inventors, from entrepreneurs such as Nate Byerley of Byerley Bicycle Blenders to students at Humboldt State University's Campus Center for Appropriate Technology (CCAT). While in Arcata I visited CCAT. Waiting to move into its newly remodeled, eco-friendly space, the organization was temporarily housed in a small ranch house stuffed with the hallmarks of student life: sagging couches, assorted near-empty bags of chips, and shelves of dusty books. Young men and women hung out in the kitchen or tinkered on an earth-friendly shelter in the backyard. One student knelt on the living room floor ironing the image of a chainring circled by the slogan "Cars Make Us Weak" onto a red T-shirt.

Years ago Bart had constructed a lab of pedal-powered devices at CCAT, and its remnants lie scattered between the back porch, an extra bedroom, the garage, and offsite storage. CCAT doesn't plan to revitalize its pedal-power program, and Bart isn't working out of their space anymore. Now he dreams of bigger projects: helping a local gym convert to generating some of their power from clients' exercise, building a playground of energy-generating equipment, hosting a bike library and teaching youth how to build bicycles and pedal-powered machines, and bringing homemade solar cookers to those in remote areas.

Foremost in his vision are the health and environmental benefits that human-powered devices offer individuals and community. He's encouraged by recent energy-efficient technologies such as LEDs and the wider applications of human power, such as discotheques lit by dancing and subways lit by commuters' footsteps. Before we parted he told me, "There's probably all kinds of ways to make this a reality and I think we're gradually seeing that. The important thing is that we don't give up hope and that we stick with it."[63]

Bikes refurbish and donate to developing nations: 5,500 and 9,000, respectively in 2006. Similar bike recycling groups exist in metropolitan areas around North America. Meanwhile, a record 20 million bikes were sold in the US in the year 2000 and annual sales since then have been close to the same.[61] How many of those have already been abandoned?

- Online sources: Focused searches of high-volume online classifieds sites such as craigslist.org or online auction sites such as eBay can lead to finding exactly the part you want in short order. Prices may not be as favorable as flea markets or rummage sales, but it's still better than buying new. Also target online vendors that specialize in the kinds of used parts

Working Bikes Cooperative

Community outreach and social change have always been central to the mission of Chicago's Working Bikes Cooperative. Lee Ravenscroft, a retired electrical engineer, founded the organization in 2001 to collect cast-off bikes from the city's alleys and garages and ship them to places like Tanzania, Ghana, and Guatemala, where they can transform lives. Several times a week volunteers wield wrenches in a giant, urban warehouse to turn the surrounding towers of bikes into functional vehicles. Some of the refurbished bikes are sold locally to help support the nonprofit.

Now the cooperative is moving beyond reassembling bikes. Instead, they're disassembling them and turning them into bike machines just as one of their partner organizations, Maya Pedal, does. However, rather than making corn grinders and macadamia nut shellers, Working Bikes has concentrated on something better suited to Chicagoans: pedal-powered electrical generators. Volunteers meet every Wednesday evening to learn about bike machines and make them for practical and educational use.

Recently Working Bikes teamed up with students and science teachers at Francis W. Parker School to create a fleet of electrical generators from recycled bikes. One teacher made the pedal-powered electrical generators part

of a physics class project. Students and volunteers spent an afternoon in the lab putting bikes on stands, attaching permanent magnet DC motors, and then wiring them to high-intensity LED lights. Later that week, students — and even the school's mascot, the Colonel — pedaled to power these stadium lights at an evening soccer game. Working Bikes volunteers have added "youth education" to their mission, and plan to continue bringing pedal power into classrooms across Chicago.

Figure 2.27 Pedal-Powered Soccer Field Lights

or devices you seek. American Artifacts (americanartifacts.com), for example, offers a curious variety of mechanical tools, scientific instruments and old, manual farm machinery, with some explanations on how they were once used.

Once you find some promising materials, how do you know whether they'll work for your human-powered machine? The following tips should help you decide:

- Stationary bikes: Look for the stationary bikes that have a wheel in the front, positioned like the front wheel on a traditional bicycle. Avoid those with wheels placed directly under the seat. Also avoid the type of exercise bikes that direct your pedaling motion to a fan to generate more resistance. Often these have names that begin with "Air-" (Airdyne, Airciser, Airgometer, etc.). It's easiest to convert stationary bikes with a front wheel to a friction or belt drive. Further, older styles with front wheels usually run on a chain drive, in case you're interested in modifying or replacing the front wheel with a custom sprocket to make a chain-driven machine. Stationary bikes with front wheels or flywheels are often older types and priced lower than more contemporary models. If you're designing a belt or chain drive, choose a stationary bike that has a heavy flywheel over one with a lightweight, spoked wheel. If you have a choice, also choose one with a large chainring over one with a small chainring.
- Frames: Find a sturdy, stable steel frame. Scratches, surface rust, and even some

dents won't affect the quality of your human-powered machines. Bends in tubes or forks that render a bicycle unsafe to ride don't rule it out as a source of parts for a stationary human-powered machine. But if you're choosing an exercise bike, make sure the frame's feet sit evenly on a level surface. Also determine whether the frame can be adjusted to suit your size.

- Chains: Used bikes and stationary bikes might have rusty chains, but that doesn't mean they're unusable. One test of whether a rusty or grimy chain can be used is whether its links still bend. Try flexing each pair of links. If the joints are locked tight, consider replacing the chain. Surface rust — the kind that has not progressed to causing pits in the metal — and grime can be scrubbed off with a stiff brush (try an old toothbrush to clean in between the links — or better, a chain scrubber specially designed for this purpose) and a solution of diluted dishwashing liquid. Alternatively, some bike enthusiasts advocate removing the chain and soaking it in a degreasing solution for at least a day, then rinsing it a few times to thoroughly clean it. In all cases, be sure to lubricate the chain well after cleaning and before using it. Chains may also suffer from wear on the inside of the links, which makes them feel loose. Chains slipping off a sprocket while in motion can indicate wear. Worn chains, in turn, can cause sprockets to wear out faster. Thus, it's best to replace a worn chain before it damages the sprockets of a chain drive.

- Sprockets: If you're designing a chain drive, be alert for worn-out sprockets on the used machinery you're eyeing. With ill-fitted or worn chains, a sprocket's teeth become sharp and eventually begin to look like the curled waves you drew as a child to represent a roiling ocean. Replace the sprocket(s) if this is the case.

"The past enthusiasm for reducing what has been called 'back-breaking' labor through the incorporation of gasoline engine- and electric-motor-powered devices has led to an almost total neglect of efforts to improve human-powered tools. In consequence, there is today an unfair competition between highly developed modern electric hedge clippers, for example, and manual shears that have not been sensibly improved for a hundred years."

DAVID GORDON WILSON[62]

- Treadle Sewing Machine Bases: Plentiful at auctions, flea markets, antique stores and in classified ads, treadle sewing machine bases are usually found in workable condition, because they were manufactured to last 100 years or more. When examining a treadle base, don't be concerned if the belt is off, stretched, dried up or missing. Belts are simple to find and replace. Try moving the treadle with the belt disengaged from the wheel. It should offer little resistance as you rock it forward and back, and it should cause the band wheel to rotate. Even if the mechanism sticks, a few drops of lubricant will probably revive it to work as well as it did when it left the factory. If you need only a treadle base, save money by purchasing one separately from a sewing machine. (These can be found for as little as $20.) Make certain, however, that the foot pedal, Pitman rod and band wheel are present and working together (i.e., no bolts or other parts are missing or hopelessly rusted). Beware of treadle sewing machine bases that have been functionally dismantled and converted into plant stands or display tables.

- Other Exercise Equipment: Though most of the examples and plans in this book are based on bicycles, exercise bikes, treadle bases or hand cranks, you could recycle other machines such as treadmills, rowing machines and elliptical steppers to turn muscle power into necessary work. Key to this conversion, of course, is translating the motion from one machine to another. However, accomplishing this translation with other machines is not as simple as adapting a stationary bike or a bike on a trainer stand. Nor in most cases — and especially when using a treadmill — would you harness your muscle power with the same efficiency.

When it comes to sourcing and vetting parts, experience is the best teacher. Search enough thrift stores and junkyards and you'll figure out which places most often carry what you need. Test enough stationary bikes and you'll discover which models are best for recycling.

Similarly, spend enough time tinkering and you'll determine what kind of drive train you prefer to make and use — and how best to make and use them.

Summary: Making Your Own Human-Powered Devices

So far this chapter has described human potential, the particular advantages and disadvantages of human-powered devices, efficient ways of harnessing human power, and examples of what others have constructed. From all of this information, you've probably come to some conclusions about the capabilities, purposes and shapes of the optimal human-powered devices. Summarized below are some key points:

- A human-powered device is appropriate when a device requires less than ¼ hp (or about 185 watts) for short durations or approximately ¹⁄₁₀ hp (or about 75 watts) for an extended period of time.

- When possible, it's preferable to power appliances such as blenders, ice-cream makers, grinders or scroll saws mechanically, rather than using your muscles to generate electricity that could then be used to power the same appliance. You'll lose less energy in the transmission process and won't have to contend with the burst of electricity a motor requires at start-up.

- Because leg muscles are larger and can generate up to four times as much power as arm muscles, pedal or treadle power should be preferred over hand power for any devices that require more than 50 watts.

- Human-powered machines are especially useful when one requires portability or operates in remote areas or where electricity is expensive or unreliable. Under other conditions, they are not always more convenient or economical than motor- or electric-powered devices. However, they can promote good health and offer a sense of empowerment.

- Compared to other drive types, chain drives capture and transmit the most muscle power. Still, belt drives and friction drives possess certain advantages, such as ease of set-up, flexibility or quietness, that make them more desirable in some cases.

- Adding flywheels and variable gearing to your invention will help you make better use of your human power and potentially drive greater loads. If you make your own flywheel, ensure that it's true and sized properly for your desired output.

- Steel is an excellent choice for custom-made frames, because of its strength, workability, durability and availability.

- If you're making your own frame and do not have the skills or tools to weld it, but are instead bolting the frame together, use nylon locking nuts to minimize the consequences of vibration over time. Check the bolts periodically to make sure they're tight.

CHAPTER 3

HUMAN-POWERED DEVICES
FOR THE KITCHEN

Perhaps no other room in the home boasts a greater abundance of human-powered devices than the kitchen. Today, still, we slice and whisk by hand. But our great-great-grandmothers also blended, pureed, pressed, ground and extruded without the aid of electricity. Motorized food preparation is a 20th-century phenomenon. And though we might occasionally play with that hand-cranked ice-cream maker we inherited, many of us left behind the manual food preparation tools.

Others, however, consider these tools necessary rather than nostalgic. A 1997 *New York Times* article featured famous chefs who preferred to do things the old-fashioned way, crushing spices with mortar and pestle, pureeing tomatoes in a hand-cranked food mill, or cooking meat on a hand-cranked rotisserie. Alice Waters of Chez Panisse in Berkeley, California, was quoted as saying, "There's a kind of information that comes from handling the food, and most modern equipment gets in the way. With all of the ease this equipment is supposed to bring, it removes you one step. Cooking is a real sen-sual thing, and you can't get the information that comes from handling the food unless you touch it, manipulate it and deal with it." Chef Eberhard Muller extolled the virtues of the hand-cranked food mill. "This is a simple instrument that has been used for centuries in Europe, and particularly in France," he said. "Most restaurants use machine-cranked ones, but when something runs fast, it whips air into the food, and the color changes dramatically."[1] I've heard similar comments from people I've interviewed who regularly use human-powered kitchen gadgets. Cooks feel more connected to the food and the process of preparing it.

This chapter includes descriptions and photos of both time-tested and newly designed human-powered kitchen devices, most of which are hand-cranked. Where possible, I've inserted notes about how and how well each device operates. First, though, in case you want to try your hand at making your own devices, this chapter offers plans for making a pedal-powered blender and for converting a hand-cranked grain mill to be pedal-powered.

Plan for Making a Pedal-Powered Blender

Many people interested in pedal power experiment first with combining a bike and a kitchen blender. A blender is an obvious choice for a human-powered machine. Its blades rely on rotary motion that can be transferred directly from a bike wheel to the blender's shaft. Mixing requires only modest amounts of power, achievable by the average cyclist. Bike-powered blenders are also a lot of fun to operate; as a result, they attract crowds at farmers' markets, concerts and green festivals.

Bikes and blenders can be combined in several ways. One is to make a universal pedal-powered electrical generator (as de-scribed in Chapter 6) and simply plug in your blender. Or you could convert the motion of the bike's wheel to the blender's shaft rotation directly, using a friction drive, as described in this plan. You may also choose from several frame types. Since this is the first plan in the book, it incorporates the simplest type of pedal-powered machine frame, a bicycle mounted in a trainer stand. This plan is further simplified by requiring you to use the base that comes with the blender, rather than crafting a custom base.

Ease of construction: Simple, using standard tools and minimal skill. For some steps it helps to have two sets of hands.

Figure 3.1 Pedal-Powered Blender

Time to make: 5 hours or less

Cost to make: $10 to $25 for scrounged parts to add to your existing bike and trainer stand

Ease of operation: Moderately easy; however, it can be a real workout if mixing thick liquids

Following is an overview of the steps in this plan:

- First, you'll disassemble your motorized blender to leave only the necessary mechanical parts.
- Next, you'll construct a shelf for the blender out of a piece of wood and two pieces of steel conduit and connect this shelf to your bike.
- Then, you'll make a shaft from a steel rod and attach that shaft to the blender's shaft with a coupling nut.
- Finally you'll fasten the blender to its shelf and add the rubber roller that will rest against the wheel and drive the shaft.

Materials

- Bike. A mountain bike will work fine, but a bike with smoother tires, such as a road bike or hybrid bike, will allow for better transfer of force between the bike's wheel and the blender shaft. (If all you have is a mountain bike, you can replace the rear tire with a smoother tread, of course.) This plan assumes that your bike has a seat-stay bridge with a center mounting hole, which is common to many bikes; however, it's easy to modify the plan if your bike doesn't.
- Bike trainer stand that fits your bike

- Blender with a square-ended, ¼" metal shaft in the base of its pitcher. I recommend finding an Oster-brand blender. New or old, these are the simplest to convert to a friction-drive bicycle blender, and I've found them to be readily available from thrift stores for $10 or less. This plan was written to be used with Oster-brand blenders, but other similar styles could probably be substituted. Avoid brands that have plastic cams in the pitcher bases. (I've discovered that Hamilton Beach and Kitchen Aid brands are more difficult to convert to bike blenders.) Blenders whose electrical systems don't work, such as those with worn-out motors, are fine for this project.
- One piece of 2 × 12 dimensional lumber approximately 12" long to act as a shelf for the blender
- Two 15" lengths of ½" or ¾"-diameter steel conduit (or tube)
- One hanger bolt, ¼"-diameter and 3" long (a hanger bolt has a wood screw on one end and a bolt on the other), plus matching washer and nut for bolt end
- Two ¼"-diameter machine screws 1" long and matching nuts for attaching the shelf and its supporting conduit tubes to the bike frame's rear rack braze-ons or eyelets
- Two wood screws 2" long for connecting the top of the conduit tubes to the wooden shelf
- Four ¼"-diameter machine screws 4" long and matching washers and nuts for mounting the blender base to the shelf
- A rubber stopper approximately 1.5" in diameter, with a pre-drilled center hole, for

the roller.* (If ordering from a lab supply company or buying at a hardware store, choose a Size 8 stopper with a single hole. While it's possible to drill a hole in a solid rubber stopper, it's very difficult to make that hole perfectly vertical and centered.) See the variations at the end of this project for alternative roller possibilities.

- One ¼"-diameter steel round stock approximately 10" long*
- One ¼" to ¼" coarse-thread steel coupling nut*
- One ¼"-diameter metal shaft collar for securing the rubber roller in place on the shaft*
- At least four fender washers no larger than 1" in diameter with ¼" holes*
- One ¼"-diameter coarse-thread hex nut for base of shaft (below roller)*

Confirm that the shaft inside your blender is ¼" in diameter before purchasing these parts. If your shaft diameter differs, change the size of the steel round stock, coupling nut, shaft collar, washers and nut accordingly.

Tools
- Measuring tape
- Permanent marker
- Pencil
- Safety goggles
- Hacksaw
- Handsaw or chop saw
- Phillips head screwdriver
- A set of hex-head socket drivers
- Wire cutter
- Drill with ³⁄₁₆", ¼" and ⁵⁄₁₆" bits
- Die stock and die for ¼" coarse thread
- Vise-grip pliers
- A large vise (on workbench)
- Allen wrench small enough to tighten shaft collars
- Pliers
- Steel square (or similar square)
- Center punch
- Workbench or other sturdy work surface

Steps for Making a Pedal-Powered Blender

1. Secure your bike in the trainer stand. (Follow the manufacturer's instructions for proper use.) Normally this simply involves lining up the rear wheel axle (or skewer) with the cups on the stand, and then tightening those cups against the axle. It's also helpful to use a piece of wood or a stabilizing block to keep the front wheel from wobbling.

2. Disengage the trainer stand's resistance mechanism. On many popular trainer stands you do this by loosening the adjustment knob until the resistance unit no longer touches the rear tire.

3. Now that your bike is fixed in place, you'll begin to convert your blender.
   Note: Do not allow the blender to be plugged in at any point during this project!

4. Remove the pitcher, blade and rubber gasket from the base of your blender and set them aside. You'll reattach them later.

5. Turn your blender's base upside down and notice how the bottom panel is attached. Typically, it's fixed with 3 or 4 screws (they may be Phillips head or socket hex head, for which you'll need a socket driver). Remove the screws and set them aside. You'll use them later.

6. After opening up your blender's base, get a sense of how the fan and motor are attached to the housing. In an Oster-brand blender, the lowermost component is the fan, then above that sits a bracket, the stator (or coil), the rotor, and another bracket. All are centered on a ¼" metal shaft. Figure 3.2 illustrates the typical arrangement of parts within an Oster-brand blender base. In the next few steps you'll remove as much of the blender's interior as necessary to free the shaft for a coupling and extension. With this as the goal, you might need to remove only a fan on your blender, or you might need to remove virtually everything in the base.

7. Using the wire cutters, snip the electrical cord where it terminates inside the blender base. Then remove the electrical cord from the blender's bottom panel and discard. (If it's not possible to pull the electrical cord out, cut it close to either side of the bottom panel.) Similarly remove any other wires that might get in your way during Step 8.

8. Remove the fan and the coil and any brackets that fix those to the blender's base. However, leave the rotor, as it likely contains bearings that will help the blender run even while pedal-powered. You will not need the screws that hold in the fan and the coil. If any screws are necessary to attach the rotor's frame to the base, keep those available for later use.

9. The very end of the blender's shaft might be threaded like a machine screw. If it is not, skip to Step 10. If the shaft *is* threaded, check to see whether it fits into the cou-

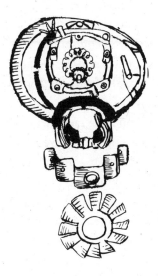

Figure 3.2 Parts Inside a Blender Base

pling nut that you bought. Chances are it's fine-threaded, rather than coarse-threaded. If that's the case, you'll need to remove the shaft from the blender and re-thread it with the die stock and die, as described in Steps 10 through 13, then put it back in the blender. However, if the base of the shaft is coarse-threaded and fits in the coupling nut, set aside the blender for now and go to Step 14.

10. Before attempting to remove the shaft from the blender, make sure no screws remain to fasten any parts inside the base. (That is, make sure the only reason the rotor remains in the base is because the shaft can't be pulled out.)

11. Lock the square metal drive stud that sticks up above the top of the base with vise-grip pliers. Grab the opposite, lower end of the shaft with pliers and unscrew the shaft from the base. This might take some strength, especially if the blender is old. You should be left with a long piece of

the shaft connected to the rotor (or whichever parts you couldn't remove from the blender's base) and the square drive stud plus a washer from the top side of the blender base. Set aside the drive stud and washer. You'll reattach them later.

12. Now that you've removed the shaft, secure it tightly in a vise on a workbench with the end that had pointed toward the bottom of the blender now pointing upward. Make sure the shaft is fixed in a vertical position.

13. Insert the ¼" coarse thread die in the die stock. Hold the die stock horizontally atop the end of the shaft, then turn it once to the right and begin to cut a new thread. Then turn it backwards to clear the metal out of the thread. (It might take a few tries to set properly.) Repeat the forward and backward rotations until you have cut approximately ¾" of new thread.

14. Using the pliers and vise-grip pliers, replace the shaft in the blender by connecting the square drive stud and washer from the top side of the base to the long shaft you just threaded that goes in the bottom side of the base. Reattach the rotor if it's held in place with screws. Set aside the blender for now.

15. Next, you'll make the blender's shelf and its supports. Hold the 2" × 12" × 12" piece of wood above the rear wheel so that its length is roughly centered over the wheel. Also hold it high enough so that its front face hits the bike's seat-stay bridge. In the next few steps you'll mark and cut this face to match the angle of the seat stays.

16. Using a marking pen, draw a line on the wood to indicate the angle of the seat stays where they will meet the 2" plane of the wood.

17. Saw the wood along the diagonal mark that you made in Step 16.

18. The board will be fastened to your bike's seat-stay bridge along the edge you cut in Step 17 with a hanger bolt. Mark a dot at the intersection of the horizontal and vertical center lines on the board face that you cut in Step 17. Also note the angle of the seat-stay bridge mounting hole, if one exists.

19. Using a ³⁄₁₆" bit, drill a hole about ¾" deep on the dot you drew in Step 18. The seat-stay bridge mounting hole is usually angled, so drill this hole at an angle that matches it.

20. Screw the wood-screw side of the hanger bolt into the hole you drilled in Step 19.

21. Now insert the bolt side of the hanger bolt in the seat-stay bridge mounting hole and affix the matching washer and nut on the other side of the seat-stay bridge.

22. The board should be held firm and level now by the hanger bolt. However, it's not yet stable enough to support a functioning blender. Next, you'll create two side supports for this shelf from the pieces of steel conduit.

23. Hold a piece of conduit so that one end is about ½" lower than the rack mount braze-on or eyelet at the bottom of the seat stay on one side of the wheel's axis (making sure that this tolerance will allow it to lie flat against the rack mount).

Rest the top end against the outside edge of the blender shelf.

24. Now angle the piece of conduit so that its outer edge just touches the back corner of the shelf. Using a marking pen, trace a horizontal line on the conduit where it meets the top of the shelf. Then trace another line at the bottom of the shelf. Also while holding the conduit in this position, use a pencil to make a temporary mark somewhere in the middle of the conduit to indicate which side of the frame it belongs on and which direction is up.

25. Repeat Steps 23 and 24 with the second piece of conduit on the other side of the wheel.

26. Now place one piece of conduit in a vise so that the horizontal line indicating the bottom of the shelf is flush with the side of the vise. Using the hacksaw, cut the piece of conduit along the horizontal line that indicates the top of the shelf.

27. Tighten the vise to flatten the last two inches of the piece of conduit. (If your vise isn't large or sturdy enough to do this, you could instead use a hammer to flatten the ends, but this takes a bit more strength.)

28. Repeat Steps 26 and 27 for the second piece of conduit.

29. Next, you'll need to mark points for drilling holes in the flattened ends of the pieces of conduit. Hold the pieces of conduit in position against the frame once more. Using the marking pen, place dots on the flattened tops and bottoms of the conduit pieces where the machine screws will attach them to the rack mount at the bottom and to the wooden shelf at the top. These should be ½" to ¾" from the end.

30. Using a center punch, punch a guide hole on each of the four marks you made on the conduit ends.

31. With the ¼" bit, drill holes through the pieces of conduit at each guide hole you created in Step 30.

32. Fasten the bottom side of each conduit tube to the frame's rack mount holes with the 1"-long ¼"-diameter machine screws and nuts.

33. In turn, hold each of the conduit tubes against the side of the shelf at the rear, where you want it to be fastened. Using the marking pen, place a dot on the wood through the center of the hole you drilled at the top of the piece of conduit.

34. With the ³⁄₁₆" bit, drill holes on the marks you made in Step 33.

35. Use the 2"-long wood screws to tighten the top ends of the conduit against the sides of the wooden shelf. The shelf should now be securely fastened to the frame of your stationary pedal-powered drive, as shown in Figure 3.3.

36. Next, you'll determine length and positioning for the homemade shaft extender. Slide the rubber stopper onto one end of the ¼" steel rod with the narrower end of the rubber stopper pointing upward. Since blender blades rotate counterclockwise, you want the rubber stopper to also rotate counterclockwise. This means that the stopper should rest against the left side of the rear wheel. (When you are facing this side of the wheel as someone's

Figure 3.3 Attached Blender Shelf

pedaling, it, too, should be spinning counterclockwise.)

37. Hold the rubber stopper tightly against the left side of the rear tire, then pivot the rod to the rear underside of the wooden shelf. Using the pencil, mark the top of the wooden shelf to indicate where the rod hits the wood (that is, the distance from the right or left edge of the board).

38. Now pivot the rod to the left side of the wooden shelf, making sure the rubber stopper rests against the apex of the wheel. Using the pencil, mark the top of the wooden shelf to indicate where the rod intersects the wood.

39. Set the rod aside and, using a square, draw two lines, one perpendicular to the edge of the wooden shelf and in line with each of the pencil marks you just made. Mark the intersection of these two lines with a dot.

40. Using a ⁵⁄₁₆" bit, drill a hole through the

blender shelf at the dot you marked in Step 39. (Before drilling, make sure that your drill bit will not approach the tire when it leaves the wood.)

41. Next, you need to determine where to drill the holes for the screws that will secure the blender base to the wooden shelf. Retrieve the bottom panel of the blender base. If it has rubber feet, remove these temporarily. Determine where the blender's shaft is located (for example, if the fan vents are in a circular pattern, the shaft would sit directly in the center of this). Align the panel so that the blender's shaft will be centered over the hole you drilled in Step 40 and, using the pen, mark the position of each of the four feet on the wooden shelf.

42. Using a ³⁄₁₆" bit, drill a hole through each of the four marks you made in Step 41.

43. Take another look at the blender base's bottom panel. Chances are that there are holes in the plastic or metal where you removed the rubber feet. If not, drill ¼" holes in these spots now.

44. You also need to create a hole for the shaft in this panel before reattaching the panel to the blender base. Depending on its age, the panel probably has metal or plastic where the extended shaft needs to come through the bottom. Use the ⁵⁄₁₆" bit to drill a hole at that position in the bottom panel. This hole needs to be wide enough to allow the coupling nut to fit through, so you might need to circle the bit around in a wider arc.

45. Now you're ready to reassemble the blender in its new form. Insert one of the

four 4"-long machine screws through the top of the blender's bottom panel feet and through the rubber feet, so that the machine screws stick out the bottom of the panel. The underside of the blender should now look like the illustration in Figure 3.4. It's almost ready to mount on the shelf.

46. Using the four screws you removed in Step 5, reattach the bottom panel to the base of the blender. The shaft's coupling should extend just to or through the hole you drilled in Step 40.

47. Align the blender base so that the coupling is centered over the shaft hole and the four machine screws are centered over their holes. Push the machine screws through the four holes so that the blender base rests flush with the top of the wooden shelf.

48. Affix the nuts to secure the machine bolts and hold the blender base tightly in place.

49. Now you're ready to create the shaft extension. Determine how long this must be by holding the shaft with the rubber roller attached up through the hole you drilled in Step 40 and tight against the coupling.

50. Adjust the rubber roller so that its side rests flush against the tire and so that its bottom edge does not quite reach the tire's rim. The more surface area touching the tire, the more power you'll transfer from the rear wheel to the blender. Below the rubber roller you need only enough length to attach one of the collars and a hex nut, or about ¾". Use the pen to draw

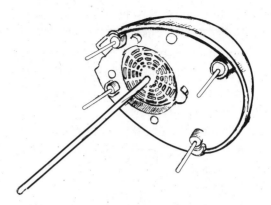

Figure 3.4 Underside of Blender Ready For Mounting

a line that indicates where the bottom of the shaft extension should fall.

51. Remove the rubber roller from the shaft extension and, using the hacksaw, cut the steel rod at the mark you made in Step 50.

52. Follow Step 13 to cut a thread on both ends of the shaft extension.

53. Insert one end of the shaft extension up through the blender's shaft hole in the wooden shelf and, while holding the small square end of the shaft that sticks up above the base in a vise grip, tighten the shaft extension into the coupler. Now your blender's shaft is extended to reach the rear tire.

54. At the other end of the shaft attach the metal shaft collar in a position just above where the top of the rubber roller will fall. Tighten it with the appropriate Allen wrench.

55. Add a fender washer below the shaft collar.

56. Next, add the rubber roller to the shaft so that it's tight against the fender washer and shaft collar above it.

57. Add a fender washer below the rubber roller. If you miscalculated and left too much room between the bottom of the rubber roller and the threaded shaft end, you can fill the space with a few additional fender washers now.

58. Finally, add the ¼" hex nut below the lower collar. Tighten securely. Try turning the rear wheel to make sure the whole shaft rotates when the wheel causes the rubber roller to rotate. If the roller simply revolves around the shaft, you need to compress it more firmly between the shaft collar, washers and hex nut. The end of the shaft should now look like the diagram in Figure 3.5.

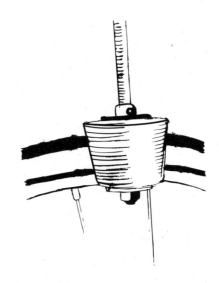

Figure 3.5 Rubber Stopper Affixed to Blender Shaft

Frederick Breeden and Just Soap

Handcrafting soap requires a lot of mixing. Frederick Breeden of Just Soap makes soaps, salves and shampoos for over 100 retailers across the US. At first he mixed the batches by hand, but as business grew, this proved too slow, not to mention exhausting. Yet he couldn't justify buying a big electric mixer. Being a passionate recreational and commuter bicyclist, Frederick knew the power of leg muscles. So he wondered whether it was possible to run a soap mixer with a bicycle. He searched local bike shops and found a skilled bicycle builder who shared his enthusiasm for the idea. Together they engineered what Frederick calls "a beautiful, wonderfully built machine." Still, it was a gamble. "I was spending all this money and we had no idea whether a human could mix in a sufficient way that the whole thing becomes homogenous and uniform."

But the bicycle blender worked well. In fact, Frederick was surprised at how easy it was to

Figure 3.6 Frederick Breeden and His Bicycle-Powered Soap Blender

59. Reposition the rubber gasket, blade and pitcher on the blender's base.
60. Get seated, cycle and test your pedal-powered blender.

Variations and Considerations

- If your bike already has a rear rack, you can use that as a base for mounting the blender on the back of the bike, rather than making a shelf from wood and supports from electrical conduit.
- If you don't have a bike trainer stand, you can make your own using angle iron or another frame-suitable material.
- The larger the wheel, the greater the gear ratio between the wheel and rubber stopper. This will help you spin the blender's shaft at higher rpm.
- Many small, round objects can be substituted for the rubber roller. To give the bike blender greater longevity and durability, some inventors use a rollerblade wheel. However, you first need to remove the central bearings from these wheels; otherwise the shaft will spin within the rollerblade wheel, and force from your bicycle wheel will not be transferred to the blender shaft. You could also make a roller out of a drum sander attachment for a drill whose shaft is the same size as your blender's extended shaft. (I've tried this with success, too.)

pedal. The only changes made to the original design were to add a fixed gear on the back to allow Frederick to pedal both forwards and backwards and to substitute a larger flywheel, thereby giving the mixer more speed.

To mix one batch of soap, or 440 pounds of liquid, he pedals between 20 to 90 minutes, often in intervals of 5 minutes of pedaling and 5 minutes of resting. Timing depends on the characteristics of each batch — and this is where pedal-powered blending trumps motor-powered blending. As the mixture of oil and lye begins to thicken, pedaling becomes increasingly more difficult, and Frederick can sense how close the batch is to being finished. "I have to be totally aware and concentrating on the soap because otherwise it's going to go past the point where I can control it…. [I'm] getting a feel for the particular batch. I like the connection." Frederick also appreciates that with no motor running, making soap is a quiet activity.

After 8 years of regular use and despite its large number of working parts, the bicycle blender has required absolutely no maintenance. It works as well today as it did on day one. "I don't know how many motors would have lasted that long or whether a commercial mixer would have lasted that long," Frederick told me.

Business at Just Soap is brisk and growing. Besides preferring Frederick's products, some customers especially admire his bike-blending process. "It definitely appeals to people who are interested in alternative ways of manufacturing, who like that I'm small-scale, but able to produce in a way that can sufficiently make the product and keep the prices low. A lot of folks like me because they're cyclists and they love seeing things done with pedal power." Frederick has even been asked whether he'd sell the machine or the plans to make it. So far his answer has been "no."[2]

- If your bike doesn't have a seat-stay bridge, you can still insert the hanger bolt as described in Steps 18 through 20. However, rather than fasten the bolt through a seat-stay bridge mounting hole, use a mending plate wide enough to span both seat stays on the opposite side of the seat stays from the blender shelf. Drill a hole in the mending plate that lines up with your hanger bolt. Then secure the mending plate against the seat stays by tightening the appropriate nut on the bolt.

- Because it's convenient to face the blender while mixing liquids, you could use a stationary bike, on which the front wheel rotates, as the pedal-power drive, creating a shelf for the blender that's suspended from the head tube and the front wheel's axle.

- If you prefer to mix while mobile, try taking your bike out of the trainer stand and blending as you cycle.

Plan for Converting a Hand-Cranked Grain Mill to Pedal Power

If you grind your own wheat berries into flour just before baking, you know how much better it tastes than purchased flour ground far away and who knows when. Grinding grain requires little enough effort to be easily human powered. However, grinding by hand can get tiresome. Some people connect their hand-cranked grain grinder to a stationary bike to make the work easier. This plan describes one way of doing that.

Several manufacturers make hand-cranked grain mills, and although they might look different, all follow a common design. A

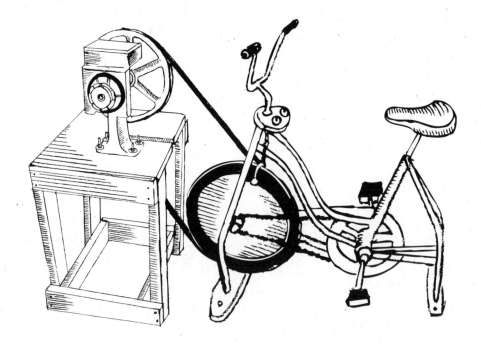

Figure 3.7 Hand-Cranked Grain Mill Converted to Pedal Power

crank turns an auger that drives wheat berries, corn kernels or other grain seeds toward grinding stones or steel burrs that crush the seeds. This plan is designed for a Diamant or Country Living brand grain mill, which, though relatively expensive, are considered by many to be the most durable, quick and effective human-powered grain mills on the market. Both are also simple to convert to pedal power, since their cranks are attached to cast-iron, grooved wheels. If you have a different mill, you can adjust the plan for its design, and such an adjustment might involve adding a pulley to the mill's crankshaft. In addition to modifying a stationary bike to act as the driving mechanism, this plan walks you through building a custom stand for the grain mill.

Ease of construction: Very simple, using standard tools and moderate skill.
Time to make: 4 hours or less
Cost to make: $30 to $40 for parts from the hardware store, assuming you have a stationary bike and grain mill
Ease of operation: Very easy

Following is an overview of the steps in this plan:

- First, you'll modify the stationary bike's front wheel to accept a pulley belt.
- Next, you'll construct a stand for your grain mill and bolt the mill to the stand.
- Then, you'll connect the stand to the stationary bike for stability.

Materials
- Stationary bike. Refer to Chapter 2's "Scrounging For Parts" section for hints

on how to choose the best type. For this plan you must have one with an accessible front wheel.
- Hand-cranked grain mill with a grooved wheel, such as the Diamant or Country Living grain mill. Measure the holes in the mill's base. The size of the four carriage bolts used to mount the mill to the stand should match the diameter of these holes. In this plan, the holes are assumed to be ⅜" in diameter.
- 1-inch wide nonskid (or "safety") tread tape — optional, and sometimes pricey; if you can't find 1-inch wide tape, you can get 2-inch wide tape (which I've found to be more common) and cut it to fit
- One A-series pulley belt, 100" long
- Seven pieces of 2 × 4 dimensional lumber cut to 18" long
- Four pieces of 2 × 4 dimensional lumber cut to 24" long
- Extra length of 2 × 4 dimensional lumber (no more than 2' long) or other wood to cut into shims
- One piece of ¾" plywood that measures 18" by 25"
- 36 wood screws 3-⅛" long
- Four carriage bolts ⅜" diameter and 3" long, with matching washers and nuts*

Tools
- Workbench
- Measuring tape
- String or twine
- Marking pen or pencil
- Steel square (or framing square)
- Handsaw or chop saw
- Circular saw

- Set of open-ended wrenches
- Two pry bars or long-handled flathead screwdrivers (optional)
- Wood chisel and mallet
- Workbench or other sturdy surface
- Drill with ⅜" bit*

*This assumes that the mounting holes in the base of your grain mill are ⅜" in diameter. If yours are different, change as necessary.

Steps for Converting a Hand-Cranked Grain Mill to Pedal Power

1. To get a pulley belt around the stationary bike's front wheel, you have to remove it. Begin by removing from the bike anything that might provide resistance or prove to be an obstacle, such as brake pads or resistance rollers (used to vary the intensity of a person's workout). Also remove the chain guard, if one exists. Further, it's important to remove any part that extends downward from the head tube or fork and that might get in the way of a pulley belt wrapped around the front wheel and the mill's wheel.

2. On some stationary bikes, the front wheel is fastened not simply with nuts on a center bolt, but with an eye bolt and plate that are perpendicular to the front axle (the plate might be part of the chain guard). In any case, remove all nuts and bolts that hold the front wheel's axle in the fork. Keep these handy so you can reattach the wheel later.

3. In order to free the wheel, you'll first have to slip off the chain that connects the front sprocket to the chainring. When you removed the nuts in Step 2, you should have

loosened the front wheel enough to swivel it slightly toward the chainring, thereby giving the chain some slack. Disengage the chain from the front wheel's sprocket.

4. Now remove the front wheel from the bike.

5. Steps 5 through 9 are optional and will work only with the type of stationary bike wheel fashioned with a tire around a rim (similar to a normal bicycle). Following these steps will help transfer the most possible power from your bike's wheel to the grain mill's wheel. However, it's not required. Remove the tire from the wheel you took off in Step 4. If it's a soft rubber wheel, you might be able to pry it off using a couple of pry bars or long-handled flathead screwdrivers. If it's a hard plastic wheel, you'll probably have to cut it off with a hacksaw.

6. Measure the inside width of your tire's metal rim (the width of the valley).

7. Next, you need to determine the rim's circumference. Hold one end of a long piece of string against any point on the rim's valley. Then wrap the string around the rim and mark where the string meets the starting point. Remove the string and then use a tape measure to measure this distance on the string.

8. Cut a piece of antislip tread tape to the width you measured in Step 6 (if the tape is wider than the inside of the rim) and the length you measured in Step 7.

9. Apply the piece of tread tape you cut in Step 8 to the valley of the wheel's rim.

10. Now you're ready to position your pulley belt. Wrap the belt loosely around

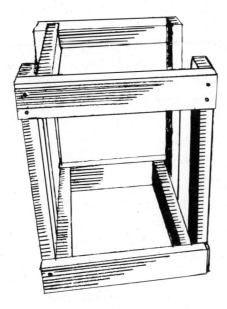

Figure 3.8 Braces Connected to Legs

the wheel and then put the wheel back in place, but don't tighten the nuts until you guide the chain back onto the front sprocket. Then tighten the nuts to fix the wheel in place.

11. Next, you'll make a stand to hold the grain mill. Of course, there are many ways to create a suitable stand. For this plan I've simply used pieces of leftover 2 × 4s, but you could also make a stand out of angle iron or even a small table. The four 24" lengths of 2 × 4 will make the stand's legs, while the seven 18" lengths will form braces at top and near the bottom of the stand. (You'll only use braces on three sides at the top of the stand, so that nothing gets in the way of the pulley belt.)

12. Using the 3-⅛" wood screws, screw the seven 18" lengths of 2 × 4 into the four 24" lengths of 2 × 4 as shown in Figure 3.8 to make the base of the grain mill stand. The

braces should meet at the very top and the very bottom of the legs.

13. Next, you'll create a slot in the plywood table top for the pulley. Place the 18" × 25" piece of plywood on top of the stand and center it, but don't screw it down yet. The wider dimension will be perpendicular to the bike's wheel and will extend 2" off the edge of the stand on each side.

14. Position the stand in front of the stationary bike with the side that's missing a top brace facing the bike. For taking the first measurement, you can place it as close as possible to the bike. Align the stand's center with the bike's front wheel.

15. Use the square to extend the edges of the front wheel to the side of the plywood and mark both edges as shown in Figure 3.9. This indicates how wide the slot in the plywood needs to be to accommodate the belt.

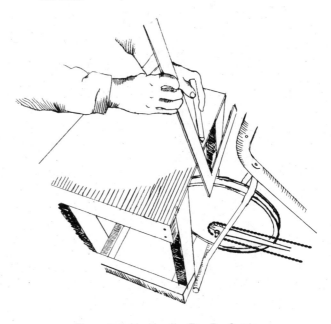

Figure 3.9 Marking the Top For Cutting

16. Using the square as a guide, extend the marks you created in Step 15 to be 12" long.

17. Next, you'll remove the portion of the top necessary to allow the pulley belt free motion. Take the top off the stand and then, at your workbench, use a circular saw to cut along the lines you marked in Step 16. Use a wood chisel and mallet to knock out the last side of the rectangle that needs to be removed.

18. Set the plywood top on the stand so that the slot you cut lines up with the stationary bike's front wheel. Affix the top to the stand with the remaining 3-⅛" wood screws, one at each corner.

19. Set the grain mill on the stand so that its grooved wheel is centered over the slot you cut in Step 17. Mark the location of the mounting holes in the grain mill's base on the top of the stand.

20. Remove the mill from the stand for now, and then drill ⅜" clearance holes at the places you marked in Step 19. The top of the stand when viewed from above should look similar to what's in Figure 3.10.

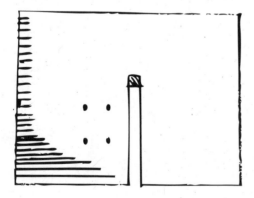

Figure 3.10 Top of Stand

21. Put the mill back on the stand, aligning its mounting holes with the holes you drilled in Step 20. Using the four carriage bolts, washers and nuts, bolt the mill's base to the stand's top.

22. Next, you'll need to determine the optimal distance between the mill stand and the stationary bike. Wrap the pulley belt around the mill's grooved wheel, then slide the stand away from the bike until the belt is taut. (This is easier to do with two people.) Measure the space between the stand's legs and the stationary bike's front feet.

23. Cut two shims from a 2 × 4 that are slightly longer than the measurement you took in Step 22. This will ensure that your pulley belt is as tight as possible.

24. With the belt still wrapped around the grain mill's wheel and the stationary bike's wheel, insert the shims so that one end presses against one of the stand's legs and the other end presses against the stationary bike's front feet, as shown in Figure 3.11.

25. Pour some wheat berries or corn kernels into your mill's hopper, and try grinding. If the pulley belt slips, try inserting slightly wider shims. (However, be careful not to use shims that are so thick that they cause the stand to tilt forward.) Maintain a moderate pace, because grinding too fast risks overheating the burrs and compromising the flour's nutritional value.

Variations and Considerations

• Rather than making a custom stand, some people bolt the grain mill to the side of a small table, so that its grooved wheel extends beyond the table's edge. You'll still need to steady the table, either by attaching it to the stationary bike, weighting it down, or affixing it to the floor or a wall.

- For an ideal pace, rather than wrapping the pulley belt around the stationary bike's front wheel, use a 3- or 4-inch pulley attached to the wheel's axle. This requires a front axle wide enough to accept the added pulley, and it might involve a visit to a machinist's shop to customize a pulley to fit on the bike's axle. Grinding will proceed more slowly, but the turning will be easier and smoother. It's best to keep the bike's wheel attached to the axle even after adding a pulley so you can take advantage of its flywheel effect, however small.
- You could use the same plan with other hand-cranked devices, like ice-cream makers or juicers, after adding a pulley wheel to their crankshaft.

Figure 3.12 shows another way to convert a hand-cranked grain mill to pedal power. Lee Ravenscroft, founder of Chicago's Working Bikes Cooperative, constructed this for a friend. The drive is made from a bike frame with its head tube and handlebars removed and turned upside-down. Lee made a stand for the rear wheel from pieces of discarded bed frames bolted together. He looped the drive belt around the bicycle's tire. Then he ensured sufficient tension in the belt by attaching it and gauging the distance between the two wheels before fully inflating the tire. The advantage to using this setup compared

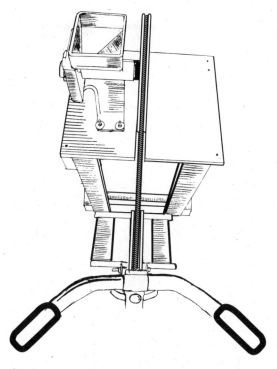

Figure 3.11 Shims Inserted for Adequate Belt Tension

Figure 3.12 Lee Ravenscroft's Pedal-Powered Grain Mill

*Figure 3.13 GSI Outdoors' Vortex
Hand-Cranked Blender*

to using a stationary bike is that it requires less space. It also allows for variable gearing. One potential disadvantage is that the pedaler is separated from the machine and therefore has to steady herself to keep from tipping back or sliding away from the device as she pedals. Given that the mill demands only a modest amount of pedaling force, however, this isn't a significant drawback.

Commercially Available Plans and Devices for the Kitchen

Despite the preponderance of motorized food preparation tools, you can still buy new human-powered blenders, mills, presses, juicers and ice-cream makers. Most of these devices also have antique counterparts. Finding one of the originals in good condition can result in significant savings. But quality, newer models often come with improved features or are crafted of materials that make them last longer.

This section doesn't attempt to cover the myriad human-powered kitchen devices. For example, it doesn't include many small, simple and inexpensive apparatuses such as apple peelers, cherry pitters, pea shellers, bean frenchers, potato ricers, pasta makers and salad spinners. But it does compare more general-purpose devices, as well as a few novel, late 20th-century innovations. Most are hand-cranked. Coffee mills, food mills and ice-cream makers, for example, are so easy to operate with arm power, there's no need to pedal-power them. Blenders, however, depending on their capacity and contents, can cross the threshold of comfortable hand-powering. Following are examples of both hand-cranked and pedal-powered blenders.

Hand-Cranked Blender

GSI Outdoors makes the Vortex hand-cranked blender pictured in Figure 3.13. The long handle can be attached to either one of two square-ended pins in the base for low power or high power blending. The casing and pitcher are made of sturdy plastic, but the base is heavy enough to stabilize the machine while you crank. The Vortex blender comes with a C-clamp for mounting to a counter or shelf. You can also buy a trailer hitch mounting kit and table to mix drinks by the tailgate. It's marketed mostly to campers, and it seems to be popular among this crowd. In 2002 a representative for the outdoor equipment retailer REI remarked that it was one of their fastest selling products.

Users of the blender, including myself, have found that it blends liquids with moderate effort at low or high speed. Crushing ice or blending thicker substances, like waffle batter, can demand significant effort and is best begun with the handle attached to the low power connector. Like any electric blender, the Vortex makes quite a bit of noise during operation. Make sure the blender is securely clamped to a shelf or counter before starting to crank.

At the time this was written GSI Outdoors' hand-cranked blender sold for $69.95 and was available direct from GSI Outdoors' online store at gsioutdoors.com (under the "Party" subcategory of products), as well as at many outdoor equipment retailers.

Pedal-Powered Blender

Although pedal-powered blenders are easy to fabricate in a home workshop or garage, some people might prefer a spiffy, mechanically optimized model with a warranty and a buyback policy in case you decide that pedal-powering your breakfast smoothies is not for you. For those folks, there's Byerley Bicycle Blenders.

Early in 2001 Nate Byerley, a self-described "bike freak," read an article that featured Bart Orlando's pedal-powered devices in use at Humboldt State University. He'd always imagined combining his love of bicycling and food in some kind of business. Inspired by Bart's pedal-powered blender, Nate cobbled together a bike blender of his own and brought it to the Critical Mass gathering in San Fran-

cisco in the autumn of 2001. He spent the day making margaritas for happy festival-goers. By the end of that tiring day, he'd pinpointed all the flaws in his design and noted ways to make the bike blender more efficient.

Nate improved his design and modified the blender's base to be mounted on an Xtracycle, a type of hitchless bike trailer. He then started a company called the Juice Peddler, which brought bike-powered blenders to festivals around the country and allowed attendees to make their own smoothies. Though not always profitable, Nate said, it was rewarding work.

More variations on his design followed. In 2006 a marketing firm working for Starbucks contacted Nate with a request to develop a stationary, *front-mounted* pedal-powered blender so that customers could mix their own Frappucinos. The design that resulted, the Fender Blender, has drawn curious crowds beyond the cafes. One man bought a bike blender to use at his daughter's wedding reception. Another bike blender became part of a Cambridge, Massachusetts politician's campaign that focused on sustainable transportation issues. (The politician won.) Nate said that although he preferred the concept of a mobile bike blender, he supported any way of attracting people to human power.[3]

Byerley Bicycle Blenders are available for purchase on the Web at bikeblender.com. At the time this was written, the B3, a bike-blender attachment for an Xtracycle trailer, cost $349. The Mini-B3, shown in Figure 3.14, is a blender with a shelf and supports that attaches to any bike as a rear rack. It cost $249. The complete Fender Blender setup, a stationary bike blender, cost $1,899. The site also allows you to order bike blender setups that include a bike.

Grain Mills

Since Neolithic times people have ground grain between stones. The earliest method of grinding involved a quern, or a stone base containing a round or saddle-shaped depression. Another stone was rolled or turned over the grain spread in that depression to crush it and make flour. (In Mexico, a quern is known as a metate.) Rotary querns, in which the user rotated the top stone with a primitive, attached handle, came along sometime around 200 BC. Besides demanding a formidable amount of work, querns had the added disadvantage of introducing small flecks of stone into the

Figure 3.14 Byerley Bicycle Mini B₃ Blender

flour. Prehistoric skeletons reveal what these stones did to teeth. Romans and Greeks improved on querns by enlarging them, grooving the stones, and using first horses or slaves, and then water or wind as milling power. Hand-cranked mills came along much later, however, because the invention of the crankshaft took place only recently in human development.

To grind grain into flour at home, you could try the Neolithic approach and crush it in a stone mortar and pestle or on a metate, still available from a few specialty cookware stores. However, I recommend embracing the invention of the crankshaft and using a modern-style grain mill. There are plenty to choose from. Of all the human-powered kitchenware described in this chapter, possibly the greatest variation and selection occur in grain mills.

Modern human-powered grain mills grind using either stone or metal burrs. In the first type, two stones aligned close together on a horizontal axis crush grain seeds between them when you rotate the crank. In mills that use metal burrs, one burr remains stationary while the other turns and crushes seed against it. Home flour grinding purists consider stone grinding superior to metal-burr grinding, since stones don't risk heating the flour and compromising its nutrition and taste as readily. The potential disadvantage to using stone grinders, however, is that moist or oily substances can clog them, and therefore they aren't recommended for pulverizing oil seeds or nuts. Also, metal burrs grind faster and will not chip if a stone comes through with the wheat berries, for example. On the other hand, grinding stones are considered self-sharpening, and they make slightly less noise during operation than burrs. However, none of these mills is quiet.

In addition to using different grinding methods, hand-cranked grain mills can differ in construction, material, cost, hopper capacity and the extent to which you can control the flour's fineness.

One highly recommended mill is the Country Living Grain Mill, which grinds with hardened steel burrs. Its body is made of powder-coated cast aluminum, its auger is steel, and it comes with a heavy cast-iron flywheel, which helps smooth the output of your cranking. The manufacturer claims that the Country Living Grain Mill is the only hand-cranked grain mill engineered with sealed bearing assemblies, rather than bushings, for greater drive shaft stability. The mill's wheel is relatively easy to rotate, but if you want better leverage, you can purchase a handle extender. And because the flywheel is grooved, it can accept a V-belt and be easily converted to pedal power. The mill's base contains four holes so that it can be bolted to a flat surface. At the time this was written, the Country Living Grain Mill, pictured in Figure 3.15, sold for about $350 and came with a one-year warranty.

Like the Country Living Grain Mill, the Diamant mill also features a heavy cast-iron flywheel and mounting holes in its base. However, the Diamant is even heavier, weighing in at 58 pounds, because of its powder-coated cast iron housing. Unlike the Country Living Grain Mill, it can be ordered with stone grinders or one of several cast iron burrs for grind-

ing flour to varying fineness. Its manufacturer claims that because of the mill's larger burrs, it grinds grain faster than other hand-cranked models. Made in Denmark, the Diamant mill sells for about $850 and comes with a one-year warranty.

A mill that grinds exclusively with stones comes from Schnitzer, a German company. As do the Country Living and Diamant grain mills, the Schnitzer Country mill has a high-capacity hopper capable of holding about four cups of grain seed. Unlike those mills, Schnitzer's mill offers a numbered fineness adjuster dial, making it easy to gauge your

Figure 3.15 Country Living Grain Mill

flour's grind and remember what setting you prefer. (The others allow adjustment, but without the numbered dial.) Users report that Schnitzer's Country Mill grinds slower than previously described burr-type mills — but bear in mind that grinding time depends on what you're grinding (corn versus wheat, hard red spring wheat versus soft white winter wheat, for example) and how fine you've chosen to grind it. It weighs almost 18 pounds and mounts to the counter with a clamp. Its casing is made of wood and stainless steel, and its funnel is made of aluminum. At the time this was written the Schnitzer Country Mill was available for approximately $430 and came with a 2-year warranty. A smaller Schnitzer stone mill is available for about $170.

A less expensive, though still effective and recommended hand-cranked grain mill is the Family Grain Mill. It uses cone-shaped steel burrs to crush the grain seed. Users report that it's slower to grind than the Country Living and Diamant grain mills, and it might require you to grind the same grain twice to obtain fine pastry flour. Another potential drawback is that its auger and housing are made of plastic. The Family Grain Mill offers several attachments, including one for grain rolling or flaking. Made in Germany, it costs approximately $120 for the base and only the flour attachment and comes with a 5-year warranty.

In case you're confused about which mill to buy, Lehman's, a retailer of goods for country and off-grid living, offers an online tool to help you determine which of the ten mills they sell is best suited to your family's needs. To access this tool, search for "grain interview" on the Lehman's site at lehmans.com. For a thorough review of all types of home grain mills, hand-cranked and electric, as well as mill use and maintenance tips, check out Marleeta F. Basey's *Flour Power: A Guide To Modern Home Grain Milling.*

If you're especially ambitious, you can craft a hand-cranked flour mill in your workshop. In 1976 Enterprise Works/VITA, a not-for-profit organization based in Washington, DC, published a technical bulletin that provides instructions. The plans specify plywood, common metal hardware, and stone for grinding "that can be found along lake shores, river banks and in open fields." Construction appears to be simple, if time consuming, though you have to round and smooth the stones into discs. Limestone is suggested as a workable, quality type of stone for this use. Request the plans from Enterprise Works/VITA via their Web site, enterpriseworks.org.

Coffee Mills

Many hand-cranked coffee mills closely resemble grain mills in their design and operation. Nearly all rely on steel burrs. In some mills the shaft spins a conical burr over another burr that's stationary. In other mills, both burrs are disks. Whether manual or electric, burr-style coffee mills create more uniformly sized particles than blade grinders, which shred the coffee beans. (Most small, inexpensive electric coffee grinders are blade grinders.) Uniformly sized grounds, as coffee brewers know, are key to a quality beverage. And as with flour milling, the speed characteristic of blade grinders is not necessarily better. By grinding beans slowly you won't risk overheating the grounds and corrupting the coffee's flavor.

One of the greatest advantages of hand milling coffee, however, is not having to listen to the high-pitched whine of a motorized coffee grinder first thing in the morning. Milling coffee requires very little effort, too. In my experience, grinding enough for a 12-cup press pot takes just under 5 minutes at an easy, half-awake pace. Of course, the finer your grind setting, the longer it will take, and this depends on your brewing method. For percolated coffee, you want very coarse particles; for press pots, a coarse grind; for drip coffee, a medium grind; and for espresso, a fine grind. Turkish coffee demands the finest grind, a virtual coffee powder. Some users of hand-cranked coffee mills complain that grinding beans for espresso seems to take forever. Others claim that their hand-cranked mills can grind coffee beans finer than any electric mill.

On a hand-cranked coffee mill you control the granularity of the grind by adjusting a knurled setting knob on the crankshaft near the handle. This knob pushes the burrs closer or allows more space between them. On some mills the knob is tightened in place with a cog wheel. (After weeks of daily use, this knob might loosen and result in a coarser grind, so check it periodically.) On most human-powered coffee mills the crank sits above the hopper on a vertical axis. On other mills it's mounted to one side and sometimes attached to a flywheel. The ground coffee collects in a drawer or capsule at the base of the grinder.

With coffee mills, quality varies widely, and you truly get what you pay for. (Though it should be noted that the best hand-cranked mills still cost much less than the best electric mills.) In general, stay away from the low-cost, decorative hand-cranked mills. Zassenhaus brand mills are considered top-notch. Made in Germany, they contain tool-grade, hardened-steel conical burrs and come with a 10-year warranty on the grinding mechanism. Zassenhaus offers several models, including a large mill that clamps to the counter, a Turkish mill that's cylindrical, and a "Knee Mill," which can be grasped between the knees and used in a sitting position. Prices for Zassenhaus mills range from $70 to $100. However, at the time this was written, several US suppliers claimed that these were difficult to obtain.

Peugeot of France began making coffee mills in the mid-1800s and still makes high-quality hand-cranked coffee mills today. Their models are box-style mills with top-mounted cranks. As in the Zassenhaus models, steel conical burrs grind the coffee. Costing between $85 and $130, each Peugeot coffee mill comes with a lifetime warranty on the grinding mechanism. If you're looking to spend less, you can find decent quality conical-burr hand-cranked coffee mills from other manufacturers, too. Examples include models made by Tre Spade and Camano, which range from $45 to $90.

While camping you probably don't want to pack your expensive home coffee mill. But if you still want to hand-grind your morning coffee, you can choose from a few portable models. GSI Outdoors makes the Javagrind Coffee Grinder, which is shaped like a flying saucer with a crank on top. The crank is large, metal, and can be folded over the side for more compact storage. An adjustment knob sits under the crank. A sliding door on the hopper allows beans to be poured in as with a standard box-style mill. Inside, conical ceramic burrs grind the coffee, but no bin exists to collect the grounds (the grinder is designed to fit directly over GSI's JavaPress coffee maker). Users report good outcomes with coarser grinds, but some instability during fine grinding. Other users complain that this mill is a bit difficult to hold steady while grinding. At the time this was written, the Javagrind Cof-

ChocoSol's Pedal-Powered Cacao Grinder

To ChocoSol founders Michael Sacco and Graham Corbett, bicycle-driven machines are "artisanal technology" and chocolate is an "energy unit," but both are also much more.

In January 2005 Michael was working on sustainable chocolate making with communities in Oaxaca, Mexico, roasting cacao beans in solar roasters and grinding them by hand. He figured there must be a better, faster way to grind. Then he learned of Maya Pedal and its bike-powered maize grinders in nearby Guatemala. After studying photos of Maya Pedal's devices, Michael designed a cacao bean stone grinder that looked similar to the bicimolino. Then in the spring of 2007, Carlos Marroquin Machàn, the chief mechanic for Maya Pedal, visited Oaxaca, and the two became collaborators. What resulted from their work together was a new and improved grinder design for both organizations, one that cost half as much as Maya Pedal's existing bike-powered maize grinder. This is one example among many of what Michael terms "co-design."

ChocoSol's philosophy supports local, community-based innovation. They do not plan to centrally manufacture and distribute cacao bean grinders. Instead, they hold workshops to help others understand bicycle technology so that community groups in Mexico can design and fabricate their own machines, using readily available materials and devising new uses and applications for pedal power according to their needs.

Graham and Michael have also brought novel bicycle technology to their hometown, Toronto. As chocolatiers, they use a pedal-powered cacao bean grinder, pedal-powered blender, and bicycle cargo trailers for delivery and transport. "We're not interested in making stuff for other people if we're not interested in using it ourselves. Where's the hypocrisy in that,

Figure 3.17 ChocoSol's Pedal-Powered Cacao Grinder

fee Grinder was available for about $20 direct from the manufacturer at gsioutdoors.com or from outdoor equipment stores.

I've tried the RusTek Traveler 2 Coffee Mill, manufactured by Clipper International and pictured in Figure 3.16. It's designed to al-low a firm grip with one hand while you crank with the other. It grinds using a conical steel burr. With a smaller, plastic handle and no bearings, this mill doesn't turn as easily as the pricier hand-cranked mills. As a result, you'll need more time to grind the same amount of

right? We're actually using these things that we're making, whether they're solar roasters or bicycle blenders or bicycle grinders, and a lot of the time it's by using them that we're constantly finding ways of making them better and making them practical. So the good thing is that the work we do ends up being transferred back through friendships and relationships with the people in Mexico." They even share their latest choco-late making recipes with their sister communities south of the border.

When I spoke with them, they'd recently held a chocolate-making party in Toronto, where at-tendees had to be virtually pried off the pedal-powered cacao bean grinder so others could try it. Graham remarked that the machine appealed to people on many levels: "One is the fact that the human is the motor, the engine. You're bring-ing your calories to produce food that then you would eat and have calories to burn. On an ener-getic level, you're tightening that gap that exists in our society about how we produce and con-sume food. [Also,] to know that you are respon-sible for grinding that bean…into a liquidy paste, that you are in fact the engine that is making that transformation into something that you've taken for granted, a substance that you've never fully understood and you've consumed since early on in your childhood, is a real transformative experience."

Michael and Graham continued to refine their cacao bean grinder. They connected with a rural Ontario man who, they said, possessed old-world mechanical knowledge after being raised among blacksmiths and millwrights and spending his career as a maker of agricultural machinery. He suggested they add pulleys and a flywheel with a weighted circumference to make better use of their leg power. Meanwhile, they've also replaced the first design's spartan, plywood seat with something more comfortable and changed the frame from a recumbent style to an upright. That gives pedalers the advantage of standing on the pedals when the grinding gets especially tough. One senses the pair will never stop im-proving their design and sharing their ideas with others.

Indeed, Michael suggested that more pedal-power innovation is exactly what our society needs. "Combustion engines came around and put research into pedal power on the back burner, and what we believe is that now, as we go into the age of sustainability, the age of envi-ronmental crisis, it's starting to look more attrac-tive again. The most thermodynamically efficient machine in the world with modern materials and designs can actually be seen as a step forward rather than a step backward. And it can be one that's both efficient and ecological."[4]

coffee. Also, the grinding adjustment is located somewhat inconveniently inside the coffee tray at the bottom of the unit and requires a small screwdriver to turn. Another potential disadvantage is that the crank must be removed in order to fill the hopper with beans. Still, it's functional, ergonomic and would be welcome at the morning campfire. At the time this was written, the Rustek Traveler 2 cost $24. A smaller version, the Traveler 1, cost $19. Both are available from the manufacturer at rustekonline.com and from outdoor equipment stores.

If you grind coffee in your hand-cranked mill daily, you should clean the grinding mechanism periodically. Tom and Maria Owen of Sweet Maria's in Oakland, California, who evaluate and sell fine coffee and coffeemaking equipment (and run what they call a "virtual coffee university" online), recommend grinding a handful of quick-cooking white rice in

Figure 3.16 Portable Hand-Cranked Coffee Mill

your coffee mill every three months. The rice will remove coffee-bean buildup from the burrs without leaving an undesirable scent or flavor.

Food Mills, Strainers, and Juicers

Food mills fall under the category of "better muscle-powered than motorized". A simple, hand-cranked device, the food mill doesn't quite puree, but pushes soft fruits and vegetables through a sieve. Turning the top-mounted crank rotates a blade that presses, for example, cooked apples into applesauce or tomatoes into puree. The sieve filters out pulp, skins and seeds. Food mills are also used to make seedless jam, homemade baby food and pureed soups. Some people call them, generically, "Foley mills," after the 20th-century brand that would have been familiar to all housewives of that era. The Foley brand, now owned by Mirro, still exists.

A food mill's advantage over a blender or food processor is in its relatively gentle touch. Potatoes that would turn gluey pureed in a food processor leave a food mill with perfect consistency. Tomatoes that would turn frothy in a blender instead become a smooth, dense sauce. One potential disadvantage to using food mills is that the peels, seeds and pulp can clog the holes or cause the rotating blade to get stuck. When this happens, reverse the blade's rotation so it acts as a scraper to loosen the excess.

Several companies make food mills, and they are all similar, but vary slightly in their designs. Most, though not all, come with a way to set them atop your favorite pan or bowl. Check before buying to make sure this feature is included. Suspending the mill with one hand while cranking with the other is tricky. Models also vary in the angle of their blades and in some cases, the choice of sieves. The best food mills come with three interchangeable disks whose hole sizes are characterized as fine, medium and coarse.

A 2003 article in *Cooks Illustrated* that compared food mills rated the Cuisipro brand, which currently sells for about $90, the best in their tests. The Foley food mill, which sells for about $30, comes with only one sieve size and was rated lower than most other brands because of its instability and difficulty to clean. Users report liking the OXO brand food mill because of its comfortable grip. It does come with variable sieve sizes and sells for about $50. The All-Clad food mill, pictured in Figure 3.18, also includes fine, medium and coarse sieves. It sells for about $105. Avoid buying a mill made of plastic. And when operating your metal food mill, avoid turning the blades when the mill is empty, as you could scratch or damage the mechanism.

Another style of food mill, which is clamped to a counter, has a hopper for holding fruits or vegetables and an auger to push them against the screens, as shown in Figure 3.19. This type is better known as a hand-cranked strainer, a tomato strainer, or a tomato machine, because of its primary use, pureeing tomatoes.

Several models of hand-cranked strainers are available, but the most popular are the Back to Basics (which used to be known as the Victorio brand, a name that longtime canners will recognize), the Squeezo Strainer, Villaware and Roma brands. All work in the same

Figure 3.18 Food Mill

way. You fill the hopper with fruits or vegetables — for example cooked apples or quartered tomatoes — and they fall into a chute. A plunger made of wood or plastic helps you tamp the food down. Cranking the handle turns an auger that drives the food into and against the edges of a conical sieve. The puree falls out into a bowl beneath. The pulp, seeds and skins are extruded out the other side of the cone.

The advantage to using a hand-cranked strainer over the "Foley mill" is that you can operate continuously without having to stop and clear the excess. This makes hand-cranked strainers well suited to long, late-summer days of making tomatoes into sauce for canning. On the other hand, they require more storage space, setup and cleanup than a food mill. However, both can be a challenge to clean. To lessen the burden, rinse the sieve disks or strainer cones immediately after use.

Brands of hand-cranked strainers differ chiefly in their materials. The Squeezo Strainer is the only one made entirely of metal. It's also the most expensive, coming in at $189 for the original version and $239 for the larger deluxe version. Those who own Squeezo Strainers, however, rave about them. The Villaware model is made entirely of plastic and sells for about $30. The Back to Basics brand (which used to be the Victorio brand) has a plastic hopper and a metal base. Still a favorite among home food processors, it sells for about $50. Very similar to the Back to Basics brand is the Roma brand, pictured in Figure 3.19, which also sells for $50. Most models offer optional accessories such as berry strainers (with a finer mesh) or pumpkin strainers (with a coarse mesh).

Juicers serve a different purpose but operate in a similar fashion to hand-cranked strainers. Fruits, vegetables or grasses are loaded in a small hopper. Turning the hand crank rotates an auger that crushes and pushes fruit or vegetable matter against a conical sieve. Excess pulp is released on the opposite end of the cone. (And if desired, you can put this pulp back in the hopper for further juice extraction.) A juicer's sieve has a finer mesh than a strainer's. This results in a more liquid product, but also means that you have to chop the fruits or vegetables into smaller pieces to avoid clogging. In fact, some juicers are labeled "wheatgrass juicers" and are guaranteed only to juice grasses. However, users of these machines claim they can also accept apples, beets and carrots, for example, as long as they're diced.

Like many manual kitchen devices, hand-cranked juicers are considerably safer to operate than their motorized counterparts. Some argue that juices made manually don't risk being heated, as they might in an electric juicer, and as a result retain a higher nutritional content. In addition, manual juicers are generally easier to clean than electric versions.

The most popular manual juicers are the Hurricane, Z-Star, Healthy Living and Back to Basics models. The Hurricane juicer is made entirely of stainless steel, and users of this juicer value its heavy-duty construction. At the time this book was written it sold for about $105. Also highly rated, the Z-Star, which sells for about $90 and is made by Tribest, has a metal base and a plastic hop-

Figure 3.19 Hand-Cranked Strainer

per and auger housing. People credit this model with thorough juicing and especially easy cleanup. It's shown in Figure 3.20. If you're looking for something less expensive, consider the Healthy Juicer, made by Lexen, which costs around $45.

Food mills, strainers and hand-cranked juicers are simple enough to operate by hand, but that doesn't mean you can't pedal-power them. The authors of *Pedal Power In Work, Leisure and Transportation* described connecting their Energy Cycle to various kitchen implements, including a food mill. Woody Roy Parker designed his own pedal-powered juicer beginning with a bike frame and tire, as described on page 143.

Cider and Wine Presses

The pressing of apples into cider (the alcoholic version) is said to have begun in the Basque winemaking regions of Spain. Traveling Celts then brought the knowledge to Northern Europe, and later, colonists brought it to the New World.[5] Over two hundred years ago nearly every farm in the eastern United States grew apples for cider. Families processed it at home or brought bushels of apples to the local cider mill for pressing. Then they casked it and kept it in the cellar. One source estimates that in Massachusetts in 1767 the annual per capita consumption of hard cider was forty gallons. And although 20th-century Prohibition threatened the alcoholic cider's future, over the last decade it has made a strong comeback.

Today, small-scale cidermaking follows the same process early farm families knew. After letting the apples sit (or "sweat") for one to two weeks, then washing them, you macerate them into a mash called pomace. Next, you crush the pomace in a press to drive the juice through a filter, such as a nylon mesh cloth, and into a tub or pot. (A bushel of apples makes approximately three gallons of cider.) You can still bring your apples to a nearby cider mill, though they're harder to find in the 21st century than in the 18th century. Or you can purchase your own cider press and make it at home. Two styles are available: those that use ratchets to push a plate and squeeze the juice from the pomace and those that use a large screw to drive the plate. These presses work equally well for crushing grapes as part of the wine-making process.

Happy Valley Ranch sells well-known, durable screw-style presses. They offer four sizes: the Yakima, a table top press, and in

Figure 3.20 Z-Star Manual Juicer

order of increasing size, the Pioneer Junior, Homesteader and American Harvester models, the last of which features a double-tub design. At the time this was written, these cider presses sold from the manufacturer for $139, $429, $599 and $739, respectively and came with a 3-year warranty. The most popular model, the Homesteader, is pictured in Figure 3.21. All feature a maple hardwood structure with a 1.5-inch Acme-thread pressing screw and come with a cast-iron grinder with stainless steel blades and a cast-iron flywheel. When squeezing pomace with a screw press, the company recommends, rotate the han-

Figure 3.21 Happy Valley Ranch's Homesteader Cider Press

dle only one quarter or one half turn, until you meet resistance, then wait before turning again. Pressing faster will result in cloudier juice. Happy Valley Ranch's cider presses come mostly assembled (they're too large to ship otherwise). The company also sells kits and parts for making your own cider press. Find out more at happyvalleyranch.com.

Another screw-style press, the Jaffrey Cider and Wine Press, is similar to those made by Happy Valley Ranch. One difference is that the pressing screw is 1 inch, rather than 1.5 inches in diameter. Some users report that the Jaffrey is less durable than the Happy Valley Ranch's Homesteader and also, that its handle doesn't allow as much leverage. At the time this was written the Jaffrey Cider and Wine Press sold for as low as $385 and came with a 1-year warranty. Like Happy Valley Ranch, Jaffrey makes elements of their press, such as the cross braces, screw handles, and pressing disks, available for separate purchase for those who want to build their own. Jaffrey also makes a tabletop screw-style press, available for as little as $136. Although you can't buy the Jaffrey presses or parts directly from the manufacturer, the company's Web site, at jaffreypress.com, provides a list of retailers.

Ratchet-style presses are considered the best way to squeeze the most juice from crushed grapes ("must") or apple pomace. Rather than turning a handle to advance the pressing disk, this style affords the user the added leverage of a ratchet. In other ways, the two types of presses are similar. Choices, however, are limited to relatively small presses, which don't come with an attached grinder. One example is the Weston Fruit and

Woody Roy Parker's Juicycle

The inspiration for Woody Roy Parker's Juicycle, a pedal-powered juicer, was a hand-cranked chipper-shredder he saw in *Popular Mechanics* in the late 1970s. He copied the design in his shop and then years later applied principles he learned while making the chipper to his Juicycle.

In his first Juicycle design a chain drive connected a modified bike's chainring to a juicer's axle. But this required a fussy alignment of the two sprockets. If the sprockets weren't perfectly aligned, the chain would jump off. After tinkering with the design in AutoCAD (which he said saved him lots of time in the shop), Woody settled on a friction-drive solution. His Juicycle now uses a regular bike tire spinning against a smaller wheel attached to the juicer's axle. As shown in Figure 3.22, Woody also beefed up the flywheel characteristics of the bike's wheel by weaving leftover chain through the spokes near the rim. Despite having a degree in mechanical engineering, Woody said that except for determining gear ratios, he rarely spends time on physics calculations. His advice for human-powered machine inventors is to improve your design by trial and error.

Woody makes Juicycle plans, complete with technical drawings, available at no cost on his Web site, juicycle.com. When we spoke he emphasized that his Juicycle design could be adapted for any hand-cranked device, including a grain mill or hand-cranked blender. His next goal is to make a pedal-powered juicer that can be attached to any bike and used on the go.[6]

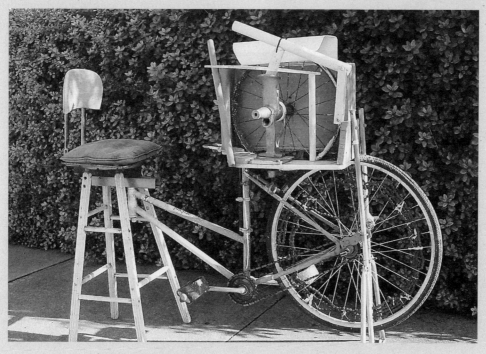

Figure 3.22 Woody Roy Parker's Juicycle

Figure 3.23 Weston Fruit and Wine Press

Wine Press, pictured in Figure 3.23, which sells for as low as $200. Many retailers, including those that sell homebrew supplies, carry this press, and some also carry even smaller, less expensive presses.

If you don't want to spend the money on a press of your own, in some areas you can rent cider presses or time at an orchard's cider press. Or you could build your own press. At a fraction of the cost, you can match the quality of the finest commercially available presses. An oft-cited plan is found in the book *Cider:*

Making, Using & Enjoying Sweet & Hard Cider by Annie Proulx and Lew Nichols. Another plan was published in the September/October 1976 issue of *Mother Earth News*. And at the time this was written, a handful of individuals had posted their own unique plans online. If you plan to build your own, bear in mind that the frame must be very rigid and capable of withstanding tremendous pressure. Also, all materials used to build your press must be food-grade. That means, for example, using stainless steel, food-grade plastic and food-grade grease.

Maverick cider makers also find alternatives for the hand-cranked grinders that come attached to cider presses. Some recommend using a garbage disposal, because it grinds the apples to a slurry, allowing for maximum cider extraction. However, a garbage disposal isn't designed for continuous duty. During long periods of use it's liable to overheat. Ben Polito, of Five Islands Orchard in Maine, had experimented with using garbage disposals in his cidermaking operation and was dismayed by its repeated overheating. Then he and his friends, who work as engineers in the alternative energy field, devised a pedal-powered apple grinder.

Shown in Figure 3.24, the pedal-powered apple grinder is a truly original machine. The inventors even honed their own cutting blades from stainless steel strap stock. The power train relies on two chain drives. One connects the bike's chainring to a cogset on an intermediate shaft. A second chain connects a sprocket on that shaft to a smaller sprocket on the grinder's shaft. A flywheel is attached to the grinder's shaft on the opposite side of the hopper to help smooth the variable forces from pedaling. The hopper is within the pedaler's reach, making solo operation possible. Ben wrote, "The effort to keep the system spinning in the absence of fruit is trivial compared to pedaling with no load at all. The effort to grind an apple is noticeable but not strenuous."[7] He estimated that alone, he could pedal-grind a bushel of apples in about 10 minutes.

In case you're inspired to try making your own pedal-powered apple grinder, Ben's blog, online at fiveislandsorchard.wordpress.com/, provides copious details about how he and his friends designed and improved the grinder.

Ice-Cream Makers

Making ice cream at home is nearly foolproof. Even if you don't follow instructions precisely, given reasonable proportions of cream, eggs, sweetener and flavorings, the results are apt to taste delicious. David Lebovitz, author of *The Perfect Scoop*, writes that you can even make ice cream in a baking dish or shallow bowl in your freezer — in fact, that's how people made it at home before the hand-cranked ice-cream maker was invented. Making ice cream this way takes about two hours and requires stirring the mixture vigorously for a few minutes every half hour. However, "the advantage to using an electric or hand-cranked machine,"

Figure 3.24 Ben Polito's Pedal-Powered Apple Grinder

Lebovitz says, "is that the final result will be smoother and creamier. Freezing anything from liquid-to-solid means you're creating hard ice crystals, so if you're making it by hand, as your ice-cream or sorbet mixture freezes, you want to break up those ice crystals as much as possible so your final results are as smooth and creamy as possible." [8]

A dish and spoon, nested coffee cans or plastic bags, gas- or electric-powered mixers, hand-cranked paddles in canisters — there are many techniques for making fresh ice cream at home. This section reviews two commercially available human-powered ice-cream makers.

Probably the most familiar human-powered ice-cream maker is one that uses a

Figure 3.25 White Mountain Hand-Cranked Ice-Cream Maker

hand crank. In fact, the design of today's hand-cranked machines differs little from Nancy Johnson's 1843 patent for an "artificial freezer," which consisted of an inner metal canister to hold the ingredients, a dasher (or rotating paddle) that fit inside the canister, an outer pail, and a hand crank that turned the dasher. Rock salt and ice are poured in the cavity between the pail and the inner chamber and help make the milk crystals inside the chamber freeze. The motion of the dasher churns the ice cream and breaks the crystals.

The White Mountain hand-cranked ice-cream maker (now owned by Rival) is not the only modern-day equivalent to Nancy Johnson's invention, but it is by far the most popular, well-constructed and highly rated. It takes approximately 30 minutes to make ice cream in this maker. During that time you'll probably have to pause to replenish the ice and rock salt in the bucket. When the ice cream becomes too thick to continue churning, you've finished. After that, you're advised to "pack" the ice cream before eating it: seal the canister and replenish the ice once more, then leave the mixture to further harden.

Prices start at $135 for White Mountain's four-quart hand-cranked ice-cream maker. (Electric versions by the same manufacturer cost at least $50.00 more.)

If you attended scout camp as a child you might recall assembling an ice-cream maker from two coffee cans. With this simple invention, you put all the ingredients in a one-pound coffee can, put on the lid and seal it with duct tape, place the coffee can within a larger three-pound coffee can, pour ice and rock salt in the space between the cans, and roll it around for a half hour or so before the ice cream is done. The Play & Freeze, a human-powered ice-cream maker from Industrial Revolution, works similarly, but it's more colorful and durable. (Some people say it resembles a hamster's exercise ball.)

An inner metal chamber holds the ice cream ingredients, and the space between this chamber and the outer polycarbonate shell is filled with ice and rock salt. The Play & Freeze ball, which is advertised as a source of entertainment for kids, is meant to be rolled, not tossed or kicked (in fact, with ingredients and ice inside, it's too heavy and potentially dangerous for children to throw). Periodically during mixing you need to open the ice cream chamber and scrape the ice cream off the sides. Users report that it takes between 30 to 60 minutes to make a batch of ice cream. Some recommend wearing gloves to protect your fingers from the cold plastic.

Figure 3.26 Play and Freeze Ice-cream Maker

The Play & Freeze comes in two sizes: the original model, which holds a pint of ice cream, and the MEGA model, which holds a quart. At the time this was written, the pint-sized version cost about $29.00 and the quart-sized version cost about $40.00.

CHAPTER 4

HUMAN-POWERED DEVICES FOR LAWN AND GARDEN

The joy of working outdoors lies in appreciating nature. But birdsong and blossom-scented breezes are too often extinguished by the racket and smell of gasoline engines. Peace is the reason, many have told me, that they opt for human-powered lawn and garden tools. Others add that many human-powered tools work just as well, if not better, and as quickly as their motorized counterparts. Watch how long it takes someone to blow leaves off a sidewalk. Could sweeping them really take longer? Not only that, but human-powered tools are often more durable. In his book *Homesteading: How to Find New Independence on the Land* Gene Logsdon writes, "The [hand-pushed] cultivator makes no noise, always starts, never breaks down…, needs no gasoline, can be controlled easily to avoid plowing out vegetables — and mine is at least fifty years old." [1]

This chapter includes a plan for a human-powered cultivator whose ergonomics and leverage are improved by combining it with a bike frame and wheel. Another plan describes how to make an inexpensive treadle water pump based on one devised by volunteers for a Haitian development organization. The second half of the chapter reviews what's available in human-powered garden and lawn care equipment, including the best push-type reel mowers and lawn sweepers. Along the way you'll learn about people who've built pedal-powered lawn mowers and even a pedal-powered snow plow.

Plan for Making a Bike-Frame Cultivator

Home gardeners might be familiar with the twisted back and cramped hands that result from hours of loosening dirt with a handheld cultivator. A cultivator attached to a modified bike frame, however, affords the gardener greater power and a more comfortable, ergonomic position. It also covers more ground in less time.

This plan is inspired by a bicycle cultivator mentioned in a 1981 issue of *Mother Earth News* magazine, though I've created a modified version that's more durable in some ways and simpler to construct. The plan doesn't call for welding skills or supplies, but if you have them, you could make your cultivator sturdier.

Figure 4.1 Bike-Frame Cultivator

At the time this was written, commercially available versions of similar wheeled cultivators sold for $85 to $130.

Ease of construction: Fairly easy; it involves minimal knowledge of (or willingness to learn) basic bike mechanics. For some steps, it's helpful to have two sets of hands. Depending on the bike, it might require special bike repair tools.

Time to make: 4 to 6 hours

Cost to make: $15 to $30, using scrounged parts

Ease of operation: Very simple

Following is an overview of the steps in this plan:

Figure 4.2 Antique, Long-Handled Cultivator

- First, you'll disassemble most of an adult bike by removing the seat, shifters, brake levers, brakes, crankset, chain, derailleurs and front wheel and sawing off the top tube and down tube.
- Next, you'll separate the front fork and steerer tube from the head tube and re-attach the front fork to the part of the frame you saved. This creates the cultivator's long handle.
- Finally, you'll attach a cultivator head to the seat tube in your modified bike frame.

Materials
- One adult-sized, steel-framed, single (not tandem) road bike, salvaged. A bike with a wheel size between 20" and 27" will work. It's okay if the frame is slightly bent or banged up. A lower-quality bike can often be dismantled with standard shop tools, whereas a high-quality bike is more apt to require custom bike tools. You probably wouldn't want to ruin a high-quality bike for this project, anyway.
- One old, long-handled cultivator, as shown in Figure 4.2. In rural or exurban areas these are common antique-store finds, usually costing less than $10. (In fact, if the handle is broken or missing, which is fine for this project, you could get an even better bargain.) However, if you can't find an old cultivator, you can substitute a modern long-handled cultivator, given some modifications to this plan. See the "Variations and Considerations" section at the end of this plan for ideas.

- Four ¼"-diameter carriage bolts, 1-½" long, plus matching washers and nuts
- One ¼"-diameter carriage bolt, 6" long, plus matching nut
- At least six fender washers which are at least 2" in diameter and whose center holes are least ¼" in diameter
- One 6" hose clamp
- One ¾"-diameter galvanized steel pipe nipple, 5-½" long* (if you're short, choose a slightly shorter one, or if you're tall, a longer one)
- One ¾" galvanized steel floor flange*
- One ¾" galvanized steel 45-degree street elbow (male-to-female)*

The size of these parts — all of which can be found in the plumbing department of your local hardware store — depends on your seat tube's inside diameter being roughly 1"; this is almost always the case, but check yours to verify its size before buying these materials.

Tools

- Safety goggles
- Permanent marker (in a color that contrasts with your bike frame)
- Set of wrenches (sizes will vary to match the sizes of nuts on your bicycle; they are almost always metric), including open-ended wrenches, socket wrenches and Allen wrenches
- Pipe wrench
- Phillip's head and flathead screwdrivers
- Hacksaw
- Drill press with ¼" drill bit and cutting oil
- Clamps
- Cable cutter

- Bolt cutter or chain link tool to sever and remove bike chain
- A bike repair stand or other method of locking bike into place (a workbench and clamps could suffice)
- Lockring tool or pipe wrench
- Optional, if your bike requires it: Crank extractor tool (or crank puller)
- Optional, if your bike requires it: Bottom bracket tool
- Optional, if you might want to re-use the chain: Chain link tool

Steps for Making a Bike-frame Cultivator

1. If you have a bike repair stand, mount the bike on the stand and clamp it securely. If not, try finding a way to clamp it tightly to the edge of a workbench, vertical post or shelf support. If you have no way of fixing the bike in place, it's best to have another person help you steady it during some of the following steps.

   Note: Refer to Figure 2.23 if you don't recall the names for various bike frame parts.

2. Remove the bike's seat, or saddle. Seats are attached to the seat post with a saddle clamp. Saddle clamps differ from one bike to another. However, in most cases removing the seat is a simple matter of removing one or two nuts and bolts or a screw.

3. Next, remove the seat post from the seat tube. The seat post is the metal tube that fits snugly within the seat tube and allows you to adjust the height of your seat. Most seat posts are fixed in place by a binder

clamp. Loosen the binder clamp (often this entails turning one screw) and pull out the seat tube.

4. If the bike has a kickstand, remove it. Most kickstands are attached to the chainstay, either near the bottom bracket or near the rear hub. Removing a kickstand might be a simple matter of removing one nut and bolt that hold the kickstand to the frame. In some cases, though, kickstands (for example, those on old Schwinn bikes) require a special tool to remove them or they might be welded onto the chainstay. If your kickstand isn't bolted on, you can either leave it attached (it won't hamper the cultivator's functioning) or use a more drastic removal tool — for example, a hacksaw or an acetylene torch.

5. If the bike has an attached bottle cage, take that off by removing the nuts and bolts that hold it to the frame.

6. Cut the chain with a bolt cutter and remove it. If you don't want to ruin it, use a chain tool to remove a link pin and free the chain.

7. Next, using a cable cutter, sever the front and rear gear cables both near the shifters and the derailleurs and slide them out of their braze-on cable guides to remove them from the frame.

8. Also use a cable cutter to sever the front and rear brake cables, both near the brake levers and near the brakes. Slide them out of their cable guides and remove them from the frame.

9. Take off the shifters and brake levers. These might be connected to the handlebars, the stem (just below the handlebars), or on older bikes, the down tube. No matter where, they're affixed to the frame with a clamp that's tightened using screws. In some cases the screws are hidden under rubber covers. Use the appropriate screwdriver or Allen wrench to loosen the clamp and then remove the shifter or brake lever. If the handlebar end grips prevent sliding off the shifters or brake levers, remove the grips (they're normally held on with friction). If the grips are stuck, try holding a wrench snugly around the handlebar just before the grip, then hitting the side of the wrench with a mallet to nudge the grip off the end of the handlebar.

10. Next, you'll release the tension in the rear brake and remove it. Depending on the type of brake, releasing the tension might involve flipping a lever, loosening a small screw or bolt, or squeezing the calipers, then pulling up on the cable that spans the two calipers. After releasing the tension, remove the brake and attached cable, if any, by threading the nut off the end and removing the bolt that holds the rear brake assembly to the top of the seat stays.

11. Repeat Step 10 for releasing the tension in and removing the front brake from the top of the front fork.

12. Remove the rear derailleur and any remaining length of the gear cable by removing the lug that holds the derailleur to the rear drop-outs (the metal ends of the rear fork, where the seat stays and chain stays intersect). It's okay to leave the cogset in place.

13. The front derailleur is attached to the bottom of the seat tube or a nearby braze-on with a bolt and nut. Remove the bolt and nut to remove the front derailleur and any remaining gear cable.

14. Remove the pedals where they attach to the cranks using the appropriate open-ended wrench. On nearly all bikes, the right-hand pedal is removed by turning the wrench counterclockwise while the left-hand pedal is removed by turning the wrench clockwise. In other words, in both cases, you would turn the wrench toward the back of the bike to loosen and remove the pedals.

15. Next, you need to remove the crank arms, chain rings and spindle — that is, everything that's left at the intersection of the seat tube and down tube. Crank arms are attached to the bike's frame via a spindle that goes through the bottom bracket. However, the attachment can take one of a few different forms depending on the bike. On many inexpensive bikes, crank arms are made of one S-shaped piece of metal, also known as a one-piece crank. These are the simplest type to disassemble, requiring only the use of wrenches and a flathead screwdriver. If you do not have a one-piece crank — that is, if your crank is attached in a more complex manner, consult a bike repair manual, such as Todd Downs' *Bicycle Maintenance & Repair for Road & Mountain Bikes* or Lennard Zinn's *Zinn and the Art of Road Bike Maintenance* to find out how to remove it. You might need to purchase a crank extractor tool (or crank puller) and bottom bracket tool to accomplish this (unless you want to try a brute force method, which might involve a pipe wrench).

16. Now the bottom bracket should be hollow. Next, you'll remove the front wheel. Since you took off the front brake earlier, you can easily remove the wheel by loosening the axle nuts on either side of the wheel and slipping the wheel off the front fork. Or, if your bike has a quick-release mechanism on the wheel — that is, a lever on one side and a cap nut on the other — loosen the nut and pull the lever outward to release the wheel.

17. Clamp the frame, by the seat tube, in a repair stand or workbench. Then use a hacksaw to cut off the top tube close to where it intersects with the seat tube.

18. Also using a hacksaw, cut off the down tube close to where it intersects with the seat tube. You should be left with a modified bike that consists of the rear tire, seat tube, seat stays and chain stays, similar to the one pictured in Figure 4.3.

Figure 4.3 Dismantled Frame

19. Remove the handlebar tube and front fork from the head post on the part of the frame that you cut off in steps 17 and 18.

20. Flip the remaining bike frame so that the bottom bracket shell is on top. Secure the frame on a bike repair stand or workbench.

21. Next, you'll attach the front fork and handlebar tube to the chain stays to create a handle. Hold the fork and handlebar tube in front of you in the same position it would be if you were riding the bike. Now rotate it 180 degrees. With its "wrong" side facing up, slide the fork over the seat stays and hold it so that the fork arms line up with the seat stays. The fork arms should also bisect the bottom bracket shell. (As shown in Figure 4.4.)

22. On each side of the fork, use the permanent marker to place a dot where an imaginary line through the center of the bottom bracket shell would intersect the fork. This is where you'll drill and insert a bolt. (If you're welding, weld the fork in place at the bottom bracket and against the seat stays. This will probably require adding some material between each arm of the fork and the bottom bracket's rim. Then skip to Step 27.)

23. On the drill press, drill a ¼" hole through the fork in each place where you made a mark in Step 22. For safety's sake, wear protective goggles while doing this and use cutting oil. To keep it steady while you drill, clamp the fork to the drill press table. Because forks are tapered, it's helpful to use a shim between the fork and the table so that it's level. Be sure to drill in the center of the fork arm, since drilling closer to the edges might compromise the strength of the arm. Also, aim to make the hole perpendicular to the face of the fork.

24. Line up the fork so that the holes you just drilled match the center of the bottom bracket. Notice the space between the fork's edges and the outer rim of the bottom bracket. Insert enough 2"-diameter or larger fender washers on either side of the bottom bracket to fill this space. Try to position them flat against the rim of the bottom bracket shell.

25. Insert the 6"-long carriage bolt through one side of the fork, the fender washers, the bottom bracket shell, the fender washers on the other side, and then the other side of the fork.

26. Add a nut to the end of the bolt and tighten securely.

27. To doubly fasten the handle in position, bind the front fork to the seat stays by wrapping a 6" hose clamp around both. Tighten securely with a screwdriver. (If you're welding, weld each side of the fork to its respective chain stay.) The fork-handle attachment should look similar to Figure 4.4.

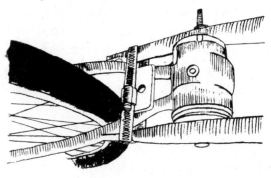

Figure 4.4 Fork Handle Attachment

28. Now you're ready to insert the handlebars back into the head tube. You probably want them to face the same way when you operate the cultivator as they would face if you were riding the bike, which means inserting them into the head tube 180 degrees opposite of the direction in which they were originally installed.

29. If you removed grips from the handlebars earlier, replace them now.

30. Setting the bike frame aside for a while, next you'll disassemble the long-handled cultivator and prepare it to be attached to the bike frame. Clamp the cultivator head onto your workbench. Using a hacksaw, cut off the metal bracket that connects the head to the wooden handle so that the remaining cultivator head has as near to a flat top as you can make it.

31. If you are indeed using an old long-handled cultivator, the tines will be bolted tight between two metal plates. In the cultivators I've picked up, there are four bolts, and the two outside bolts are spaced 2-⅜" apart on center. This happens to match exactly the distance between opposite holes in the pipe flange. If the bolts on your cultivator head do not line up, or if you are using a cultivator head whose tines are fastened in a different manner, you'll have to make your own bracket from two steel plates, measuring where best to put bolts and drilling holes for the bolts to go through.

32. Remove two bolts and nuts on the exterior of old cultivator head plates.

33. Attach the floor flange to the top of the cultivator head by inserting new 1-½"-long ¼"-diameter carriage bolts through the holes on the exterior. Add matching washers and nuts and tighten firmly.

34. Now screw the 45-degree pipe elbow onto end of the floor flange. Use a pipe wrench to screw it in so that it's tight.

35. Next, screw the 5-½" pipe nipple into the 45-degree elbow. Use a pipe wrench to screw it in so that it's tight. The cultivator head and its attachments should look like the illustration in Figure 4.5.

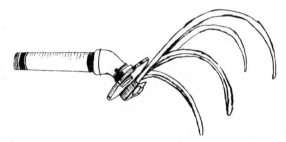

Figure 4.5 Modified Cultivator Head

36. Unfasten the bike frame from its stand or workbench and flip it over, so that the seat tube is facing up and the handlebars are resting on the floor. Insert the end of the 5-½" pipe nipple (and the attached, modified cultivator head) into the seat tube. Tighten with a pipe wrench. The curved ends of the tines should be pointing toward the wheel and away from the handlebars.

37. Flip the bike-frame cultivator over and try it out.

Variations and Considerations

- If you can't find an old-fashioned, long-handled cultivator to dismantle for this project, you can buy new five-tine cultivator heads manufactured by Beaver Manufacturing (for attachment to their push garden plows) for about $25. Because these are designed differently than the antique types, you'll have to adjust the means of attaching the head to the floor flange at the bottom of the bike frame cultivator.

- Rather than using an old cultivator head, one variation on this plan uses recycled bike forks as cultivator tines.

Plan for Making a Treadle-Powered Water Pump

In 1983, VITA (Volunteers for Technical Assistance), now EnterpriseWorks, published plans for homemade pumps in a bulletin titled "Six Simple Pumps: A Construction Guide." That booklet includes instructions for making several types of pumps: chain-and-washer, diaphragm, screw, inertia and two different piston pumps. (You can order the bulletin via the organization's Web site at enterpriseworks

Treadle Pump Designed for Haitian Growers

CODEP (Comprehensive Development Project) is part of The Haiti Fund, Inc. (haitifund.org), a North Carolina-based ecumenical group working to better the lives of poor Haitians. Recently the organization's director recognized the need for simple crop irrigation in Haiti's isolated highlands. Ready water supplies would improve the yields from small plots and also the lives of peasants who tended them. However, no one could find a source for treadle pumps that would ship to the United States (a situation I was able to confirm while writing this book). The only pump they found was a commercial model imported from India, and that cost $300, including shipping and other fees. CODEP's director challenged several people in the group to create a less expensive alternative. Jim Sylivant, an electrical engineer and longtime CODEP board member, accepted that challenge.

Jim said his specifications called for an inexpensive pump that could draw water from lower elevations to fields located on mountain sides. He called on engineer and former coworker Larry

Figure 4.6 Treadle Pump

.org.) Other resources for appropriate technology professionals also describe the construction of simple chain-and-washer or screw pumps. However, guides for making a simple treadle pump are scarce.

What follows is a plan for making a dual-piston treadle pump from materials you can find at nearly any hardware store. The pump, capable of pumping about 15 gallons per minute, would be useful if you wanted to, for example, water a garden from a shallow well or cistern, transfer water from a pond to a holding tank, raise water from a cistern to an elevated tank, or drain a pool of water. It's extremely easy to use. At first glance it might seem as if the pump requires the effort of a Stairmaster, but in fact, it relies only on the operator's body weight to push the pistons down. Pumping water is simply a matter of shifting your weight from side to side.

Since this plan is the most complex in the book, its materials and steps are divided

Shannon to collaborate on the design. After months of experimentation and trial runs, including pumping water out of the pond in Jim's yard to the end of his 1,000-foot driveway, they arrived at a design. It cost $35 to $40 in parts, not including the investment in tools.

The treadle pump, shown in Figure 4.6, is made mostly from dimensional lumber, PVC and commonly available hardware. It functions just like the treadle pumps described in Chapter 1's "Appropriate Technology" section. In this pump, the seals inside the pistons are made of leather cups. Jim told me that he remembered using pitcher pumps — which have always used leather seals — as a child. And although the two didn't know the inner workings of a treadle pump then, while they constructed theirs, Larry said, "It felt like we were learning things that we sort of already knew."

After perfecting their design Jim said he hoped to teach a few talented craftsmen in remote areas how to make their own pumps. He envisioned giving them the necessary tools so they could set up small enterprises and make pumps for their communities. It might prove a steep learning curve, however. The people CODEP serves live in remote areas, where people aren't familiar with the construction techniques used to make the pump. Until the most appropriate method of distribution can be determined, Jim and Larry have maintained a blog that chronicles the development of their pump (treadlepump.blogspot.com). In response, they've received requests from around the world asking for plans and specific dimensions.[2]

When I talked with them, they were in the process of writing up detailed plans for making their pump. You can now find their plans, plus photos of the pump construction process, at treadle.pump.googlepages.com/buildyourown treadlepump.

The treadle pump plan that follows in this chapter is largely based on Jim and Larry's pump, but it's slightly simpler and somewhat less portable.

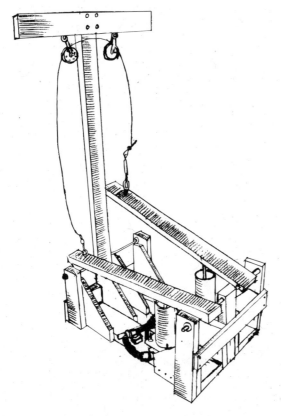

Figure 4.7 Treadle Pump

according to pump components: frame, piston and cylinders, valves and tubing.

Many thanks to Larry Shannon and Jim Sylivant for sharing their treadle pump dimensions and construction techniques, which form the basis of the plan below (though I've taken some liberties with their design).

Ease of construction: Challenging. In fact, making the pump isn't difficult, but because of the number of parts and steps, it takes some forethought, organization and time.

Time to make: One day
Cost to make: $80–$100
Ease of operation: Very simple

Following is an overview of the steps in this plan:

- First, you'll assemble the frame for the pump, which includes the wooden support members, treadle mechanism, cross piece and cable assembly.
- Next, you'll create the pistons (including their rods and seals) and cylinders and attach those to the frame.
- Then, you'll make four one-way valves that will regulate the flow of water in and out of the pump's cylinders and connect them to the pump.
- Finally, you'll modify hoses and connect those to the valves to act as the pump's inlet and outlet.

Safety Precautions
- Always wear safety goggles when operating a drill or power saw.
- Use PVC cement only in a well-ventilated area.
- Keep fingers, hair, loose clothing and jewelry away from the pistons where they could get caught, resulting in harm.

Materials
For the Frame and Cable Assembly
- Two pieces of 2 × 6 dimensional lumber 34" long for the base
- Eight right-angle triangles of ¾" plywood, 12" × 12" × (roughly) 17" for the side braces

- Three pieces of 2 × 4 dimensional lumber 16" long for rear uprights
- Two pieces of 2 × 4 dimensional lumber 12" long for the front uprights
- Two pieces of 2 × 4 dimensional lumber 37" long for the treadles
- One piece of 2 × 4 dimensional lumber 67" long for the vertical member of the pulley support, or "mast"
- One piece of 2 × 4 dimensional lumber 27" long for the horizontal cross piece on the pulley support
- Two pieces of ¾" plywood 20-¼" × 5" for the front and rear braces
- One length of ½" round bar stock 22" long for the rear axle
- One length of ½" threaded bar stock 22" long for the front axle
- Four ½" nuts and washers for front axle
- One 7" or longer ½" pipe nipple cut into four 1-¾" long pieces for spacers on rear axle
- Two ½" washers for rear axle
- Two ⅛" cotter pins 1" long for rear axle
- Four ⁵⁄₁₆" carriage bolts 3-½" long, plus matching washers and nuts
- Four ½" eye bolts 2" long for cable assembly
- Two 3" garage door pulleys with forks
- One 8' length of ⅛" safety cable with loop ends (designed for use with garage doors)
- Two ¼" quick hook links
- One ¼" × 4" eye-to-eye turnbuckle (a slightly shorter or longer one would also work)
- One ⅛" wire rope clip

- Two 6" zinc-plated hinge straps (not the ornamental kind) designed for use with ½" bolt hooks; each hinge strap should have holes for two ⅜" bolts
- Four ⁵⁄₁₆"-diameter bolts 1-½" long
- Four ⁵⁄₁₆" tee-nuts
- About 50 wood screws 2" long
- At least 8 wood screws 3" long

Note: Where the plan calls for dimensional lumber, use exterior grade — that is, treated — lumber if you're concerned about the pump's longevity when exposed to the elements.

For the Pistons and Cylinders

- One piece of 6" PVC pipe at least 5" long (for making disks)
- One 9" × 12" sheet of 6-mm thick "craft foam" (available at craft supply stores), or neoprene, for the seals
- Two ½" × 8" bolt hooks (the threaded type)
- Four ½" washers and bolts (in case these don't come with your bolt hooks)
- Two pieces of 4" diameter PVC pipe 10" long for the cylinders (if you cut these yourself, use a file to clean off the cut edges)
- Two squares of ¾" plywood 5-½" × 5-½"
- Two 4" PVC slip caps (not threaded, and with flat tops, not domed tops)
- Eight ¼"-diameter carriage bolts 6" long, plus matching washers and nuts

For the Four Check Valves and Tubing

- Eight 1-½"-male-to-¾"-female PVC pipe threaded bushings
- Four 1-½" PVC couplings

- One piece of 1-½" PVC pipe at least 9" long (for cutting into spacers and X-shaped stoppers)
- Four ⅞"-diameter lightweight plastic balls. Following Jim and Larry's recommendation, I used acetyl (Delrin®) balls from Salem Specialty Ball company, but you might find a less expensive alternative (at a toy store, for example). Consider that, if the pump will be used often with gritty, murky water, the balls need to be tough enough to withstand constant abrasion.
- Four ¾" close pipe nipples
- 7' of flexible agricultural spray hose, capable of withstanding 200 psi (see the "Variations" list for other options, if you can't find this)
- Four plastic ¾"-to-¾" NPT male adapter barbed fittings (with one male, threaded end and the other a barbed end)
- Two ¾" plastic barbed Tee fittings
- Ten 1" hose clamps
- Teflon tape

Note: For all the PVC pipe and plumbing parts I used Schedule 40 PVC, but another grade of PVC would probably also work.

Tools

- Workbench, clamps and vises
- Marking pen or pencil (thin)
- Permanent marker
- Straight edge
- Drawing compass with pencil
- Screwdrivers
- Set of open-ended wrenches
- Hammer
- Goggles
- Cable cutter
- PVC pipe cutter, hacksaw or chop saw to cut PVC pipe
- Drill press or drill with ⅛", ⁵⁄₁₆", ⅜", ⁷⁄₁₆", ½", ¹⁵⁄₁₆" (or ⁵⁹⁄₆₄", if you can find it) bits, plus ½" countersink and ½" spade bits
- Cutting oil
- 4" hole saw
- ¾"-14 NPT tapered pipe tap
- Optional: Lathe
- Calipers
- Scissors
- Half-round bastard file
- Flat bastard file
- PVC cement
- Oven
- Baking sheet
- Two pieces of scrap lumber at least 6" wide and 1' long

Steps for Making a Treadle Pump
Making the Frame

1. Begin with the two 34" lengths of 2 × 6 dimensional lumber, which will form the base of the treadle pump stand. Mark one side of one board "Right – Top" and mark one side of the other board "Left – Top." Then, on the tops of each, mark one of the 6" ends "Front" and the other end "Back."

2. On the top side of each 2 × 6, mark a line across the width that's 9" in from the end marked "Back." Next, draw a line that follows the center of the board along its length. Where these two lines meet indicates the center point of the cylinder.

3. Using a drawing compass, mark circles with a radius of 2-¼" around the center points you found in Step 2. These circles

indicate roughly where the exterior of each cylinder will fall.

4. On the top of each board, mark a line across the width that's 6-¼" in from the end marked "Back."

5. On the top of each board, mark a line across the width that's 11-¾" in from the end marked "Back." The two lines you just drew mark the edges of the 5-½" square cylinder collars.

6. Now place a dot between the circle and each corner of the squares that mark the collar position (you can eyeball this). The marked end of your board should resemble the one shown in Figure 4.8.

7. Drill ⁵⁄₁₆" holes through the 2 × 6s at each of the eight dots you marked in the previous step.

8. Use the ½" countersink bit on the undersides of the boards to countersink each of the eight holes you drilled in the previous step.

9. Next, you'll create holes for the rear axle through the three rear upright pieces. Clamp together three of the 16" long 2 × 4s so that the center board is perpendicular to the two outside boards. The center board's face should be aligned with back edges of the outside boards.

10. Using the ⅛" drill bit make a pilot hole that's 1" from the top of each upright and centered along the width of the pieces. Using the spade bit, drill a ½"-diameter hole over that pilot hole through all three pieces.

11. Repeat Steps 9 and 10 for the front three uprights (two 16" 2 × 4s plus the 67" 2 × 4 mast in the middle). Note that the hole will pass through the outside 2 × 4s at about 1" from the top, but will pass through the center mast about 50" from the top.

12. Now cut the pointed tips off each of the eight triangles approximately 2" in from the end of the tip and perpendicular to the straight edge. (See Figure 4.9, where they're already attached, to get a glimpse of their finished shape.)

13. Next, use four 2" wood screws to attach a supporting triangle to the front of the left-hand side (or inside) of the 2 × 6 marked "Left." The narrow edge of the front triangle should be flush against the front edge of the board.

14. Repeat Step 13 to attach a supporting triangle to the rear of the left-hand side of the 2 × 6 marked "Left." The narrow edge of the triangle should be flush against the back edge.

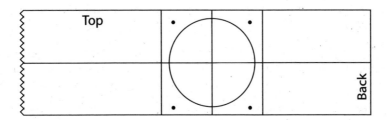

Figure 4.8 Marking the Base

15. In the same manner, attach a supporting triangle to the front and rear of the right side (inside) of the 2 × 6 marked "Right."

16. Now you're ready to attach the 2 × 6 bases and triangles to the center uprights. Align the 2 × 6 marked "Left" with the 16" 2 × 4 upright that has a hole drilled through its width (the one that was in the middle of the three you drilled in Step 10) so that the edge of the attached rear triangle is flush with the rear face of the upright. Use two 2" wood screws to connect the triangle to the upright.

17. Repeat the previous step to connect the front 67" 2 × 4 mast to the *front* of the 2 × 6 marked "Left."

18. Then connect the same uprights to the supporting triangles on the 2 × 6 marked "Right."

19. Soon you'll be ready to thread the front and rear axles through the holes you drilled earlier. First, though, you need to make corresponding holes through one end of the treadles. Using a ½" bit, drill through the center (along the width) of each treadle about 1" in from one end.

20. To make sure the rear axle doesn't slide out while the treadle pump is in use, you'll hold it in place with a cotter pin on both ends. Using the ⅛" bit and some cutting oil, drill a hole for a cotter pin within ¾" from each end of the piece of round bar stock (not the threaded stock).

21. Insert the 22"-long ½"-diameter round bar stock through the hole in the rear center upright that's already been attached to the 2 × 6 base boards. Roughly center the rod from left to right, and then on either

side of the upright, add one of the 1-¾" spacers cut from a ½" pipe nipple.

22. Next, on either side of the spacers, add a treadle, threading the axle through the holes you drilled in Step 19. Since the treadles are identical, it doesn't matter which one goes on which side of the center upright.

23. Add another spacer to the axle on the outside of the treadles you added in the previous step.

24. Now you're ready to attach the outside supports. On the rear outside of the 2 × 6 marked "Left," position a supporting triangle so that it's flush with the rear edge of the board and also parallel to the inside supporting triangle that you attached in Step 14. On top of that triangle, position one of the remaining 16" 2 × 4s so that its width is flat against the supporting triangle and its depth is flush against the rear edge of the 2 × 6. Obviously, you'll want to thread the axle through the hole you drilled in the 16" 2 × 4. (See Figure 4.9 for more details.)

25. Use two 2" wood screws to connect a supporting triangle directly to the 2 × 6, then use two 3" wood screws to connect the upright 2 × 4 plus the triangle to the 2 × 6.

26. Repeat steps 24 and 25 for the 2 × 6 marked "Right," attaching a supporting triangle and one of the 16" uprights to the rear of the board.

27. Insert a cotter pin through the holes at each end of the rear axle to keep the axle from shifting side-to-side.

28. Now insert the threaded ½" bar stock through the front mast. Because the trea-

dles are not connected to this axle, you don't need spacers.

29. You do, however, need a nut and washer on the inside and outside of each 2 × 4 upright. Add a ½" nut and washer to each end of the front axle and turn each nut until it's about 2-¼" in from the end.

30. Next, attach the exterior supporting triangles and a 12" length of 2 × 4 to the outside front of the right and left 2 × 6s, in the same manner as you attached the rear triangles and uprights. Match the holes in the 2 × 4s to fit over the axle before screwing the uprights and triangles to the 2 × 6s.

31. Attach a ½" washer and nut to each end of the front axle. Then, on both the right and left sides of the axle, use two wrenches to tighten the nuts simultaneously against the 2 × 4 upright.

32. Now attach one of the 20-¼" × 5" pieces of plywood to the rear of the frame by screwing it into the three rear uprights.

This brace should be positioned so that its top edge is roughly even with the top edges of the triangle supports, but this positioning isn't critical.

33. Attach the second 20-¼" × 5" piece of plywood to the front of the frame by screwing it into the three front uprights. This brace should be positioned so that its bottom edge is even with the bottom of the 2 × 6s and 2 × 4 uprights. The frame should look like the one shown in Figure 4.9.

34. Next, you'll prepare the mast to support the pulleys and cables. Place the 27" 2 × 4 across the top of the mast so that the boards are perpendicular and the shorter board's length is flush against the top end of the longer board. In the square where they meet, drill four ⅜" holes, evenly spaced.

35. Insert a 3-½"-long ⁵⁄₁₆"-diameter carriage bolt into each of the four holes you drilled in the previous step, then add the matching washers and nuts and tighten.

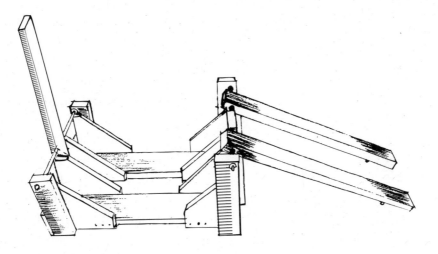

Figure 4.9 Treadle Pump Base

36. On the top side of each treadle, mark a spot that's in the center of the board's width and 4" from the front edge of the board. Screw in an eye bolt at this mark.

37. On the horizontal cross piece of the pulley support, mark a point about 5-¼" out from the right edge of the mast. Do the same on the left side. These marks should line up roughly with the eye bolts you screwed into the tops of the treadles. Adjust their positions as necessary so that they do. Then, at each of these points, screw an eye bolt into the underside of the cross piece.

38. Next, you'll hang the 3" pulleys from the eye bolts you just screwed into the cross

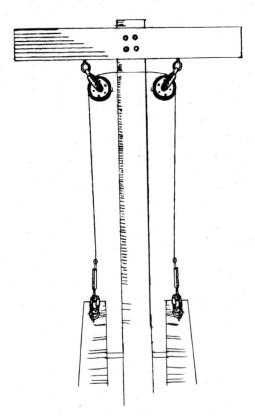

Figure 4.10 Pulleys and Cable

piece. To do this, detach the fork (sometimes also called a yoke) from the center of each 3" pulley. (This usually involves removing a nut from the pulley's center bolt.) Then thread one end of the fork through the bolt's eye, then reattach it to the center of the pulley by replacing the pulley's center nut.

39. Use the cable cutters to lop off one end of the ⅛" garage-door cable so that the remaining cable is 72" long. The opposite end of the cable should retain its loop.

40. Open one of the quick hook links and thread the looped end of the cable over it. Then thread the link through the eye of the left-hand treadle's eye bolt. Screw the link tight to close it.

41. Thread the free end of the cable around both pulleys so that it spans the crosspiece between them and then hangs down over the right-hand treadle.

42. Create a loop on the free end of the cable by inserting it through the wire rope clip and tightening.

43. Open one end of the eye-to-eye turnbuckle and thread it through the loop you created in the previous step. Tighten the turnbuckle to close it.

44. Now open and then thread the opposite end of the eye-to-eye turnbuckle through the eye bolt sticking up from the right-hand treadle. Tighten the turnbuckle to close it.

45. The pulleys-and-cable assembly should now resemble the one pictured in Figure 4.10, and your frame is complete. If you want to adjust the position of the treadles, you can twist the turnbuckle in the appro-

priate direction to shorten or lengthen the cable span. Ideally, when the treadles hang even with each other, they should be parallel to the ground.

Making the Pistons and Cylinders

46. The 8"-long ½"-diameter bolt hooks will make up the piston rods. In the following steps you'll create the disks and seals that need to be added to those rods. Begin by using a PVC saw or hacksaw to cut a slit through the side of the 5"-long piece of 6"-diameter PVC.

47. Preheat your oven to 300°F. When it's warm, put the piece of 6" PVC on a baking tray and put it in the oven. Leave it there for about 5 minutes to soften.

48. Remove the PVC from the oven and immediately unroll it, sandwich it between two pieces of scrap lumber, lay the sandwiched pieces on the floor, and then put weight on the lumber (for example, kneel on it).

49. Wait for just a few minutes until the PVC has cooled. You should now have a flat piece of PVC.

50. Use the 4" hole saw to cut four 4"-diameter disks from the piece of PVC you just flattened.

51. The disks you just made need to fit snugly within the 4"-diameter PVC cylinders. Use the calipers to measure the inside diameter of the 4" PVC pipe. (You can also test whether the disks you made will fit inside the cylinder before proceeding.) The disks will probably need to be reduced to a slightly smaller diameter. One way to do this is to clamp them together on a lathe and hold a file against the disks' circumferences as they spin. Keep filing down the exterior evenly until the disks fit within one of the 4" PVC cylinders but are not so small that they wobble around.

52. Next, drill a ½" hole in the center of each plastic disk.

53. Now you're ready to create the seals. Use the drawing compass and pen to draw a circle on the sheet of (neoprene) craft foam. The circle should be about ¹⁄₁₆ of an inch *larger* than the 4" PVC pipe's inside diameter you measured with the calipers. Draw and cut out two of these circles. (Leave extra room on the foam sheet in case these seals don't work and you need to cut more.)

54. Cut a ½"-diameter hole through the center of each foam disk. Using a drill or drill press is overkill for this, but you still want a perfectly round hole. What worked for me was clasping the foam disk between the PVC disks and turning the ½" drill bit by hand through the center of the foam disk. This way, the holes you already drilled in the PVC disks help guide the bit.

55. You're ready to test your pistons. Attach the following to one of the bolt hooks in this order: nut, washer, PVC disk, foam disk, PVC disk, washer, nut, as shown in Figure 4.11. Tighten the nuts so that the foam disk is held firmly between the disks.

56. Try pushing the piston into the 4" PVC cylinder. Because the foam seals must be tight, it's okay if you have to first tilt the piston assembly to get it in. Keep testing and adjusting the diameters of the plastic

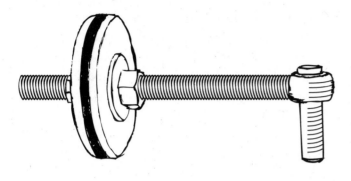

Figure 4.11 Piston Assembly

disks or foam disk as necessary so that the foam disk is pressed tightly against the inside walls of the 4" PVC pipe and the plastic disks don't prevent up-and-down movement within the cylinder. (If your foam disk is only slightly too small at this point, you can increase its diameter by further tightening the nuts on either side of the plastic disks, thereby compressing the foam.)

57. When you've determined the disks' proper size and spacing, make the second piston assembly to match the first.

58. Now you're ready to modify the cylinders to accept the valves. The 4" caps will form the bottom of the cylinders. Use the PVC cement to attach a cap to one end of each cylinder.

59. After the PVC cement has cured, you can drill holes for the threaded ends of the valves. Each cap will need two holes, positioned about ½" above the base of the cap and in a V-formation with about 36 degrees of separation, as is evident in Figure 4.14 (which shows the valves and hoses already inserted). Ideally, you would use a $^{59}/_{64}$" bit to drill these holes, but if you can't find that, you could use a $^{15}/_{16}$" bit. Clamp the cap and cylinder in a vise before drilling, and be sure to wear goggles.

60. Next, using the ¾" pipe tap, tap the four holes you drilled in the previous step. Make sure that the tap is straight as it enters the PVC and turn slowly, then back off periodically, to clean out the plastic you've removed.

61. With the cylinders ready to accept the valves, you can now attach them to the treadle base and hold it in place using the cylinder collars. To begin, place a 5-½" × 5-½" piece of plywood on one of the base's 2 × 6s. Align it with the lines you drew on a 2 × 6 in Steps 4 and 5. From the underside of the 2 × 6s, put a thin marking pen or pencil through each of the $^{5}/_{16}$" holes and make a dot on the plywood collar to indicate where to drill holes for the bolts. Do the same for the second 5-½" × 5-½" piece of plywood.

62. Drill $^{5}/_{16}$" holes through the plywood collars at the marks you made in the previous step.

63. Use calipers to measure the outside diameter of your PVC cylinder. Saw a hole in the center of each 5-½" × 5-½" piece of plywood slightly larger than that diameter. Make sure the hole is centered, as the collars aren't wide enough to give much room for error.

64. Position the cylinders on the 2 × 6s with the caps facing down and the centers 9" in from the back edge of the frame (the circles you drew in Step 3 should roughly in-

dicate the exterior of the cylinders). Turn the cylinders so that the valve holes are facing the front of the treadle pump.

65. Place a plywood collar over each of the cylinders. Thread the 6"-long ¼"-diameter carriage bolts from the underside of the 2 × 6s through the 2 × 6s and plywood collars. Fasten in place with the matching washers and nuts.

66. Now you're ready to add the hinge brackets to the underside of the treadles. The hinge brackets accept the bolt hooks, or piston rods, so setting up the pistons will help you determine exactly where to place the hinge brackets. Insert a piston assembly into one of the cylinders (with the disks downward and the L-shaped end of the bolt hook on top). Then slide the hinge bracket onto the shorter arm of the bolt hook. Position the piston so that the seal is approximately halfway to the bottom of the cylinder. Pull down the treadle until it meets the hinge bracket. Mark on the underside of the treadle where the hinge bracket's two bolt holes fall. (The bracket itself will be positioned toward the outside of the board.) Repeat this process for the other treadle and hinge bracket.

67. Drill ⁷⁄₁₆" holes at the points you marked in the previous step.

68. Attach the hinge straps to the bottom of the treadles using the 2"-long ⅜"-diameter bolts and, on the opposite side, the tee-nuts. The hole, which is slightly bigger than the bolts, should accommodate the flanges on the exterior of the tee-nuts. Use a hammer to force the nuts into the wood if necessary.

Making the Check Valves and Routing the Hoses

69. To begin, cut four ⅛"-wide spacers from the 9" length of 1-½"-diameter PVC pipe. It helps to hold the pipe in a vise if you do this with a handheld PVC saw or hacksaw, because it's hard to cut such a small piece accurately. Alternatively, you could use a chop saw. Set aside the four spacers for now.

70. Next, saw a slit along the length of the remainder of the 1-½" pipe.

71. Preheat the oven to 300°F, then put the 1-½" pipe in for 5 minutes. As soon as you remove it, flatten it between two boards and hold it fast for a few minutes, until the PVC has cooled.

72. Next, you'll make four X-shaped stoppers like the one shown in Figure 4.12. These stoppers catch the balls that allow water to flow in one direction, but not the other. First, use a PVC saw or hacksaw to cut four squares whose sides are 1-½" long.

73. Make an "X" on each square by drawing diagonal lines from corner to corner.

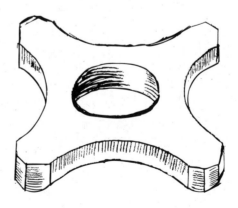

Figure 4.12 X-Shaped Stopper

The intersection of these lines indicates the square's center point. Drill a ½" hole through the center point of each square.

74. To allow a ball to rest tightly against the center hole of each square, you'll want to create a bevel on one side of the hole. Use a ¹⁵⁄₁₆" drill bit lightly against, but not all the way through, one side of each hole to create a bevel.

75. Use a half-round bastard file to create the rounded depressions between the corners of the stopper, as shown in Figure 4.12. The depressions should be about ³⁄₁₆" deep.

76. Also use the file to round off the corners of each square, so that it fits snugly within a 1-½" coupling.

77. Before assembling the valves, use a permanent marker to draw an arrow on the outside of each of the four couplings. This arrow will indicate the direction of water flow through the check valve.

78. Each check valve should consist of these parts in the following order, from upstream to downstream (that is, toward the arrow's head): bushing, ball, ⅛" spacer,

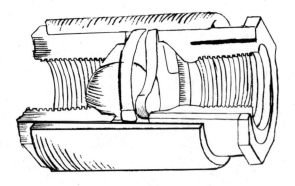

Figure 4.13 Cross-Section of the Homemade Check Valve

coupling, X-shaped stopper with beveled end on the left so that it can accept the ball, and then the other bushing. (Note that the arrow on the bushing should be pointing to the right.) After verifying that your valve parts fit together, use PVC cement to fasten the bushings tightly within the coupler. Figure 4.13 provides a cross-sectional view of the complete check valve.

79. After assembling all four valves, you can attach them to the cylinders. Wrap Teflon tape around both threaded ends of each of the four ¾"-diameter close pipe nipples. Screw a pipe nipple into each of the four holes you tapped in the cylinders.

80. For each cylinder, screw one of the valves onto a pipe nipple so that its arrow indicates an upstream-to-downstream flow — this will be the water intake valve. Screw the other valve on so that its arrow indicates a downstream-to-upstream flow — this will be the water output valve. From one cylinder to the next, alternate the input and output valves so that two of the same type aren't next to each other in the middle.

81. Now you're ready to prepare the hoses for routing. The agricultural spray hose is used to route the flow of water into and out of the cylinders because it's flexible and can make the relatively tight curves necessary to connect the inflow and output valves from each cylinder. Yet it's tough enough to withstand the suction the pump will create. From the 7' length of flexible agricultural spray hose, cut two 22" pieces and two 14" pieces.

82. Spread a little liquid soap on the insides of the ends of each piece of hose you cut in the previous step. This will make it easier to slide them onto the barbed fittings.

83. Put a hose clamp loosely over one end of one of the 22" lengths of agricultural hose, then push it over the barbed fitting attached to the left-hand cylinder's input valve. Once it's pushed in as far as possible, tighten the hose clamp around the connection.

84. Put a hose clamp loosely over one end of the other 22" length of agricultural hose, then push this end over the barbed fitting attached to the right-hand cylinder's output valve. Once it's pushed in as far as possible, tighten the hose clamp around the connection.

85. Put a hose clamp loosely over one end of one of the 14" lengths of agricultural hose, then push this end over the barbed fitting attached to the right-hand cylinder's input valve. Once it's pushed in as far as possible, tighten the hose clamp around the connection.

86. Put a hose clamp loosely over one end of the other 14" piece of agricultural hose, then push this end over the barbed fitting attached to the left-hand cylinder's output valve. Once it's pushed in as far as possible, tighten the hose clamp around the connection.

87. Now you're ready to connect the two input and output hoses. Slide the ends of the two output hoses over two prongs of one barbed Tee fitting. Fasten the hoses in place with hose clamps.

88. Slide the ends of the two input hoses over two prongs of the second Tee fitting. Fasten the hoses in place with hose clamps. (Refer to Figure 4.14 to see how the hoses should look when attached.)

89. Now your pump should be complete. To test it, attach one hose to the open end of the intake barbed Tee fitting and attach another hose to the open end of the outflow barbed Tee fitting. Then run the intake hose to a water source that's more than a foot deep. Step on the treadles and shift your weight from side to side to pump.

Variations and Considerations

• Rather than making your own check valves, you could purchase sump pump check valves from the hardware store and use those. They would work just as well. However, in my experience doing so added over $100 to the cost of the pump, not because the valves were expensive,

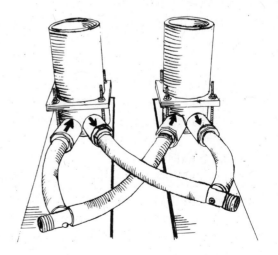

Figure 4.14 Routing the Hoses

but because of the cost of additional connectors necessary to insert the valves. Also, these connectors increased the bulk of the input and output lines where there isn't much free space.

- The engineers who designed the treadle pump for Haitian growers inserted bushings into the rear axle (over the round stock and inside the 2 × 4 treadles and uprights). This will help the device operate smoothly for a longer time. They also drilled multiple holes horizontally through the three front uprights and used a separate 2 × 4 for the mast. This means the mast and pulleys can be raised and lowered to adjust to the height of the operator. And finally, they added brackets to the front and back through which you can slide the mast to make a handle. This way, the pump is more portable.

- Rather than baking and flattening PVC pipes, you can also buy PVC flat stock — that is, sheets of PVC. However, I found that the flat stock didn't come in small sizes and in the larger sizes, it was expensive.

- If you can't find agricultural spray hose capable of withstanding high pressure, you could use a different kind of hose for connecting the inlet and outlet valves. However, the hose needs to be flexible. Both I and the engineers who designed the pump for Haitan growers experimented with inexpensive poly hose, but found it too inflexible for the hoses that exit the valves. Jim and Larry recommend using automotive type heater hose. It's flexible, but unfortunately, it's also liable to collapse under the pressure generated by the pump. To make sure the hose stays open, you can insert a long compression spring or even a coil of 10-gauge wire that you make yourself (for example, by winding it around a ¾" mandrel, such as round bar stock). In the same way a stent keeps an artery from collapsing during medical procedures, this metal coil will prevent the hose from collapsing under pressure. You would only need to insert the coil on the intake hoses.

- Rather than using 4" PVC pipe for the cylinders and slip caps, you could use 3" PVC. The difference between the 3" and 4" cylinders is that the latter is capable of pumping more water.

- If you want to human-power your pump, but don't want to go to the trouble of creating your own from scratch, you can purchase a simple hand-powered pump. For example, Lehman's, which sells supplies for self-sufficient living, carries several types of pitcher pumps as well as a plastic hand-cranked transfer pump (often used for moving fuel from one container to another). Tool suppliers and farm stores carry rotary transfer pumps, too. With minor modifications, you can convert these to be pedal-powered. For example, Lee Ravenscroft of Working Bikes Cooperative in Chicago (featured in Chapter 2) was commissioned to create a kid-friendly pedal-powered pump for the Root River Environmental Education Community Center in Racine, Wisconsin. Lee connected a sprocket to the axle of a transfer pump. Then he ran a chain from a bike's chainring to this sprocket. Before installing it at the environmental learning center, he'd created a safety shield around the chain drive. He estimates the pump will transfer about 10 gallons per minute.

Commercially Available Plans and Devices For Lawn and Garden

Lawn and garden care is an area where using human power can truly benefit the environment. According to the US Environmental Protection Agency (EPA), each year approximately 17 million gallons of fuel, mostly gasoline, are spilled while refueling lawn equipment. That's more than the amount of oil spilled by the Exxon Valdez in the Gulf of Alaska. In addition, the agency warns, "gasoline-powered landscape equipment (mowers, trimmers, blowers, chainsaws) account for over 5% of our urban air pollution."[3]

In the following pages you'll read about modern versions of machines that have been used to cultivate, hoe and mow for centuries. But thanks to advanced materials and manufacturing, these human-powered devices come with significant advantages over the antique versions. They're lighter weight, better designed, and easier to use. If you commit to tending your lawn or garden with human power, invest in one of the contemporary devices described below.

Push Seeders and Cultivators

If you grow food on a scrap of land in the city or a sprawling farm on the prairie, then the push seeders and cultivators described in this section probably aren't appropriate tools.

They're targeted to market gardeners or home gardeners with relatively large plots. If that describes you, then the human-powered rotary seeders and cultivators (as well as their hoe and plow attachments) can save hours of straining and bending over.

Push seeders, such as the one pictured in Figure 4.15, can also result in more uniform plantings, which means less thinning and potentially higher yields. As you push, the seeder plows a furrow, drops seeds from a hopper at prescribed intervals, and then covers and packs the seeds with soil. Before planting, you have to choose and insert the disk, or plate, that matches your seed type. The size of and distance between holes in the plate will determine how much seed can drop at once and how frequently seeds are dropped. Planting depth is adjusted by moving the wedge-shaped "ground opener" up or down and then fixing it in place.

Figure 4.15 Push Seeder

Push seeders work best for planting many rows of relatively large-seeded crops such as corn and beans. You couldn't, for example, use them to plant potatoes, hills of squash, or, needless to say, transplant seedlings. And their performance tends to be less reliable with tiny, lightweight seeds such as lettuce and carrots. They work best in freshly tilled, rock-free soil. Some users complain of unevenly distributed seeds or clogs, and to some extent, this can be controlled by properly sizing the seed plate to what you're planting. Also make sure that the seed chute is free of debris and that seeder plates are not warped.

One popular push seeder is the EarthWay Precision Garden Seeder. At the time this was written, the EarthWay seeder was available for as little as $70 and came with a 90-day warranty. Six seed plates (sweet corn, radish, carrot, peas, beans and beets) are included, but additional plates, like those for lettuce, broccoli and lima beans are available for an extra $4.50 each. (Bear in mind that some seed plates can do double-duty. Flower gardeners, for example, might use the beet seed plate for planting zinnias.) Or you can buy one of EarthWay's blank plates and customize it by drilling the size and spacing of holes you require. The EarthWay seeder also comes with a row marker that attaches to the side and drags a line parallel to the row you're seeding to indicate your next row. Another optional accessory for this seeder is a fertilizer attachment that allows you to apply fertilizer above or below ground.

For covering more ground, consider combining multiple seeders into one implement. Gene Logsdon, in his book, *The Contrary*

Farmer, describes how he bolted together his two Earthway planters using three pieces of scrap wood and hardware. Similarly, Andrew Lee, in his book *Backyard Market Gardening*, describes how he connected three Earthway seeders on a common axle. Such an implement, he claims, enables one person to plant at least two acres in one day.[4]

Compared to the EarthWay seeder, the Cole Planet Jr. Hand Seeder, another popular model, is a premium machine. It looks similar and operates on the same principle. Like the EarthWay seeder, it plows a furrow, drops seeds from a hopper and through the appropriate seed plate, then covers them with dirt. It also comes with a row indicator arm and allows for simultaneous fertilization and planting. The main difference, however, is in its construction, which is almost entirely steel, rather than partly plastic. Also, the Planet Jr. comes with a handle-mounted cutoff lever, so that you can stop the flow of seeds while rounding a corner and before beginning another row. And finally, its combination of multiple seed plates and the ability to customize which holes are used on each plate allows for a wider variety of planting with less fuss. At the time this was written, the Planet Jr. sold for about $500. Market gardeners credit this model with long life and excellent precision, even when sowing lightweight seeds such as lettuce. In fact, the Planet Jr. seeder is an old brand that some might remember from the early 20th century. You can still find antique versions of this seeder, and as long as the wheels aren't too rusted and the wooden handles remain firm, it might be worth your investment.

The gravity-fed plate seeders are not the only types of push seeders on the market. Others, such as the Stanhay Precision Belt Seeder and Seedburo Equipment Company's Cone Push Seeder are more complex and precise human-powered machines. But with prices starting at $1,300 and $4,500, respectively, they're not typically marketed to home gardeners.

Before planting it's often beneficial to loosen the soil. And if you're a human-powered gardener, push cultivators, sometimes called high wheel cultivators, can help you do this. They're designed to loosen soil or free shallow-rooted weeds between rows. And as described in this chapter's plan for a bike-frame cultivator, which is very similar, they provide added leverage for slicing through the ground. However, they aren't strong enough to till or plow through sod or heavy clay soil. Push cultivators, and their close cousins, push furrowers or plows, are old inventions. (You might have seen them in country yard displays, surrounded by rocks and flowers.) The modern versions, as shown in Figure 4.16, vary little in design from the antiques (unlike push mowers, for example, which have been greatly improved since the early 20th century).

In addition to its push seeder, EarthWay makes a high wheel cultivator. Its frame and 24-inch wheel are made of steel, and its long handles are made of oak. It comes with three steel attachments: a five-tined cultivator, a moldboard plow (or hilling plow), and a furrow plow (or furrower). These are easily interchangeable with the adjustment of one bolt. At the time this was written, the EarthWay High Wheel cultivator was available for as low as $75 and came with a 90-day warranty. You could also buy an optional slicing hoe attachment for an additional $14.

Another high-wheel cultivator, from Beaver, shares the same characteristics as the EarthWay cultivator, including the three attachments, which this company calls: a five-tine cultivator, a double-pointed shovel (or moldboard plow), and a turn shovel (or furrower). The Beaver high wheel cultivator with all three attachments sold for about $95.

A unique multipurpose, pushed garden tool comes from the Swiss company Glaser Engineering. It sells a single- and a double-wheeled hoe whose head can be replaced with different implements, including a spring-loaded seeder, a three-tined cultivator, and

Figure 4.16 High Wheel Cultivator

furrower. The wheel on this device isn't as large as the Earthway or Planet Jr. models, and its seed hopper is also smaller. At the time this was written, Glaser's single-wheeled seeder cost about $140 while the three-tined cultivator cost $63 and came with a 2-year warranty.

Reel Mowers

Manual mowers are making a comeback. Also known as push mowers or reel mowers, they're based on an 1830s British device invented to replace the scythe. (Although some electric- or gas-powered reel mowers exist, for the sake of simplicity, the term "reel mower" used in this section refers to the manual type.) For over a century they were the only kind of lawn mowers. But shortly after World War II gasoline-powered mowers, perceived as faster and more powerful, quickly replaced them. Recently, however, interest in reel mowers has surged. A spokesperson for American Lawn Mower Company, the largest producer of reel mowers in the United States, estimated that annual sales of reel mowers today are seven times higher than they were in the 1980s.[5] Granted, that still represents only 2% of all lawn mower sales. However, people who convert are convinced of the manual mower's benefits, particularly when it comes to air quality.

The California Air Resources Board calculated that "2006 lawn mower engines contribute[d] 93 times more smog-forming emissions than 2006 cars."[6] This is largely because the companies that make mower engines have long refused to add catalytic converters, citing potential safety hazards. (Legislation to mandate catalytic converters on lawn equip-ment engines took effect in California in 2007, and at the time this was written, the EPA was considering a similar national standard.) A Swedish study concluded that running a gas-powered mower for one hour emitted polycyclic aromatic hydrocarbons (classified as probable carcinogens by the US Centers for Disease Control and Prevention) equivalent to those emitted by driving a car about 93 miles (150 km).[7]

Today's reel mowers rely on the same mechanical principles as those from the 19th century, but come with a few improvements. Thanks to newer materials, modern reel mowers weigh about half as much as their predecessors — from 15 to 55 pounds, depending on the model. The lighter weight and addition of bearings found in the more sophisticated models makes them easier to push. Also, many of today's reel mowers come with blades that stay sharper with less maintenance compared to antique versions.

Reel mowers cut grass differently than power mowers. In a reel mower, several spiral-shaped steel blades rotate along a horizontal axis. As the blades turn, they draw grass in and then snip it against a stationary blade in a scissoring action. By contrast, power mowers use a blade mounted parallel to the ground that tears off grass with brute force. (For this reason, they must spin faster than reel mower blades and are more dangerous.) Most of the comments I've gotten while using our reel mower have been from elderly men who reminisce about their early lawn mowing days and assure me that these mowers are more effective than power mowers and lead to healthier lawns. Indeed, some reel mower manufacturers claim the ragged edges caused by a power mower leave the grass more vulnerable to disease. The reel mower's scissoring action cuts a clean edge and discharges small clippings, not clumps, that can easily return nitrogen to the soil. Finally, reel mowers generally cost less than gas-powered mowers, and they never refuse to start.

Until you've tried a reel mower, you might expect using it to be hard work, but in fact, a new reel mower provides very little resistance. The amount of effort also depends on your lawn. Flat, homogenous turf with few weeds is easy to cut. Twigs thicker than a knitting needle will stop a reel mower in its tracks, and the mowers tend to run over, rather than slice, thick-stemmed plants such as dandelions. Hilly, overgrown lawns can be a workout. Don't let the grass grow more than 6 inches without cutting. You'll also work much harder, pushing and pulling the mower over the same patch of grass, if your blades are dull.

Companies manufacturing or selling reel mowers in North America include American Lawn Mower (which markets the "Great States" and "Scotts" brands), Brill and Sunlawn. The best resource I've found for comparing the features of the most commonly purchased reel is a chart posted by David Temple, who runs the People Powered Machines Web site at peoplepoweredmachines.com. David, a teacher, became interested in reel mowers after he moved from New York City to a house outside Boston that came with a one-acre lawn. Due to health and environmental concerns, he "absolutely" didn't want to use a gas-powered mower. He and his wife searched for the best human-powered mower

and discovered Brill's Luxus model. So enthusiastic about the machine, he agreed to resell it to hardware stores on the east coast. Shortly thereafter, he started his Web site, and sales took off. He told me he sells a few thousand reel mowers each year, in addition to other human-powered lawn tools. Business is strong enough that he quit his teaching job this year to focus full time on it. And he still tests every product for at least a year in his own yard before agreeing to sell it.[8]

David still prefers mowers made by the German company Brill. Their latest model, the RazorCut 38, shown in Figure 4.17, sells for about $250. It has a 38-inch-wide cutting reel that contains five spiral blades precisely

Figure 4.17 Brill Razorcut Reel Mower

engineered to pass within one millimeter of each other. It weighs only 17 pounds and boasts a recommended eight-year interval between sharpening. Brill mowers are considered premium models. If you're interested in a more economical solution, I've found that the Scotts Classic and Great States mowers, though heavier and in need of more frequent sharpening, work fine as well. They sell for about $160. In terms of weight, features and cost, Sunlawn's reel mowers fall somewhere in the middle. If you're interested in buying a Brill or Sunlawn mower at lower than retail prices, you can probably find a refurbished model.

Several resources can help you decide which mower is best for you. If your local home supply or hardware store doesn't carry a selection, go online and check out David Temple's People Powered Machines site, or Push Mowers 101 at pushmowers101.com, or the Guide to Using a Reel Mower, at reelmowerguide.com. Clean Air Gardening, cleanairgardening.com, is another business that sells reel mowers and

Figure 4.18 Richard Ehrlich's Pedal-Powered Lawn Mower

provides comprehensive product information about the models they carry.

Many people have dreamed of using a pedal-powered lawn mower. At the time this was written, none were commercially available, but enough examples had been made and their photos circulated for the determined inventor to get ideas. Some people experiment with simply replacing a bike's front wheel with a reel mower. However, Richard Ehrlich, a pedal-powered lawn mower inventor who tried this, pointed out that an upright design takes a lot of traction to get started and is apt to tip when turning. Richard's second attempt was a recumbent-style mower. With the help of a local machinist, he used square steel tube to make a frame for a front-wheel-driven, rear-wheel steered recumbent mower. He attached the 36" reel from an old mower to the driveshaft just forward of the seat (which, incidentally, is made from a folding chair). He also added a flywheel to the reel's axle. The bike uses two chain drives: one that connects a chainring and cogset to allow for variable gearing and another that turns the cutting reel. Richard cited as inspiration a recumbent-style mower built in 1973 by Michael Shakespear as an undergraduate thesis project at MIT under the supervision of David Gordon Wilson.

Richard's mower, pictured in Figure 4.18, weighs about 110 pounds, is very stable, comfortable, easy to pedal and maneuvers well. After more than 10 years he still uses it to mow his one-acre lot in Ontario, Canada. He told me his dogs walk alongside him as he mows, probably thinking he's taking a very long and boring bike ride.[9]

Push Sweepers

Push sweepers fall into one of two categories: those designed for sidewalks, commercial carpets, and other relatively hard surfaces and those designed to be used on lawns. The first type, known as surface sweepers or sidewalk sweepers, have two brushes oriented parallel to the ground. When you push the sweeper, the brushes rotate toward each other and direct debris into a bin behind them. The brushes can pick up not only leaves and twigs, but also small stones and trash. The debris collects in a hard-plastic bin attached to the back of the sweeper.

Surface sweepers are less common than reel mowers. You probably wouldn't find them at your local hardware store. Models range from inexpensive residential types to expensive versions designed for places like movie theaters. On the residential side are the Swooper and SooperSwooper brands. Both are relatively inexpensive. At the time this was written the Swooper, which has a 6-gallon debris container, cost as low as $80. The Sooper-Sweeper, which can accept up to 7.2 gallons of refuse, cost about $100. Both feature adjustable height and a sweeping width of under two feet. These products get mixed reviews. Some users have reported troubles operating them and question their craftsmanship. Powr-Flite, a commercial cleaning supply company, offers a 32-inch wide manual surface sweeper with a 9-gallon holding capacity and adjustable height for about $235. (The company also sells refurbished models at lower cost.) Similar high-quality surface sweepers come from German-based Haaga. At the time this was written, Haaga offered two models, a 55-cm

(21.6") one, shown in Figure 4.19, which sold for $269, and a 75-cm (29.5") model, which sold for $359.

In fact, surface sweepers can be used to sweep lawns, too, but when people refer to a lawn sweeper they typically mean a slightly different machine. A lawn sweeper, also called a leaf sweeper, resembles a reel mower, but instead of spiral cutting blades, the reel

Figure 4.19 Haaga TopSweep 55

Pedal-Powered Snowplows

David Gordon Wilson, emeritus professor of engineering at MIT and author of *Bicycling Science*, a singular work devoted to the history, physiology, mechanics and physics of cycling, has given a lot of thought to snow removal. He writes, "Shoveling snow is another example of a heavy task involving the use of the muscles of the arms and back and of having the back bent uncomfortably. It would be more efficacious and put less stress on the body to use the big muscles of the legs and to have a more natural posture; presumably this would also be less likely to overstrain the heart."[10] He designed a human-powered snow plow called a "snovel," which looks like a long-handled plow blade on wheels. With it, he told me, he can "charge into a snow bank and push" the snow away.[11] Meanwhile, his neighbors take twice as long to clear their similar-sized driveways with snowblowers. Dave also wrote, however, that we "need better human-powered snow-removal devices, efficient, fun to use even for older or nonathletic people, and compact when stowed."[12]

Kevin Blake, a mechanical engineer who works for Trek Bikes in Wisconsin, had seen a photo of the snovel and read Dave Wilson's call to build a better human-powered snow removal device. In fact, he'd been thinking about a pedal-powered snow plow for more than 10 years before he went to his workshop and began sketching. His building process matches that of many human-powered machine inventors. He'd draw something, make it, try it out, change what didn't work, then test it again. He spent considerable time perfecting the V-shaped blade, the chain tensioner, and a custom cogset to allow variable gearing. (Having access to the company shop was a big plus.) He finished the pedal-powered snow plow in February 2004. On the night after he completed it snow fell, and Kevin was late for work the following day because he was having so much fun plowing snow.

Kevin said his snow plow works best in powdery snow less than 6 inches deep, and he uses it often in the Wisconsin winters. With heavy or packed snow, he admitted, it's less effective, and it can suffer traction loss on ice: "The true advantage of this machine is the fact that it clears large areas without having to bend and lift over and over again with a shovel." And with the V-shaped blade, it takes only one pass to clear a sidewalk.

Kevin's coworkers at Trek were enthusiastic about the snow plow, and some offered suggestions for improvement. He's also received a few inquiries about building pedal-powered snow plows for purchase, but suggested that when people discovered how much a plow would cost, they'd change their minds. Instead, he's decided to redesign the snow plow from scratch with off-the-shelf parts. Then he'll write plans for that design so anyone can build it. He's also interested in designing a child-sized plow. I proposed adding a snowball launcher to that version, and he began sketching.[13]

Figure 4.20 Kevin Blake's Pedal-Powered Snow Plow

spins brushes that drag clippings, leaves and other debris into a catcher. (The catchers, or hampers, on lawn sweepers are not hard-shell cases as they are on surface sweepers, but are made of a material similar to a poly tarp.) Lawn sweepers offer an earth-friendly alternative to gas-powered leaf blowers and vacuums, as well as hours of raking leaves. If you use a reel mower, consider using a lawn sweeper first to remove small twigs that could catch in the reel mower's blades. As with reel mowers, lawn sweepers work best on flat surfaces. No matter what the brand, operating one on hilly surfaces is challenging and often ineffective. Also, be sure to adjust the height properly for your ground and what you intend to sweep up — for example, higher for pine cones and lower for pine needles. All brands of push lawn sweepers mentioned next allow you to adjust the height of their brushes.

Agri-Fab and Craftsman make the most common push lawn sweeper, and in fact, though the names are different, the item marketed by both companies is the same. It has a sweeping width of 26 inches and a hopper capacity of about 7 cubic feet. At the time this was written, the Agri-Fab version sold for as low as $110, and the Craftsman version sold for as low as $100. Mid West Products, Inc., makes a similar push lawn sweeper available for $110. The company also makes what it calls a Deluxe Push Lawn Sweeper — which has an 8.1 cubic feet hopper, much larger than other push lawn sweepers' — in two different widths: 26" and 31". The 26" model costs as low as $240 and the 31" model as low as $270. In addition, Mid West Products offers a "baler," which can supposedly double the hamper capacity, for about $20.

CHAPTER 5

HUMAN-POWERED DEVICES FOR HOUSEWORK

lthough pedal-powering a blender, for example, might seem more like amusement than work, we're probably less eager to relinquish the labor savings that electrical appliances bring to housework. In fact, long before homes had electricity, inventors were designing machines that could ease the homemaker's burden. These early human-powered machines were not always successful, however.

Consider vacuuming, for example. One of the first vacuum cleaners, patented in 1869 and known as the Whirlwind, was human-powered. It required the user to turn a crank on a wheel connected by belt to a fan, which generated a vacuum. (It did not come with a brush roll.) Unfortunately, cranking and pushing the vacuum simultaneously was awkward, and no doubt the amount of effort and time involved exceeded what it would take to simply sweep the carpet. Little is known about the Whirlwind's popularity, as most were sold in the inventor's hometown of Chicago and destroyed in the great fire of 1871. Yet it wasn't the only human-powered vacuum. "Later devices used the motion of the wheels as they advanced along the carpet to turn a fan or pump a set of bellows," writes journalist Curt Wohleber. "It was a clever idea, but either the user had to move the sweeper frantically back and forth to generate enough sucking power, or else pushing the machine required superhuman strength."[1]

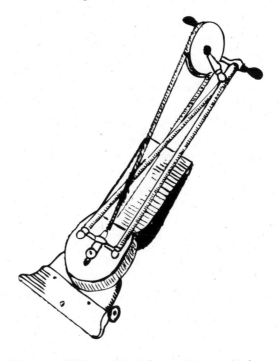

Figure 5.1 Whirlwind Hand-Cranked Vacuum Cleaner

Still, some modern day human-power enthusiasts have devised novel ways to accomplish housework. David Butcher (featured in Chapter 6), for example, uses his pedal-powered electrical generator to charge a low-wattage robotic vacuum cleaner called the Roomba. He told me, "That's my favorite toy to charge. I like to think about the Roomba doing something I don't like to do. I like to pedal but I don't like to vacuum, and it likes to vacuum."[2] Meanwhile, Alex Gadsden has invented a sleek pedal-powered washing machine that he calls the Cyclean, described in more detail later in this chapter.

Others, like Anne Kusilek, regard what would traditionally be considered housework as a pleasure, rather than a chore, and wonder why anyone would choose to motorize these tasks.

Plan for Converting an Electric Sewing Machine to Treadle Power

After reading about Anne Kusilek's enthusiasm for treadle sewing machines maybe you're inspired to try treadling yourself. This plan guides you through converting a mid-20th-century electric sewing machine to be treadle powered. One advantage of using a newer-model sewing machine rather than an original treadle machine is that it provides a wider variety of stitches. At the same time, using a treadle allows you to sew free from the grid. This plan is the simplest in the book, and after you've learned how to make the conver-

Anne Kusilek's Treadle Sewing Business

Anne Kusilek is a professional seamstress in northern Wisconsin whose business, Finely Finished, caters to a niche market — those who want their pieced quilt tops finished on treadle sewing machines. In fact, she sews exclusively with treadle or hand-cranked sewing machines and has ten, each threaded with different color of thread, ready to use at any moment.

Her devotion to treadle machines began 18 years ago when she and her husband picked up an antique sewing machine at an auction simply because they liked its oak cabinet, which complemented the woodwork in the bungalow they were restoring. She threaded it for kicks and discovered that it worked. Not only that, but she enjoyed using it. "I loved the idea that I wasn't dependent on electricity," she said. In fact, she has sewn during power outages. "I won't even notice

the power was out until I see the numbers blinking on the clock." It's been 12 years since she's used an electric sewing machine.

But more important for Anne is that treadle machines aren't fussy, don't wear out fast, and are easy to clean and oil. Durability and reliability are benefits frequently mentioned by those who prefer these machines made of cast iron and case-hardened steel that were designed to withstand a generation of heavy use. Many machines are still going strong after 100 years. Compare that to the planned obsolescence after 7 to 10 years of light use that characterizes today's sewing machines. As Anne said, "Computer-run machines are tricky to repair. When the computers go, they don't try to fix the problem, they just pop in a new motherboard. And they're not cheap." She admitted feeling cynical about the modern

sion, you could do it in 5 minutes or less for a friend.

The parts list includes a sewing machine with an external, belt-driven motor. Though the criteria are very specific, you won't have any trouble finding machines that fit this description. And providing they don't have a special feature that collectors covet, you can get a good, used machine for $20 to $40. Because these machines were manufactured to last generations, and because they don't rely on electronics, virtually all of them still function well. (You might also find a bargain on a machine whose motor is faulty; since you'll be removing the motor, it doesn't matter whether it works.) For optimal performance, consult a sewing machine maintenance manual and

Figure 5.2 Electric Sewing Machine Converted to Treadle Power

sewing machine industry. "They try to convince women that they need new things. But we need to discern the difference between improvements and change for change's sake." She doesn't consider the electric motor an improvement, much less all the fancy stitches. "I need a machine that does one stitch really well every single time."

Another advantage to human-powered sewing machines is the control they allow the user. On a hand-cranked machine, for example, a person can be so precise as to make one stitch per turn of the crank. Or, on a treadle sewing machine, given strong needles, one can sew through extremely thick material, as legs can push the machine to continue past the point when an electric motor would stall. Anne has sewn even leather horse bridles on her treadle machine.

Finally, human-powered sewing machines are easy to use. Anne told me, "Once you get this big flywheel going just a nudge of the toe is all it takes to keep it in motion. If it's hard to use, there's something wrong. It should be nearly effortless." It's rare that sewing on a treadle machine strains joints or muscles. In fact, one physical therapist recommends treadle sewing to clients as a gentle way to keep joints loose.

In addition to sewing professionally, Anne teaches workshops on using and maintaining treadle sewing machines, though it's so quick and simple, she told me, people are generally underwhelmed. Many who seek her advice have their grandma's treadle sewing machine in the basement and, fueled by nostalgia, want to make a quilt with it. She responds, "Why stop at one?"[3]

clean and oil the machine properly before use.

Treadle bases — the stand that contains the cast-iron treadle drive and a wooden table, sometimes with drawers on both sides — are also easy to come by. Prices depend on condition, but average about $50. Make sure the treadle apparatus is whole and working. Some treadle bases have been converted to side tables or plant stands, their drives dismantled, and of course, these will no longer operate a sewing machine.

Ease of construction: Very simple, using standard tools and minimal skill

Time to make: 1 hour or less

Cost to make: $75 to $125 for used sewing machine and treadle, plus new belt

Ease of operation: Very easy

Following is an overview of the steps in this plan:

- First, you'll remove the electric sewing machine from its case, then take off its attached motor and light, if it has one.
- Next, you'll place the sewing machine in the treadle base.
- Then, you'll thread the new treadle belt through the handwheel and band wheel and measure it for cutting.
- Finally, you'll cut the treadle belt to length, connect the two ends and test your converted treadle sewing machine.

Materials

- A sewing machine with an external belt-driven motor, such as one manufactured between the 1930s through 1950s. It should (and given the vintage, probably will) have a rectangular base that measures 14-½" by 7". In other words, make sure it's a regular, full-sized flat-bed machine and not a small portable or child-sized machine. As examples, Singer models 66, 15, 99 and 27 are good choices, but many others also meet the criteria. Avoid machines whose motors use friction drives in the form of a motor-driven spindle that rubs against the handwheel as it turns. The machine you choose needn't have a working motor or foot pedal, but verify that its mechanical parts function. In particular, check to make sure the needle moves up or down when you turn the handwheel.
- A treadle base for a sewing machine with a standard-sized opening that measures 14-½" by 7". These dimensions are typical of the most popular Singer treadle bases made between 1900 and 1960, for example. Avoid those designed for sewing machines with fiddle back or ¾-sized bases. Verify that the entire drive, including the treadle, Pitman rod and band wheel, is whole and functional.
- A treadle belt. These are available from several online suppliers and at some sewing machine repair shops. Most are leather, but one made of rubber or polyurethane will also work. Make sure the belt comes with the hook, or staple, used to fasten the two ends of the belt together. The standard length of approximately 72" is suitable.

Tools

- Flathead screwdriver
- Permanent marker

- Wire cutters (or a heavy-duty pair of scissors)
- Two pairs of pliers
- Hammer
- Small nail with a fine point
- Workbench or other sturdy work surface

Steps for Converting an Electric Sewing Machine to Treadle Power

1. If your sewing machine came in a carrying case (or cabinet), take off the cover. Then remove the sewing machine head from the case. Usually this means tilting it back (away from you) and pulling it up to disengage the machine's base from the two hinge pins mounted on the rear panel of the cabinet.

   Note: For safety's sake, do not allow the sewing machine to be plugged in at any point during this project!

2. If your machine has a light, take it off by removing the screw or screws that hold it to the back of the machine.

3. Now examine the sewing machine to determine how the electric motor is attached. Usually, it's supported by a bracket that's fixed to the machine with a single, large screw. Use the screwdriver to remove that screw and bracket, as shown in Figure 5.3.

4. Take off the rubber belt that connects the handwheel to the electric motor. This might require prying the belt out of the groove with a screwdriver or similar implement.

5. For some electric sewing machines, removing the light, motor and belt is enough to release the entire electrical assembly (including the foot pedal and cords). However, on other machines the cord is attached to the sewing machine's base. If this is the case on your machine, use the wire cutters or scissors to cut the cord where necessary. Set aside the motor, foot pedal and cords. You won't need them again.

6. Take a look at your treadle base. If a belt is still intact, notice how it's looped around the band wheel (sometimes also called a balance wheel or drive wheel), through the metal loop on the rear of the drive (the belt guide), through the holes in the wooden base and metal plate on top of

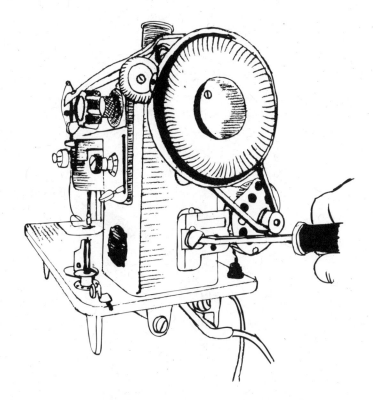

Figure 5.3 Removing the Sewing Machine Motor

the base and also through the metal loop on the front side of the treadle drive (the belt shifter). Remove it by severing it with the wire cutters or scissors, and then pulling it off the machine.

7. Place the sewing machine head into the treadle base. If the machine was held in a case with hinge pins, as described in Step 1, it will probably fit into the corresponding hinge pins in the treadle base. (If your sewing machine's base is too small for the treadle base, you'll need to create a shelf for it. A piece of ¾" plywood works well. Set the plywood on top of the treadle base, then measure and mark where you need to cut holes for the treadle belt, right above the holes in the metal plate that's on the treadle base. Do this now, before threading and measuring your treadle belt, because the added height of the plywood will add to the belt's length. If your sewing machine is wider or longer than the treadle base opening, you may set it

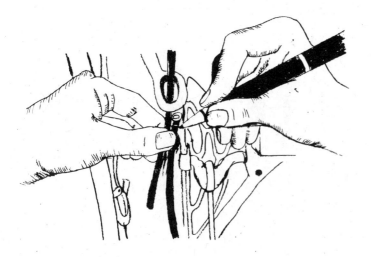

Figure 5.4 Measuring the Belt

on top of the treadle base or make a plywood shelf for it.)

8. Wrap the new belt around the groove in the handwheel where the motor's rubber belt rested previously. Then thread one end of the belt down through the front hole in the metal plate on the treadle base, through the open slat in the front of the wood base, then through the belt shifter and around the band wheel. Thread the other end of the belt down through the rear hole in the metal plate on the base, through the open slat in the rear of the wood base, then through the belt guide. Draw the ends together. They should overlap by at least a few inches.

9. Tug on the ends until the belt is as tight as possible around the band wheel, as shown in Figure 5.4, then use the permanent marking pen to mark where the end that has the staple in it meets the end without a staple.

10. With the wire cutters or scissors, cut the belt where you marked it in Step 9.

11. Unthread the belt from the machine and place it on a workbench or other work surface.

12. Next, you'll need to punch a hole in the end of the belt that doesn't contain the staple. You could use an awl or tool designed especially for this purpose, but I've found that a small nail and a hammer works fine. It's helpful to first pound the free belt end with the hammer to flatten it against your work surface, as if you were tenderizing meat. Then position the point of the small nail where the staple will enter, about ¼" in from the edge of the cut end.

Hold the nail steady while you hammer it through the treadle belt. Attempt to center the hole between the sides of the belt.

13. Thread the belt through the treadle drive again, just as you did in Step 8.

14. Next, you're ready to connect the two ends. (If your staple came wrapped with a piece of tape, remove that.) To loosen the belt so that you don't have to wrestle with tension while you fasten the staple, slip the belt off the band wheel.

15. With a pair of pliers in each hand, thread the open end of the staple through the hole that you made in Step 12. Insert the staple fully, but don't cinch it closed yet.

16. Put the belt back on the band wheel.

17. Now test the tension in the belt. While sitting at the sewing machine, start the needle by turning the handwheel, then push the treadle to continue operating the machine. If the belt slips or sags, it's too loose, and you'll need to remove the staple from one end, then repeat Steps 9 through 15. It might take a few attempts before getting the right amount of tension in the belt.

18. When you've determined that the belt is sufficiently taut, you'll need to cinch the staple closed. First, though, release the belt from the band wheel by pressing the lever on the belt shifter and pulling the belt away from the wheel. Then find the staple and, holding the closed-staple end of the belt with one pair of pliers, clamp the open staple down tight with the second pair of pliers, as shown in Figure 5.5.

19. After you've used your treadle-powered machine with its new belt for a few weeks, you might have to reduce the length of the belt again, as it will loosen the most during initial use. After that it should remain relatively stable.

Variations and Considerations

- Dick Wightman, an expert on treadle sewing machines who shared his insights with me for this plan, advises replacing the solid handwheel on a belt-driven electric machine with a spoked handwheel. He says spoked handwheels like those found on original treadle machines are 20 percent heavier than the solid handwheels found on electric machines. Therefore, they are better at maintaining momentum and smoothing out the variable force applied when treadling. If you want to replace your machine's solid handwheel, choose an old, cast-iron handwheel rather than a newer aluminum or plastic type. For more information on replacing handwheels and on using and maintaining treadle sewing machines, check out Dick's Web site,

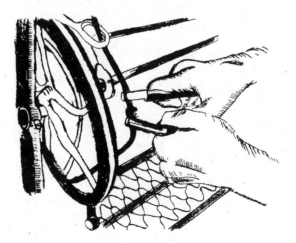

Figure 5.5 Connecting the Belt Ends

treadleon.net. You can also connect with other treadle sewing machine enthusiasts through his site's forum.

- Although the plan suggests using a sewing machine built no later than the 1950s, it's often possible to convert electric sewing machines manufactured between the 1960s and 1980s to be treadle-powered, too, because most of these also rely on a belt drive. However, their motors might be installed internally, rather than externally. If that's the case, conversion to treadle power will not be as straightforward as the process described in this plan. To convert a late-20th-century sewing machine to treadle power, first confirm that it's belt-driven and not computer-controlled, or electronic. Then determine how to disengage the motor. If the motor is internal, you might have to take off the sewing machine's face or side panel and remove the drive belt. Other machines allow you to disengage the motor simply by pulling the handwheel out and away from the machine. Next, you need to figure out how to secure the treadle belt on the handwheel. If the handwheel doesn't have a groove, consider replacing it with a handwheel that can accept a belt. Finally, make sure that the sewing machine's cover or right-hand panel is not so wide that it will obstruct the belt.

- If the belt on your treadle-driven machine continues to slip even after you've made the belt tight, check to make sure the band wheel groove is free of debris, dust or oil. Wipe it clean with alcohol, if necessary.

Plan for Making a Pedal-Powered Washing Machine

For some reason people interested in human-powered devices are especially attracted to the idea of making a pedal-powered washing machine. Maybe it's because both rely on rotary motion, making them seem like an obvious pairing. Or maybe it's because a washing machine appears to be a simple thing to construct or modify, or because doing laundry is an elemental chore that until recently in our evolution has demanded a lot of labor. Whatever the reason, many inventors have experimented with ways of combining bikes and washing machines, and several designs have resulted. One of the most sophisticated is the bicilavadora, or bike-powered washing machine, devised by MIT students in collaboration with Maya Pedal in Guatemala. In Figure 5.7, Steven Gray, a Canadian volunteer with

Figure 5.6 The Professor's Pedal-Powered Washing Machine From "Gilligan's Island"

Maya Pedal, gets some help with ballast as he operates the bicilavadora.

One of the requirements for Maya Pedal's bicilavadora was that it must use parts readily available in remote areas of Guatemala. Thus, a steel drum mounted on a horizontal axis acts as the exterior washing tub, and a punctured plastic drum inside the steel drum serves as the inner tub (the one that spins). The frame is made of recycled bike tubes, plywood and steel angle. The drive is made from a bike's chain drive. Instead of the cogset being attached to a bike's rear wheel, however, it's attached to the washing machine's shaft.

As when riding a bike, the bicilavadora operator can vary pedaling difficulty and speed by shifting into higher or lower gears. In Mayan country the bicilavadora has the potential to save hours of back-breaking labor at the community washing stations, or pilas, and to save women's hands from harsh detergents.

In the Western World, we're blessed with even more cast-off materials to reclaim, including untold numbers of wringer washers sitting in junkyards, flea markets and antique stores. One antique dealer I know confided that the common, early-to-mid-20th-century models aren't very popular with today's

Figure 5.7 Maya Pedal's Bicilavadora (Washing Machine)

antique buyers, and so they sell for modest prices. I've found them in good condition for between $10 and $50. But in pristine condition, or sporting a feature valued by collectors, they can sell for much more. Because wringer washers are heavy, you'll want to find a source nearby to avoid shipping charges and bring someone to help you get the machine home.

This plan, which is based on a device built by Bart Orlando, uses a wringer washing machine because it provides a simple means for applying pedal power to clothes washing. The advantage of using a wringer washer is that it doesn't have a spin cycle. Modern washing machines are typically too difficult to pedal-power because of the power required by their spin cycles. Bart told me that his building a

pedal-powered washing machine "was in response to the need to have clean clothes and trying to do it with an eco-ethic." He didn't want to deal with modern, power-hungry machines and he got sick of laundering his Levis in a bucket.[4] Be aware, though, that pedal-powering a washing machine, even without a spin cycle, is not an easy task. (A simpler, and less taxing, human-powered means for washing clothes would be to use one of the hand-powered machines featured later in this chapter.)

Ease of construction: Moderate
Time to make: 4 hours or less
Cost to make: Under $100, using a cast-off wringer washer and stationary bike
Ease of operation: A real workout!

Following is an overview of the steps in this plan:

- First, you'll modify the stationary bike's front wheel to accept a pulley belt.
- Next, you'll remove the wringer washer's belt from the motor pulley, leaving it looped around the agitator pulley.
- Then, you'll create an intermediate drive shaft that includes two smaller pulleys: one that will be connected with a belt to the stationary bike's front wheel and one that will connect to and drive the washing machine's agitator. You'll also create a wooden base for the intermediate drive shaft.
- Finally, you'll position the intermediate drive shaft, washing machine and stationary bike to form a complete pedal-driven wringer washer.

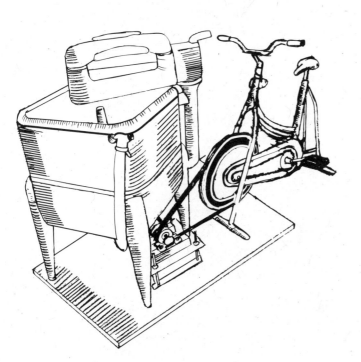

Figure 5.8 Pedal-Powered Washing Machine

Materials

- A stationary bike. Refer to Chapter 2's section "Scrounging For Parts" for hints on how to choose the best type. For this plan you must have one with an accessible front wheel.

- An electric wringer washer, such as a Maytag from the 1920s or later, which uses a belt-and-pulley style motor. Make sure that the pulley is mounted on a horizontal axis. All Maytag wringer washers include pulleys aligned in this way, but some other brands, such as the Montgomery Ward wringer washers, don't. Before buying a machine, look underneath to make sure the pulley is not mounted on a vertical axis — that is, make sure the pulley is not oriented parallel to the floor. A gas-powered washer, rather than an electrical one, could work, but removing the engine would require more effort. For this plan I used a model "J" Maytag from the 1950s. Even better candidates for pedal-powering are Maytag wringer washers manufactured from the 1920s through 1930s of the type that have a short, cast-aluminum tub, such as the models 60, 70 and 91. Unlike the more commonly available type used in this plan, these older washers have very accessible pulleys. That means that you could omit the use of an intermediate drive shaft, thereby simplifying the conversion and making the machine more efficient. However, finding one of the early models in good shape for a reasonable price can be challenging.

- Two pillow blocks and insert bearings with ½"-diameter bores (as long as the insert bearings have ½"-diameter bores and fit inside the pillow blocks, the size of the pillow blocks isn't important)

- One 14" length of ½" round steel bar stock

- One 4" single V-groove pulley (which will accept an A-series V-belt) with a ½" bore diameter and a hollow head set screw to hold it fast to a shaft.

- One 3" single V-groove pulley (which will accept an A-series V-belt) with a ½" bore diameter and a hollow head set screw to hold it fast to a shaft.

- Two shaft collars with ½" bores

- Four ⅜" carriage bolts 3" long (this assumes that the mounting holes in your pillow blocks accept a ⅜" carriage bolt; if the mounting holes in your pillow blocks differ, change this dimension accordingly)

- One piece of ¾" plywood 10" × 12"

- Two pieces of 2" × 2" dimensional lumber 8" long

- One piece of ¾" plywood 40" × 30" to serve as the platform for both the washing machine and the front of the stationary bike

- Two pieces of 2" × 12" lumber approximately 10" long

- Four ⅜" carriage bolts 6" long, with matching washers and nuts (preferably nylon lock-type nuts, to resist loosening with continued use)

- One 100"-long A-series V-belt (depending on the size of your stationary bike's wheel, this might need to be longer or shorter)

- Two 1" conduit clamps for holding the stationary bike to the plywood platform;

if your stationary bike's feet are not steel tube or a different size, adjust the size or style of the clamps as necessary

- Four ½" wood screws

Tools

- Marking pen or pencil
- Drill or drill press with a ⅜" bit and ¾" countersink bit
- Allen wrench to tighten set screws in pulleys and pillow block bearings
- Open-ended wrenches to tighten nuts
- Steel square (or similar square)
- Circular saw (a hacksaw would also work)
- ½" or 1" wood gouge and mallet

Steps for Making a Pedal-Powered Washing Machine

1. You'll need a fair amount of space for this project, so clear an area large enough for

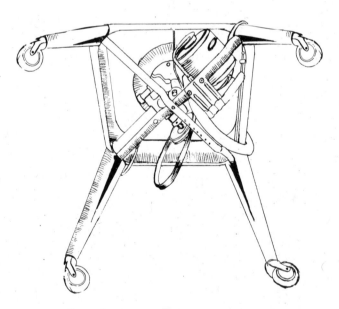

Figure 5.9 Washing Machine Agitator Pulley

the washing machine and stationary bike to stand next to each other.

Note: For safety's sake, do not allow the washing machine to be plugged in at any time!

2. First, prepare the stationary bike to be part of a belt drive by following steps 1 through 10 of the plan for converting a hand-cranked grain mill to pedal power featured in Chapter 3. (The difference with this plan, however, is that the V-belt you'll loop around the stationary bike's front wheel is not as long as the one used in the grain mill conversion plan.)

3. Now gently turn the wringer washer on its side. In order to keep the washer stable while you pedal-power it, remove the casters from its feet. If you're lucky, this is a simple matter of grabbing each one and pulling it out. However, given the machine's age, the casters might require some coaxing with a flathead screwdriver and hammer.

4. With the washer still on its side, remove the belt that connects the agitator pulley to the motor pulley from the motor pulley. You can leave it hanging loosely on the agitator pulley, as shown in Figure 5.9. After you've removed the casters and disengaged the belt, restore the washer to its upright position.

5. Next, you'll begin creating the intermediate drive shaft. Put the insert bearings inside the pillow blocks. Usually this involves sliding them into the pillow block opening perpendicular to the circumference of the opening, then turning them 90 degrees until they snap into place.

6. Slide the 3" pulley onto the piece of ½" round steel bar until it's about 6" from the right-hand end. (If necessary, loosen the set screw first.)

7. Use the appropriate Allen wrench to tighten the 3" pulley's set screw and fix it in place.

8. Now from the left side of the round steel bar shaft, slide the 4" pulley onto the piece of ½" round steel bar until it's next to the 3" pulley.

9. Use the appropriate Allen wrench to tighten the 4" pulley's set screw and fix it in place.

10. Now that the pulleys are in place, you're ready to connect the shaft to the pillow block bearings. Thread the right end of the shaft through one of the pillow block bearings so that at least 2" of the shaft extends beyond the edge of the pillow block. The two pulleys should be on the left of this pillow block.

11. Slide one of the shaft collars onto the right end of the shaft until it's tight against the pillow block. (If necessary, loosen the shaft collar's set screw first.)

12. With the shaft collar held tight against the pillow block, use the appropriate Allen wrench to tighten its set screw.

13. Next, add the second pillow block onto the left end of the shaft, leaving approximately 2" of the shaft free on the left-hand side of the second pillow block.

14. Slide the second shaft collar on the left side of the shaft (loosening the set screw first, if necessary).

15. With the second shaft collar held tight against the left-hand pillow block, tighten

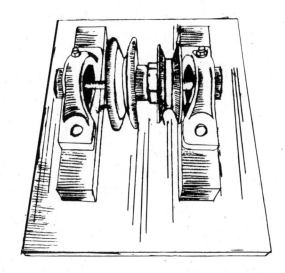

Figure 5.10 The Intermediate Drive Shaft

its set screw. The completed intermediate drive shaft should resemble the one shown in Figure 5.10.

16. Now you need to create a support for the intermediate drive shaft. Begin by centering each pillow block on an 8"-long piece of 2 × 2 lumber. Mark the center of each mounting hole on the wood.

17. Drill ⅜" holes through the pieces of 2 × 2 at each place you marked in Step 16.

18. Line up the 2 × 2s on the 10" × 12" piece of ¾" plywood with the long edges parallel to the board's 12" edges. Separate the 2 × 2s by approximately 6".

19. Now use a thin marking pen or pencil to mark the center of the holes you drilled in Step 17 on the plywood board.

20. Drill ⅜" holes through the plywood at each place you marked in Step 19.

21. On one side of the plywood, use the ¾" countersink bit to drill a wider area around each hole.

22. From the underside of the plywood, insert the 3" carriage bolts in the holes you drilled in Step 20.

23. Set the 2 × 2s on the plywood, threading the carriage bolts through the holes you drilled in Step 17.

24. Now align the pillow blocks on the 2 × 2s so that their mounting holes meet with the carriage bolts, but don't add the washers or nuts to the ends of the carriage bolts yet.

25. Next, you'll create a slot in the plywood to allow clearance for the belt that connects the 4" pulley and the stationary bike. Use a square to draw lines on the 10" × 12" plywood mounting board that indicate the left and right sides of the 4" pulley. Make the length of this slot extend from the front edge of the plywood and about 4" toward the pulley.

26. Remove the carriage bolts, drive shaft and 2 × 2 supports from the plywood. Use a circular saw or hacksaw to cut along the lines you drew in Step 26. Use a gouge and mallet to free the third side of the cutout.

27. Replace the carriage bolts, 2 × 2 supports and the intermediate drive shaft on the 10" × 12" piece of plywood. Add the matching washers and nuts to only one side of the intermediate drive shaft and tighten only enough to keep the pillow block in place. (Later, you'll need to lift up one of the pillow blocks to loop the belts around the pulleys.)

28. Next, you'll attach the intermediate drive shaft and its mounting blocks to the plywood base below the washer and stationary bike. A challenge when using two belt drives is properly positioning the intermediate driveshaft so that the belts are aligned and taut between both drives. To begin, set the wringer washer on the 40" × 30" piece of plywood so that it's as close to one of the 30" sides of the board as it can be with no danger of sliding off if it's jostled. You should have at least another foot of space on the board opposite that side.

29. Now place the two pieces of 2 × 12 on top of each other on the plywood beneath the washing machine. Set the intermediate drive shaft and its wooden base on those.

30. Get under the machine and adjust the intermediate drive shaft's position so that the 3" pulley is in line with the washer's agitator pulley. This will determine the angle at which the intermediate drive shaft is oriented.

31. Bring the stationary bike near the wringer washer and set its front supports on the large piece of plywood. Position the stationary bike so that its front wheel is in line with the 4" pulley on the intermediate drive shaft.

32. Connect the belt from the stationary bike to the 4" pulley on the intermediate drive shaft. (This requires you to lift one of the pillow blocks to slide the belt underneath.)

33. Connect the belt from the agitator pulley to the 3" pulley on the intermediate drive shaft. (This requires you to lift one of the pillow blocks to slide the belt underneath. Replace the pillow block on the carriage bolts afterward.)

34. For this step, it helps to have two people. Pull the intermediate drive shaft toward the stationary bike, with the two pieces of 2 × 12 underneath for support, until the belt between the agitator pulley and the 3" pulley is taut while still aligned. Keeping it taut, trace around the edges (or at least the corners) of the intermediate shaft's mounting board on the plywood base. Also trace around each of the washer's feet on the plywood so that you can reposition it properly.

35. Remove the belts from the pulleys on the intermediate drive shaft, then take the drive shaft and its mounting board to your workbench.

36. Next, you'll mark four points for the bolts

Figure 5.11 Aligning the Pulleys

that will hold the intermediate drive shaft to the plywood platform. Measure 1" from the tip of each corner at a 45-degree angle from either of the board's sides, then mark the spot.

37. Using the ⅜" drill bit, drill a hole through the 10" × 12" plywood mounting board at each mark you made in Step 36.

38. Now remove the washing machine and stationary bike from the 40" × 30" piece of plywood and take the plywood to your workbench.

39. Make marks on the 40" × 30" plywood base that correspond to the marks you made on the intermediate drive shaft's mounting board in Step 36.

40. Using the ⅜" drill bit, drill holes through the plywood base at the points you marked in Step 39.

41. Using the ¾" countersink bit, create larger holes around the holes you drilled in Step 40.

42. Insert the 6" carriage bolts from the side of the plywood platform where you created the countersink holes.

43. Now reassemble the pedal drive with the plywood base beneath the washing machine, the two pieces of 2 × 12 on the plywood, and the intermediate drive shaft and its base on top of those. Reattach and align both pulley belts, as shown in Figure 5.11. Ensure that the pulley belt connecting the agitator pulley to the intermediate drive shaft is properly aligned and stretched tight.

44. Thread the long carriage bolts through the holes you drilled in Step 37, then add the washers and nuts and tighten.

45. Add the washers and nuts to the carriage bolts holding the pillow blocks to the intermediate drive shaft's base and tighten.

46. The only remaining task is to position the stationary bike so that its belt connection to the intermediate drive shaft is taut. Once you're satisfied with the bike's placement, put a conduit clamp over the front horizontal steel tube support on both the left and right sides of the wood screws to screw them into place. If your stationary bike has a base that's flat or made of a different sized steel tube, adjust your style or conduit clamp diameter accordingly. Or, if you judge that the weight of the bike and a rider is sufficient to prevent it from moving, you can skip this step.

47. Finally, try out your pedal-powered washing machine. Remember that your muscles can't deliver the same amount of horsepower that the washer's motor would provide, so keep your loads small. Also, seek instructions for using a wringer washer safely. If you plug in the machine and use the wringer, be aware that it can catch hair, jewelry, loose clothing or fingers and cause serious injury.

Variations and Considerations

- A more efficient machine could be made by eliminating the intermediate drive shaft. As mentioned in the list of materials, one means of accomplishing this is to use a 1920s or 1930s version of a Maytag wringer washer whose pulley is unobstructed by the machine's housing. But if you can't find one of those, you could raise the washer on a platform approximately one foot high. This would allow the belt from a stationary bike's front wheel to connect directly to the washing machine's agitator pulley without obstruction.

- Because powering this machine requires a significant amount of effort, you might want to replace the stationary bike's front wheel with a heavy flywheel. As described in Chapter 2, flywheels can be made from cast concrete, cast iron, solid wood, a wheel rim wrapped with rebar, or a tire whose tube is filled with sand, for example.

- Also, because operating this machine requires significant effort, you might benefit from experimenting with different drive ratios.

Commercially Available Plans and Devices for Housework

Though a modern version of the human-powered vacuum cleaner has yet to be released — nor did the hand-cranked dishwasher survive to the 21st century — you can still find new, improved versions of the human-powered devices that have played a role in housework for centuries. The following pages describe commercially available treadle sewing machines and human-powered washing machines, many of which are used by Amish or Mennonite customers who maintain a traditional lifestyle. People living off the grid also contribute to demand for these products.

Treadle Sewing Machine

Singer stopped making treadle-compatible sewing machines for the US market in the 1960s. (It manufactured the machines in

Japan as late as the 1970s, but most were destined for use in developing countries.) Today, companies in India and China still turn out millions of simple, inexpensive treadle sewing machines, but sell them only in regions where electricity is scarce or unreliable. Generally speaking, since the 1960s, sewers in the Western world who wanted to use a treadle machine had to buy an antique, or combine a new machine with a treadle base as described at the beginning of this chapter.

Then in 2004 sewing machine manufacturer Janome released its model 712T, a modern sewing machine that fits into a treadle base. In fact, the 712T is simply a treadle-adapted version of a flat-bed sewing machine

the company had sold for years. The Janome 712T, shown in Figure 5.12, comes with zig-zag and reverse, variable stitch sizes and patterns, and buttonhole and zipper attachments, among other features. It also weighs less than half as much as most antique treadle heads. The company does not provide a treadle base with the machine, but claims that the 712T will fit into any Singer treadle base manufactured since the 1880s. (This is true with some exceptions. Treadles built for machines with fiddle bases or ¾-sized machines, for example, would not be compatible with the 712T.)

At the time this was written, the Janome 712T retailed for $379, and a Janome spokesperson confirmed that most of their

Figure 5.12 Janome 712T Treadle-Compatible Sewing Machine

customers are Amish. Sales have been modest, but steady, averaging just under 2,000 units sold each year.[5] Amy Smith of Brubaker's Sewing Center in New Holland, Pennsylvania, told me her store sells several per month. And before Janome released their treadle sewing machine head, her business specialized in custom treadle sewing machines. "We were converting so many Janome machines to treadle with our own conversion that Janome started building their own machine specifically for treadles." (She pointed out that Pfaff was another popular brand for conversion. And of course, no matter what the brand, computerized machines are not candidates for treadle heads.) Brubaker's Sewing Center does not sell the treadle bases, however, and Amy confirmed that her customers, mainly Amish, usually have these. Few others buy the Janome 712T today, but she did witness a rise in sales to non-Amish buyers during the "Y2K scare."

Amy admitted that older treadle machines are probably more durable, as they were built to last 100 years, but pointed out that their features were extremely limited. "The modern machines make everything so much easier and so much more professional, and so converting a modern machine to a treadle is like having the best of both worlds."[6]

More good news for fans of treadle sewing machines is that because of the dependable demand from Amish communities, Janome plans to continue selling its 712T for the foreseeable future. In fact, at the time this was written, the company was considering the development of new treadle-compatible sewing machines.[7]

Manual Washing Machines

Washing clothes off-grid can be done in ways much less taxing than pedal-powering a wringer washer as described earlier in this chapter. Some people put their clothes, water, and soap in a trash can, seal the can, then leave it in the back of the pickup while they run errands. Others use household plungers to agitate clothes in a mop bucket, bathtub or old-fashioned wash tub. (The wringer on a commercial grade mop bucket can also act as a clothes wringer.) Even better is using a plunger like the Rapid Washer, available for about $15, which is made of galvanized metal and lined with a baffle to help thoroughly mix your soapy water and laundry. But some seek a more complete human-powered laundry solution. This section describes three manual washing machines available for purchase today: the James Washer, the Wonder Clean and the Wonder Wash.

The James Washer, shown in Figure 5.13, has been available with little change to its design since the 1940s. It consists of heavy-gauge stainless steel tub shaped like a drum split lengthwise, plus a pendulum-style agitator. When the handle is pushed and pulled, the agitator, a long steel bar, sweeps an arc along the bottom of the drum to keep the laundry moving. The manufacturer claims that given hot water, soap and only 7 minutes of agitating, clothes will get as clean as those washed in any motorized washing machine. Of course, you still need to rinse and wring the laundry. The tub has a drain for releasing soapy water. To rinse, fill again with clean water, swish, then drain again. The attached wringer, used to squeeze water from the washed clothes, is hand-cranked.

The James Washer is available from Real Goods (realgoods.com) and other retailers. At the time this was written it was still made in the US and cost $439 without the wringer. With the wringer, prices started at $618. Lehman's (lehmans.com) carries a nearly identical machine called the Lehman's Hand Washer that retails for $499 without the wringer and $639 with the wringer.

The Wonder Wash and Wonder Clean are more compact hand-powered washing machines. Pictured in Figure 5.14, the Wonder Clean consists of a molded plastic drum on a stand, plus a hand crank for turning the drum. The drum holds about 5 pounds of laundry, which translates to two pairs of adult jeans. Fill the drum with hot water, soap and clothes, and then spin it for 2 minutes. The manufacturer claims that with agitation and the heat of the water, pressure builds up inside the drum that helps water penetrate and force grime out of dirty laundry. This washing machine is marketed especially to RV-dwellers and others who value water and space conservation. At the time this was written, the Wonder Clean sold for as little as $45.

The Wonder Wash is nearly identical to the Wonder Clean, but it includes a drain and hose connected to one end of the drum. Also, its lid is now made with a brass fitting for improved durability. At the time this was written, the Wonder Wash cost about $43.

Users report mixed results with these portable, pressurized washing machines. Some of those who purchased one to save water and

Figure 5.13 James Washer

Figure 5.14 Wonder Clean Washing Machine

effort were surprised that rinsing and wringing were additional steps for which the washer offered no help. Others complain of parts that broke within a few loads of washing and then difficulty obtaining replacements. But positive reviews mention the simplicity of the design and its ease of use, in addition to its minimal use of water (about two quarts) and detergent (about two tablespoons). Also, both the Wonder Clean and Wonder Wash cost a fraction of the price of a James Washer.

If you're inspired to make your own hand-powered washing machine, rather than use one of the models described here, you can purchase plans that tell you exactly how to go about it. The development organization Enterpriseworks/VITA publishes a technical bulletin with instructions for making two simple plunger-type washing machines from lumber and metal hardware. Connect to their Web site at enterpriseworks.org to order this publication.

One alternative for getting the water out of clothes after rinsing would be to use a pedal-powered laundry spinner, such as the one pictured in Figure 5.15. This laundry spinner

Alex Gadsden's Cyclean

No invention has been more continuously modified and improved in the history of patent law than the washing machine.[9] Some variations recorded in the US have included a machine operated by children on a seesaw (1895), one that can be fastened onto the side of an automobile tire to agitate and spin clothes as you drive (1952), and more recently, a sophisticated electronic version with a built-in MP3 player (2007). Historians presume that many more unique washing machines have been designed for personal use, their plans perhaps passed from friend to friend, but never patented.

It's in that neighborly, and eco-conscious, spirit that British tinkerer Alex Gadsden created his pedal-powered washing machine, the Cyclean. He told me he found a washing machine in the garbage and it occurred to him that a person could power it with a bicycle. Too, he said, "I wanted to challenge myself by achieving the impossible." He fit the front-loading drum

and its shock absorbers into a frame made of square steel tubes. He added a Plexiglas water tank above the drum for filling the machine and then extended the drum's axle to connect it to the shaft of a bike-powered drive. The drive consists of a regular bike set into a stand that's connected to the washing machine's frame. The bike's rear tire is removed so that a belt can be

Figure 5.16 Alex Gadsden and the Cyclean

was built by a fellow from Ann Arbor, Michigan, who calls himself "Homeless Dave." For years Dave washed his clothes with the James Washer, but he didn't like using the wringer. He wrote, "Ordinary items like shirts require vigilance to avoid jamming, and certain items, like jeans or garments featuring cord-locks, are virtually impossible to feed through. At the very least, such items require a wrestling match with wet laundry." He also found that wringing didn't remove as much moisture as a motorized washing machine's spin cycle. He envisioned creating a "gigantic salad spinner"

Figure 5.15 Homeless Dave's Pedal-Powered Laundry Spinner

placed around the rim. This belt is connected to the rim of a tractor wheel on the drive shaft. Every component of the machine was recycled.

It took Alex at least 5 months to construct a workable version of the Cyclean. Stability was the main challenge. While pedaling through the spin cycle, especially, the machine would jump around and cause an early version's chain to slip off. He replaced the bike's chain drive with a more flexible belt drive that could withstand more jostling. But still, the apparatus was unsteady. After some time Alex happened on the idea of using a universal joint (or U-joint) to connect the two drive shafts. This coupling allowed the bike drive and the washing machine to move independently. Alex's advice for aspiring inventors: "Keep going if you don't succeed on your first try. If you fail, sit down, have a cup of tea, rethink the situation, then later on have a look again."

The Cyclean can launder about 5 kg (11 pounds) of clothes in one load. Pedaling through the spin cycle is a workout, but not impossible, Alex told me. A front-loading, or horizontal axis, washing machine is key to the invention's usability. A top-loading machine would be more difficult to pedal-power.

Alex said he routinely washes his own clothes in the machine. He also takes it to area festivals, where people drop off their laundry or try pedaling the washer themselves. He called the response from those who've seen and tried the Cyclean "amazing." In fact, he's inspired others to build similar models from cast-off washers. Alex estimated that close to fifty people have sent him stories and photos of their successful inventions and he continues to receive e-mail inquiries from those around the globe who want to do the same. He will not attempt to patent his design or sell plans, but will make them freely available via his Web site, cyclean.biz.

Why? "Because we all have to do our bit for the planet," he said.[10]

which would spin the water out of clothes. Then he remembered that's exactly how washing machine drums work. So he found a cast-off washing machine and made the necessary modifications to power its drum with a bike in a trainer stand. Find out more details about this conversion from Dave's Web site at home lessdave.com. Before embarking on the project, however, heed his observation: "It takes above-average strength and conditioning to pedal this configuration."[8]

CHAPTER 6

HUMAN-POWERED DEVICES FOR RECREATION AND EMERGENCY PREPAREDNESS

Pedal power was conceived first for entertainment, not work. The bike began as a wheeled version of a hobby horse, to which treadles, and then later, pedals, were added. For the most part, only the daredevils of the time rode these early predecessors of modern bicycles. They didn't have brakes, rubber tires or shock-absorbing frames, and the high-wheel bikes predominant before variable gearing were so tall that taking a spill could result in serious injury. Mark Twain famously wrote, "Get a bicycle. You will not regret it. If you live."

Mechanical and manufacturing lessons from the bicycle industry led to treadle-powered tools, which enabled hobby woodworkers to use equipment such as scroll saws, lathes, rip saws and formers that were previously available only to factory owners. When electricity became widely available, these treadle-powered machines fell out of favor. However, some are still around and in use today, as described later in this chapter. The chapter also includes a plan for pedal-powering a modern-day bench grinder.

Meanwhile, even as electricity supplanted muscle power in the early 1900s inventors began devising ways to generate electricity by turning pedals and hand cranks. Later, during the oil crisis of the 1970s, modifying bikes to create power became a skill to be admired among handy environmentalists. The back-to-the-lander's journal of the day, *Mother Earth News*, published plans for a pedal-powered electrical generator in its March/April 1981 issue.

Now, whether due to a desire to conserve energy, be self-sufficient, power devices in extreme circumstances, or simply satisfy scientific curiosity, once again people are intrigued by powering electrical devices with muscles. This chapter presents a plan for a simple pedal-powered electrical generator and explains numerous options and variations for the plan. It also refers to other plans, some of which are more sophisticated, and describes two commercially available pedal-powered electrical generators, in case you don't feel like making one. Finally, the chapter reviews a variety of off-the-shelf hand-powered consumer electronics. Along the way you'll learn about people such as David Butcher, Jason Moore and Eric Hollenbeck, whose passion for treadle or pedal-powered machines goes far beyond a hobby.

Plan for Making a Pedal-Powered Electrical Generator

Given a bicycle or stationary bike, a few wires and a motor of some sort, you can find many ways to generate electricity. This plan offers instructions for one simple method. At the end of the plan you'll find a list of variations that you might want to incorporate into your design. Later in the chapter you'll read about a few different homemade pedal-powered electrical generators as well as commercially available alternatives.

Before beginning, take time to understand some basic principles and precautions about generating electricity using pedal power.

Transforming muscle power to electricity is best accomplished by using a permanent magnet DC motor as a generator. A motor converts electrical energy to mechanical energy. A generator, conversely, creates electricity from mechanical action. By spinning the shaft on a permanent magnet DC motor you generate electricity.

You can transfer motion from a bike wheel's to the motor's shaft via several different configurations, using chain drives, belt drives or friction drives. This plan uses a friction drive because it's simple to make, and with it, you can easily achieve a large gear ratio between the bike's wheel and a spindle attached to the generator's shaft.

Only certain types of permanent magnet DC motors are suited to pedal-powered electrical generators. Since even the fittest athlete cannot sustain 1 hp for more than a minute, and a more plausible output for an extended pedaling session is closer to ¼ hp, there's no need to choose a motor capable of more than ⅓ hp. Also, you don't want a motor that will require very high rpm to generate power. Even with a 1:15 gear ratio between your spindle and bike wheel, for example, you'll struggle to sustain 1,500 rpm. Permanent magnet DC motors can be purchased new or, if you know what you're looking for, scavenged. See the list of materials for more details.

Most pedal-powered electrical generators include a means for temporary energy storage, such as a battery or an ultracapacitor. These enable your human-powered device to continue operating when you step off the machine briefly (for example, to allow someone else to take your place). They also make your electrical generator more forgiving. If your output is inconsistent or briefly flags, the battery or ultracapacitor will correct for that. Practical types of batteries to use for this plan include 12-volt auto or marine batteries. Ultracapacitors (not used in this plan) should be sized according to the amount of current you expect to generate. The drawback to using a battery or an ultracapacitor is that these energy storage devices add inefficiency to the system. However, without them, it's very challenging to deliver current with the consistency that electrical devices require.

Pedal-powered electrical generators that use a battery or ultracapacitor should also include a diode in the circuit between the generator and the temporary storage device. A diode acts as a one-way gate for electrical current. In this plan's circuit it allows current to flow from the pedal-powered generator to the battery, but prevents flow in the opposite direction. If you did not use a diode, the battery (assuming it has any charge) would power the generator, thus turning it back into its original function as a motor, and spin your bike wheel. Diodes are a small, but critical, part of the circuit.

The trickiest part of generating electricity with a bicycle is regulating your output voltage. If you do not carefully monitor your output voltage you risk causing yourself harm! Please follow the safety precautions mentioned here and use common sense. In the following plan I specify using a multimeter to continuously gauge your output voltage and avoid overcharging your battery. This requires you to watch the meter as you pedal to ensure that voltage does not exceed 14 volts. When you reach 14 volts, stop pedaling. Otherwise, you may overheat the battery, which can lead to acid leaks or explosions. More sophisticated means of voltage regulation are described in the "Variations" list at the end of the plan. It's extremely important that you provide a means for regulating voltage in your pedal-powered electrical generator.

This plan also requires an inverter. An inverter is a device that converts DC electricity to AC electricity. Inverters are commonly used in conjunction with alternative power systems, such as solar panels and windmills, that supply electricity in DC form. They can also be used to drive AC devices from a car battery (some come with cigarette outlet connectors for this purpose). Many types of

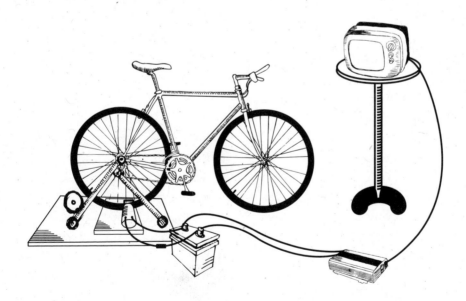

Figure 6.1 Pedal-Powered Electrical Generator

inverters exist, and they all accomplish basically the same tasks. See the list of materials for recommendations on inverter sizes.

The wattage one can produce with this generator will vary from person to person. At the end of this plan I've added a section on how to calculate roughly how much electricity you'll generate. Once you know that, you can determine how long it will take you to fully charge a nearly depleted battery, for example, or how challenging it will be to keep your small TV running.

Ease of construction: Requires some mechanical skills and close attention to safety precautions

Time to make: 3 hours or less

Cost to make: Given your own bike and trainer stand, from $50 to $350, depending on whether you can scavenge a suitable permanent magnet DC motor and 12-volt battery or whether you have to buy them new

Ease of operation: From easy to challenging, depending on wattage requirements of the device you're powering or whether you choose to simply charge the battery

Following is an overview of the steps in this plan:

- First, you'll prepare the generator platform and set up your bike in its trainer stand.
- Then, you'll attach the weld-on hub to the motor's shaft.
- Next, you'll create a wooden base for the motor, screw it into the base, and create slots in the base for an adjustable connection to the pedal-powered generator's mounting board.
- Then, you'll situate the motor base on the mounting board so that the spindle fits snugly against your bike's tire.
- Next, you'll create a simple circuit that includes the generator, a diode, a battery and an inverter.
- Finally, you'll test your circuit, plug an electrical device into the inverter and pedal.

Safety Precautions

- Charge only lead-acid rechargeable batteries with your pedal-powered generator.
- Be extremely careful to not charge the battery beyond its capacity. Overcharged batteries can get hot, release hydrogen gas, and present a situation where combustion or even explosion might occur.
- Study and follow all battery manufacturer's safety precautions for using, connecting and disconnecting the battery.
- Do not operate your pedal-powered electrical generator in hot environments or near potentially flammable materials, dusts or vapors, including solvents or fuels.
- Never smoke or allow a spark or flame near your pedal-powered electrical generator system.
- Operate the pedal-powered electrical generator only in a well-ventilated area.
- Avoid wearing loose clothing and jewelry while using your pedal-powered generator.
- For the utmost safety, have a certified electrician wire your circuit.

Materials

- Your favorite bike. Since the rear wheel will be part of a friction drive, a bike with smooth, rather than knobby, tires works best.
- A bike trainer stand that fits your bike
- A 12- or 24-volt permanent magnet DC motor. Nearly any size will work, but one that's rated for ¼ to ⅓ hp at no more than 5,000 rpm is best. Its shaft should be ½" or ⅝" in diameter (preferably with one flat side) and at least 2" long. Choose a motor with holes for mounting in its housing or attached brackets. Popular permanent magnet DC motor manufacturers include Leeson and Dayton. Discarded treadmill, motorized wheelchair and scooter motors, for example, can work. Also, Windstream Power makes and sells permanent magnet DC motors that are designed to work with pedal-powered electrical generators. For this plan I used a Windstream Power model # 443542 High RPM Permanent Magnet DC Generator with a ½" shaft. Because permanent magnet DC motors can be expensive, however, I encourage you to find something similar from a source of used equipment.
- A weld-on hub with a round bore whose diameter equals the shaft diameter of your permanent magnet DC generator (either ½" or ⅝"), as shown in Figure 6.2. This will act as the driven wheel of your friction drive. An outside diameter of less than 2" is preferable, but this dimension is not critical. You can compute your drive ratio by comparing the spindle's diameter to your wheel's diameter. The smaller the spindle compared to the bike wheel, the more rotations the spindle will take each time you complete one revolution of the pedals.

  Weld-on hubs contain set screws so that you can easily secure them to shafts. They're available from hardware stores, in particular those that carry agricultural machinery parts, for about $7.00. This heavy metal hub's weight helps it to act as a small flywheel once you begin rotating it. However, many other cylindrical parts could act as a suitable spindle. See the "Variations and Considerations" section at the end of this chapter for spindle alternatives.
- A multimeter to monitor your output voltage. As long as yours can measure DC voltage up to 50V, it will work.
- A 300-watt or higher 12-volt DC to 110-volt AC inverter that comes with alligator clips to attach to a battery's terminals. These are often found in the automotive section of hardware or home supply stores.
- Four feet of 10-gauge stranded copper

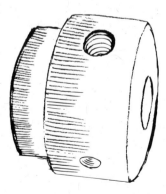

Figure 6.2 Weld-on Hub

wire with a flexible insulating jacket (for example, marine-grade wire) in black, plus an additional 4 feet of the same type of wire in red

- One piece of ¾" plywood 40" × 30" to act as the pedal generator's platform.
- One piece of ½" plywood 12" × 12" to act as a mounting base for the motor
- Hardware for mounting your generator to the piece of wood acting as its base. For the #443542 High RPM Permanent Magnet DC Generator, use four ¼"-diameter machine screws. Check your motor to find out what mounting hardware it requires.
- Four ⅜"-diameter carriage bolts 2" long, with four each matching fender washers, lock washers and wing nuts.
- Two 1" conduit clamps for attaching your trainer stand to the large plywood platform. Check the diameter of your trainer stand's horizontal supports (the part that rests on the ground) to make sure 1" clamps will fit. Your trainer might require slightly larger clamps.
- Four ½"-long wood screws
- Two plastic (either vinyl or nylon) insulated butt splice connectors (the crimping type) that are compatible with 10-gauge wire. (In fact, you can use any one of a handful of different wire connectors in your circuit. Using crimp-type butt splice connectors keeps this plan simple and avoids the need for soldering or heat-shrinking. Standard twist-type connectors, sometimes called "wire nuts," would also work, though they are typically less reliable than butt splice connectors.)

- Two plastic (either vinyl or nylon) insulated push-on wire terminals that are compatible with 10-gauge wire
- Approximately 10 insulated wire staples
- One 6-amp 50-volt diode
- A 12-volt auto- or marine-type lead acid battery. A deep-cycle battery is best. If you use a recycled battery, ensure that it's in excellent shape — for example, that it's not cracked or leaking and that its terminals are not corroded. Also, do not begin with a battery that's lost all its charge; it will be next to impossible to pedal it back to life. If you recycle a "dead" battery, use a battery charger to get it started.
- Optional: Two crocodile clips

Tools
- Small Allen wrench to tighten set screw in weld-on hub
- Marking pencil
- Safety goggles
- Drill with ¼" and 7/16" bits, plus ¾" countersink bit
- Screwdrivers
- Steel square (or similar square)
- Center punch and hammer
- Router with ½"-diameter plunge-cutting bit that's at least 1" long
- Wire cutter
- Wire crimper
- Wire stripper

Steps for Making a Pedal-Powered Electrical Generator
1. Mark one face of the 40" × 30" piece of ¾" plywood "Up" and mark one of the 40" edges on that face "Front."

2. Next, you'll measure and mark positions for two holes on the "Up" face of the plywood platform. Use a square to mark vertical lines the full length of the board at 10" and 16" from the right edge of the board.

3. Mark the positions of two holes: one at 12" from the "Front" edge along the left-hand line you drew in Step 2 and another at 12" from the "Front" edge along the right-hand line you drew in Step 2.

4. Using a $\frac{7}{16}$" bit, drill the holes you marked in Step 3.

5. Use the $\frac{3}{4}$" countersink bit, drill countersink holes on the underside (or "Down" side) of the plywood platform where you drilled holes in Step 4.

6. Now position the board on the floor where you want the back of the pedal-powered electrical generator to sit (with the side marked "Up" facing up, of course).

7. From the underside of the plywood platform, insert a $\frac{3}{8}$" carriage bolt through each of the holes you drilled in Step 4.

8. Center your trainer stand on the plywood platform and adjust the legs of the trainer to ensure that it's stable.

9. Set your bike in the trainer stand and secure it following the trainer stand manufacturer's instructions. For optimal energy transfer, pump up your rear tire to its maximum recommended tire pressure. The ends of the carriage bolts should appear approximately 4" and 10" to the right of the rear tire as you face the front of the bike.

10. Disengage the trainer stand's resistance device. Usually this involves turning a knob on the back of the resistance mechanism to loosen it.

11. Next, you'll prepare the permanent magnet DC motor to act as a generator. Ensure that the bore diameter of your weld-on hub matches your motor's shaft diameter. If your motor came with a sprocket or pulley attached to the shaft, remove it now.

12. Use the appropriate Allen wrench to loosen the set screw (or screws) in the weld-on hub, then slide the hub onto the shaft.

13. Use the appropriate Allen wrench to tighten the hub onto the shaft. Spin the hub with your finger to make sure the motor's shaft spins with it.

14. Now you're ready to mount the motor on its 12" × 12" plywood base. In the case of Windstream Power's #443542, mounting requires four $\frac{1}{4}$" machine screws whose centers are spaced 7-$\frac{1}{2}$" by 2" apart. Check your motor to verify how many and how far apart your mounting holes are.

15. Mark one face of the 12" × 12" piece of plywood "Up" and one edge on that face "Front."

16. You'll want to situate your motor on the 12" × 12" piece of plywood at least 2" in from the edge marked "Front" and centered from left to right. On the face marked "Up," use a steel square to measure precisely where to drill holes for your motor's mounting screws (based on the measurements you took in Step 14), then mark those holes with a pencil.

17. Because the position of these holes must be precise, use the center punch and

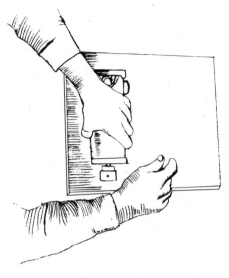

Figure 6.3 Attaching Motor to Base

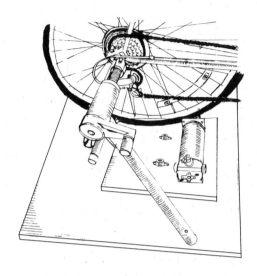

Figure 6.4 Positioning the Motor

hammer to indicate the center of the holes you marked in the previous step. Then drill the holes with a bit that matches the size of your motor's mounting holes. If you're using Windstream Power's #443542 generator, for example, use a ¼" drill bit.

18. Align the motor on the plywood mounting base so that the holes you just drilled match up with the motor's mounting holes. Then use the appropriate screws to attach the motor to the 12" × 12" plywood base, as shown in Figure 6.3.

19. Next, you'll create slots in the motor's base that will accept the carriage bolts you inserted in the plywood base. Use the router and a ½" plunge-cutting bit to gouge out slots that are exactly 6" apart on center, perpendicular to the motor, and at least 6" long. The slots should begin approximately 2" from the motor and extend toward the rear edge of the motor's plywood base. They should also be centered within the motor's length. (Depending on your router setup, you might have to remove the motor from its plywood base to do this. If so, reattach the motor before continuing.)

20. Place the motor and its base on the plywood platform. The slots you just created should fit over the 2"-long carriage bolts.

21. Now you're ready to adjust the motor's position, along with the bike's, to create the friction drive. Push the motor and its base back toward the wheel until the weld-on hub is pressed snugly against your bike's tire as shown in Figure 6.4. Make sure the motor is exactly perpendicular to the tire. Test the drive by turning the pedals and checking to see that spinning your bike tire also spins the generator shaft.

22. Attach the fender washers, lock washers and wing nuts to the ends of the two carriage bolts, but don't tighten the wing nuts yet.

23. With the trainer stand centered and stable, put a conduit clamp over the stand's rear horizontal steel tube support on both the left and right sides. Use the four wood screws to fasten the two clamps tightly to the plywood platform.

24. Test-drive the alignment of your rear wheel and motor spindle. It helps to have two people for this. While someone sits on the bike and pedals, the other person can adjust the motor's position so that the spindle and the tire make the most complete surface contact without pressing into the tire. Once you're satisfied with the motor's position, tighten the wing nuts on the carriage bolts.

25. Now you're ready to create the circuit. For the utmost safety, leave this task to a certified electrician and do not allow anyone to turn the bike's crankshaft until you've completed and tested your circuit. Also for safety's sake, make sure to leave some slack in your wires so they can't be yanked out if they're bumped. One way to do this is to tack the wire to the plywood base after making the connection generously long. Use a hammer and insulated wire tacks to do this for each of the connections you make in the following steps. An overview of the circuit appears in Figure 6.5.

26. Every permanent magnet DC motor provides a positive lead and a neutral lead. Check the documentation that came with your motor to determine which is positive and which is neutral. (Usually on a DC motor, the positive, or hot, wire is red and the neutral is black. Sometimes the hot wire is white.) It's critical to be certain of this now.

27. Cut an 18" length of red 10-gauge insulated wire and strip ⅜" of the jacket off each end.

28. Use a plastic-insulated butt splice connector to connect one end of the wire you stripped in the previous step to the positive lead from the motor. (This assumes that the motor's lead ends with bare wire and not another type of connector. Depending on your motor, you might need to adjust this step. If your motor's leads terminate with a male or female coupler, for example, you can crimp a corresponding female or male coupler to one end of your 10-gauge wire and interconnect the two push-on terminals.) Crimp both sides of the connector to ensure a solid connection.

29. At the opposite end of the 10-gauge red wire, attach a plastic-insulated push-on terminal that will accept one end of the diode.

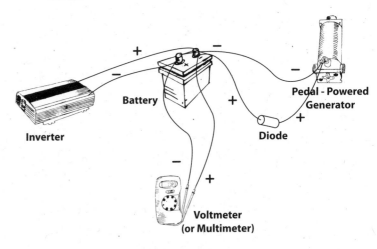

Figure 6.5 The Pedal-Powered Electrical Generator Circuit

30. Now you're ready to add the diode to the circuit. Since diodes act as one-way gates for current, you need to know in which direction yours operates before adding it to the circuit. Every diode has an anode end, indicated by an "a", and a cathode end, indicated by a "k". The cathode end is usually marked with a stripe. Refer to the documentation that came with your diode to confirm the anode and cathode sides on your diode. Insert the anode side of your diode to the push-on terminal you added to the red wire in Step 29.

31. To the opposite (cathode) side of the diode, connect a second push-on terminal.

32. Cut another 18" length of red 10-gauge insulated wire and strip ⅜" of the jacket off both ends of the wire.

33. Connect one stripped end of this wire to the push-on terminal you added to the cathode side of the diode in Step 31.

34. Next, you'll create the neutral side of the circuit. Strip ⅜" of the jacket off both ends of your 3-foot long black 10-gauge wire.

35. Connect one end of the black 10-gauge wire to the neutral lead on the permanent magnet DC motor using a butt-splice connector. Crimp both sides of the connector to ensure a firm connection.

36. At this point you can use your multimeter to test the functioning of the pedal-powered generator. Turn on the multimeter and make sure it's set to measure DC voltage. (If you need to set a range, set it to nothing less than 50 volts; some multimeters automatically choose the appropriate voltage range.) Hold or clip the red (positive) lead to the red 10-gauge wire that leaves the diode and hold or clip the black (neutral) lead to the black 10-gauge wire that you connected to the motor in Step 35. Now turn the crank arm on the bike to rotate the spindle on the motor's shaft. The multimeter should indicate the amount of voltage you're generating. If the multimeter registers zero voltage even after you turn the crank arms at a good pace, reevaluate your connections. In particular, make sure your diode is pointing in the proper direction. If your multimeter registers negative voltage, you have reversed the positive and neutral connections at some point. Make sure that you are touching the red (positive) multimeter probe to the positive side of the circuit and the black (neutral) probe to the neutral side of the circuit.

37. After ensuring that your pedal-powered generator creates voltage, set aside the multimeter.

38. Connect the free end of the red 10-gauge wire (the end that leaves the diode) to your 12-volt battery's positive terminal using a spade terminal.

39. Connect the opposite end of the black 10-gauge wire to the neutral terminal on your 12-volt battery with a spade terminal.

40. Now you're ready to connect the multimeter to the circuit. If your multimeter doesn't end in crocodile clips, but straight probes, you'll want to connect those probes to crocodile clips or find another means of easy, semipermanent attachment to battery terminals. Clip the multimeter's positive (red) lead to the battery's positive terminal, which is marked with

a "+", and clip the multimeter's neutral (black) lead to the battery's negative terminal, which is marked with a "−".

41. Next, connect the inverter to the battery by clipping the inverter's red (positive) lead to the battery's positive terminal, which is marked with a "+" and clipping the inverter's black (neutral) lead to the battery's negative terminal, which is marked with a "−".

42. Now your circuit should be complete and you can test the battery's voltage. Turn on the multimeter and make sure it's set to detect DC voltage in up to no less than 50 volts. Depending on the charge present in your battery, you should see a voltage readout between 0 and 14 volts. (If your battery reads more than 12 volts, let some of the charge dissipate, either by waiting or by using it to charge a device — for example, a laptop plugged into the inverter — before attempting to charge it with your pedal-powered generator.)

43. Assuming the battery has some voltage, test its connection to the inverter by turning on the inverter, then plugging in an electronic device or appliance such as a laptop, inkjet printer or small fan that requires no more than 300 watts.

44. With the multimeter and inverter still powered on, get on the bike and pedal. Over time, the multimeter's voltage measurement should slowly increase and your electrical device should continue to be powered by the inverter. Keep an eye on the multimeter to make sure that your total voltage never exceeds 14 volts. Remember that with this setup, watch-

ing the multimeter is your only means of voltage regulation. For safety's sake, when your multimeter's reading exceeds 12 volts, stop pedaling and use the battery until it releases some of its charge. Review the safety precautions at the beginning of this plan to make sure you're not risking harm to yourself or your appliances.

Variations and Considerations

- A permanent magnet DC motor can be mounted close to the bike's rear tire in many different ways. For example, if you don't have ready access to boards and tools such as a router to make the slots in the plywood platform, you could use perforated angle iron to create supports for the motor, then bolt the angle iron directly to the trainer stand. Such a mounting method is described by Brad Whaley in his online plans available at science shareware.com.

- As mentioned earlier, you could replace the battery in the circuit with an ultracapacitor. Ultracapacitors store a charge in a different way from batteries. Although they have a lower energy density than batteries, they accept and release a charge much more quickly. Thus, in a pedal-powered generator circuit, they're more efficient and allow you to direct more of your effort to the device you're powering. (However, since they store less energy, they aren't useful in a setup where you want to pedal first, then operate a device later on the energy you generated and stored, for example.) If you use an ultracapacitor, place a fuse in the circuit between the generator and the ultracapacitor to avoid overloading and destroying it. Also, be very careful when handling ultracapacitors, as they can release their charge suddenly.

- Some people wonder whether you could skip the battery or ultracapacitor altogether and instead connect the generator directly to an inverter. It's theoretically possible to do this, but in my experience the inverter will not function reliably. Most inverters, including the one specified in this plan, expect a continuous 12 volts. (Inverters designed to convert 24-volt DC to AC expect a continuous 24 volts.) Pedaling slower and thus supplying lower voltage might cause the inverter to suspend operation. Pedaling fast and supplying higher voltage risks damaging the inverter. At best, with this configuration you could attach a multimeter to the inverter's terminals, watch carefully as you pedal and aim for a steady and precise 12-volt output. However, doing so can be difficult.

- Adding even a small, heavy flywheel to the shaft of the generator will help to smooth your output. Some permanent magnet DC motors, including many found in treadmills, come with such a flywheel. Many motors, however, don't have shafts long enough to accept an added flywheel. In that case, you could devise a way of extending the shaft.

- Using a heavy flywheel in place of your bicycle wheel will help to smooth your output, too. As described in Chapter 2, flywheels can be made from cast concrete, cast iron, a wheel rim wrapped with rebar, a tire whose tube is filled with sand, or a disc of solid wood, for example.

- Many different parts could be used in place of the weld-on hub specified in this plan. Some people recommend skateboard or inline skate wheels. To use these, though, you either have to remove the bearings and then reduce the bore diameter to fit your shaft or disable the bearings. You could also use a small bushing or rubber drive roller available at an automotive parts store. The advantage to using a weld-on hub is that you don't need to modify its bore size, nor add shaft collars to fix it in place.

- If you wanted to make a pedal-powered electrical generator based on a belt drive, you could replace the weld-on hub in this plan with a small pulley, and then connect the bike's wheel to the motor's spindle with a belt. Obviously, this would require a different spacing between the bike and motor than is described in this plan.

- If you wanted to make a pedal-powered electrical generator based on a chain drive, you could replace the weld-on hub in this plan with a small cog, and then connect the bike's chainring to this cog with a custom-sized chain. This would require different spacing between the bike and motor than is described in this plan. Be careful to align the cog and chainring along the same plane. Also make sure the bike on its stand remains immobile once you've aligned the two, to prevent the chain from slipping off.

- If you don't have a bike trainer stand, you

can make a stand from angle iron, for example. The purposes of the trainer stand in this plan are to suspend the rear wheel, freeing it for power generation, and fix the bike in place. If you make your own, ensure that it's strong enough to support your weight and steady enough to remain stable as you pedal.

- If you happen to find a motor that's capable of producing many more volts than your battery can accept and you predict you'll pedal hard enough to generate that voltage, you can arrange several batteries in series to store the extra voltage. (Test your output voltage with a multimeter before connecting the generator to a battery.)

- If you have DC adapters for your devices, or if you are powering DC appliances, you don't need to go through an inverter, but can connect the DC adapter right to the battery. (Doing so might require more wiring, as DC adapters are often designed to plug into a car's cigarette lighter.) In the case of DC appliances, you could also skip the battery. However, you would have to watch your voltmeter very carefully and continuously to make sure you don't issue stronger current than the device can handle, thereby ruining it.

- Consider replacing the battery and inverter in this plan with a portable power pack, also known as a charger, such as one of the Xantrex-brand Powerpacks. These combine batteries and inverters in one unit and offer receptacles for both AC and DC appliances. Many also include overvoltage protection.

- Some people use car alternators, rather than permanent magnet DC motors, to transform pedal power into electricity. The advantage to using an alternator is that they condition incoming power before passing it on, and so voltage regulation is less of a concern. Conveniently, an alternator has a pulley that can be used to attach it in belt-drive formation to a bike wheel. However, car alternators are extremely inefficient compared to permanent magnet DC motors acting as generators.

- It's also possible to connect the wires from a permanent magnet DC motor acting as a generator directly to the wires that run a small electrical appliance if that appliance uses a universal motor that can accept AC or DC power (many do, including most blenders). However, don't do this with any appliance you value! Without a battery and inverter or some means to regulate voltage, you risk damaging or destroying the appliance.

- For more sophisticated voltage control — that is, if you don't want to keep an eye on the multimeter as you pedal — you can purchase a voltage regulator. A voltage regulator accepts current of varying voltage, such as that produced by your pedal-powered generator, and modifies it to create an outgoing current of fixed voltage. In the circuit described in this plan you would place the voltage regulator between the diode and the battery or ultracapacitor.

- You can, of course, use a frame type other than a bike in a trainer stand. For

David Butcher's Pedal-Powered Prime Mover

David Butcher says of pedal power, "It's an obsession." More than 30 years ago he'd begun to think about pedaling to generate electricity, and then he noticed the book *Pedal Power In Work, Leisure, and Transportation* (now out of print) in a natural foods store. Although he didn't buy the book, seeing the chain-and-belt-drive transmission on the cover gave him confidence that human power could be harnessed and put to use. He immediately took on three projects: a pedal-powered canoe, a pedal-powered pickup, and a pedal-powered electrical generator.

Decades later, he's still perfecting his pedal-powered electrical generator, which he calls a Pedal-Powered Prime Mover (PPPM). He's used it to power TVs, computers, lights, printers, amplifiers, a breadmaking machine, a washing machine and his Roomba, a robotic vacuum cleaner.

In the last few years, David's gotten serious about improving his generator's design and riding it regularly. Each morning he pedals for about 30 minutes to juice up a battery bank, which then powers his computer monitor, lights and cell phone charger. After 2 years of this he's lost 30 pounds — he now weighs what he did in high school — and quadrupled his power potential. In fact, he's had to modify his PPPM so it can accept the increased amount of power he's able to generate.

Many people have queried David about building their own pedal-powered generator. He wanted to help them achieve their goals, so in 2006 he wrote instructions for making his PPPM, which calls for commonly available parts and tools. Since then he's revised the plan almost 20 times and supplied it at a nominal cost to hundreds of people via his Web site at los-gatos.ca .us/davidbu/pedgen/plans.html. Many who've used the plan to build a generator have sent David photos and even movies of their PPPM in action. "It's like magic to see it reappear in a different part of the universe like that. It's fantastic," he said.

The PPPM follows a unique design. It's not based on a bicycle in a training stand or an exercise bike. In fact, David thinks that although an electrical generator made from a bike is simpler, he estimates such machines are 25 % less efficient than his PPPM. (Of converting bikes to electrical generators, he said, "That's a terrible thing to do to a bicycle. It should be outside on the road.") His invention is supported by a custom frame made of steel shelving supports. It uses a friction drive in which a 36"-diameter

Figure 6.6 David Butcher and His PPPM

wood flywheel (actually, a table top) rubs against a small polyurethane roller. He chose the friction drive because it was much quieter than a chain drive. The size of the flywheel and the gear ratio between the flywheel and the roller are optimized for maximum energy generation. By contrast, a bicycle wheel isn't wide or heavy enough to act as a good flywheel. Nor could it create such a large gear ratio with the same sized roller. David pointed out that if all you want to do is charge your cell phone, you needn't worry about maximizing the machine's efficiency. But if you want to stretch your power output, you should use the best design possible.

In addition to electrical generators, David has made some mechanical human-powered devices. He recently completed the prototype for a pedal-powered hacksaw that was two years in development. A rod connects the top of the hacksaw's handle to the PPPM's crank shaft. Another rod connects the bottom of the handle to a workbench. Pedaling at an easy pace causes the saw to move forward and backward. In a demonstration he cut steel frame material for another PPPM, which means that he's on his way to using a PPPM to make a PPPM.

When we spoke he said he was surrounded by piles of sketches and notes for new pedal-powered machines. I asked how much time he spends on conceiving, researching and testing these devices. He answered, "I should be spending more time on my job."[1]

Figure 6.7 David Butcher's Pedal-Powered Hacksaw

example, David Butcher recommends building a pedal-power drive from scratch with metal shelving supports, a table top, plumbing fixtures, plus a few bicycle components.

How Much Electricity Can You Generate?

How long must you pedal to charge your laptop battery? How difficult will it be to power your portable music player? The answer in both cases is the same: it depends.

To make rough calculations, it's first helpful to understand some basic principles of electricity. The generator (or motor acting as a generator) will issue current, measured in amperes, or amps, at any rotational speed. The amount of current is directly related to the rotational speed of the generator's shaft. In other words, the faster you pedal, the more electricity you generate.

Voltage, measured in volts (V), reflects the pressure of a current. It's often compared to the pressure of water flowing through a hose. In this analogy, amperage (A), would represent how fast the water flows. Wattage (W) is a measure of power and can be calculated if you know voltage and amperage with the following equation: $V \times A = W$. Obviously, too, if you know how many watts your appliance requires at 110 volts (the standard for AC appliances in the US), you can determine how many amps you need to generate to run it.

Suppose you followed this chapter's plan for a pedal-powered generator, including a 12-volt, 20-amp permanent magnet DC generator. Just because a generator is rated for 12-volt output doesn't mean that's how much

it always produces. Again, it depends on how fast its shaft spins. Consult the manufacturer's documentation to find out how many volts your generator produces with varying rpm. Windstream Power's model 443542, for example, is rated to output 12 volts at a speed of 2,250 rpm.

Knowing the desired rpm, you can determine how fast you should pedal to produce 12 volts and provide a steady charge for your battery. For example, if your bicycle's rear tire has a diameter of 26 inches and you've attached a 1-inch-diameter spindle to the generator's shaft, then the spindle and shaft will make 26 rotations each time the rear tire completes one revolution. Now, your tire's spinning rate depends on your gearing. For simplicity's sake, assume you choose a chainring that's exactly twice as large as your cog. Each time your pedals and chainring revolve once, your cog and rear wheel will revolve twice. For example, if you pedal at a cadence of 44 revolutions per minute, your rear wheel will spin 2×44, or 88 times per minute and spin the generator's shaft 88×26, or 2,236 rpm. That's fast enough to produce about 12 volts with this generator.

Any bicyclist would tell you that a 44-rpm cadence doesn't sound like much work. However, remember that unlike biking down the street, on the electrical generator you're pedaling against substantial resistance from loads on the circuit, including the battery. If you're athletic and predict you'll want to pedal faster even with these loads, use a 24-volt or higher generator in your system. (Alternatively, if you already have a 12-volt generator, you could add more resistance, like another 12-volt battery, to the system.)

If you can estimate your personal power output, you can also estimate how much current you'll produce. As mentioned in Chapter 2, NASA rates the long-term power output for a healthy adult male at 75 watts. If you exert 75 watts and generate 12 volts, you'll be issuing current of $^{75}/_{12}$, or 6.25 amps. (This assumes a perfect system.)

Given the setup described in this chapter's plan for a pedal-powered generator, it's challenging to calculate how much raw power you need to run an appliance. That's because you're charging the battery, not running the appliance directly. A simpler calculation results from a hypothetical, direct generator-to-appliance arrangement. (I don't recommend this, but I know people who do it. Also, bear in mind that on the whole, AC appliances require higher wattages than DC appliances.)

Let's say you want to power a 12-volt coffeemaker that's rated to use 10 amps of current. Ignoring inefficiencies in the circuit, the coffeemaker would require 12 × 10, or 120 watts of power to operate. An adult in decent shape could probably sustain that for as long as it takes to brew a pot of coffee.

How many Calories (kilocalories) would you need to add to your breakfast to supply this much power? As with previous calculations, variables abound. The answer depends partly on your body's metabolism, which depends on your genes, age, gender and fitness level. (See Chapter 2's "Human Power Potential" section for more details.) Assume that the coffeemaker takes 6 minutes to brew a pot of coffee. That means that it requires .1 hours × 120 watts, or 12 watt-hours of energy. To convert watt-hours to Calories, multiply by .86. In other words, 12 watt-hours equals about 10.3 Calories. Now suppose you're a reasonably fit young man and that your metabolism is optimally efficient and can convert 25% of your fuel intake to work. To make up for the Calories you expended while powering the coffeemaker, you'd have to consume an additional 41.2 Calories. Grab a kiwi or an extra slice of whole wheat bread.

Plan for Making a Pedal-Powered Tool Sharpener

Tool sharpeners, or grinders, have been pedal-, treadle- or hand-powered for centuries. Hand-cranked models, which clamp on to workbenches, are still widely available in antique stores and at flea markets. The pedal- and treadle-powered styles are generally less common and more expensive.

Figure 6.8 Pedal-Powered Tool Sharpener

Cast-off, electrical bench grinders are also plentiful. This plan describes how to recycle an older dual-wheel bench grinder to be human-powered. (A new bench grinder would work, too.) For this project, the bench grinder need not have a working motor. Because of the arrangement of the stand and the use of a stationary bike, this pedal-powered tool grinder requires two people to operate — one to pedal and one to sharpen the tool.

Note that to keep this plan simple, I've recommended using bolts to hold together the steel frame. However, if you have access to welding tools or know a welder, you might prefer welding together the stand to make it stronger and more durable. In that case, you needn't use perforated steel angle, but can use solid steel angle.

Ease of construction: Requires modest mechanical skill

Time to make: 3 hours or less

Cost to make: Given your own stationary bike, under $50

Ease of operation: Easy

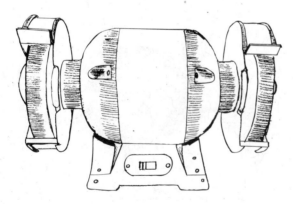

Figure 6.9 Dual-Wheel Bench Grinder

Following is an overview of the steps in this plan:

- First, you'll modify the stationary bike's front wheel to accept a pulley belt.
- Then, you'll remove the buffer, wire wheel or grinding wheel from one end of the dual-wheel bench grinder so that that end of the shaft is free, while the grinding disk you wish to use remains attached to the opposite end.
- Next, you'll attach a pulley to the free end of the grinder's shaft.
- Then, you'll make a stand for your grinder from perforated steel angle and plywood.
- Finally, you'll affix a pulley to the free end of the shaft and connect it to the stationary bike with a V-belt.

Materials

- A stationary bike. Refer to Chapter 2's section "Scrounging For Parts" for hints on how to choose the best type. For this plan you must have one with an accessible front wheel.
- At least 3 feet of 1"-wide non-skid (or "safety") tread tape — optional, and sometimes pricey; if you can't find 1"-wide tape, you can get 2"-wide tape (which I've found to be more common) and cut it to fit.
- A dual-wheel 6" bench grinder, similar to the one pictured in Figure 6.9. I recommend finding an inexpensive castoff. It doesn't matter whether the motor works, and the diameter of the wheel can vary. If you can't find a second-hand grinder, you can buy one new for $20 to $50. For this

project, I used a grinder whose shaft diameter measured ½", a common shaft diameter. However, yours might be ⅝" or 10 mm. If so, choose a pulley with a bore diameter that matches.

- One 2"-, 3"- or 4"-single V-groove pulley (which will accept an A-series V-belt); the pulley should have a bore diameter that matches your bench grinder's shaft diameter (in the case of this plan, the pulley's bore diameter is ½") and come with a hollow head set screw to hold it fast to a shaft. The smaller your pulley, the greater the gear ratio between it and your bike wheel, and thus, the faster you can spin the grinder's shaft with each pedal revolution.
- One 100"-long A-series V-belt
- Four 36" lengths of 1-¼" by 1-¼" perforated steel angle (the type I used for this project was made of 12-gauge steel and had ⁵⁄₁₆"-diameter holes)
- Eight 15" lengths of 1-¼" by 1-¼" perforated steel angle
- Four 3" lengths of 1-¼" by 1-¼" perforated steel angle
- One piece of ¾" plywood 24" × 28"
- One piece of ¾" plywood 15" × 15"
- Twelve ⁵⁄₁₆"-diameter bolts ½" long, with matching washers and nuts*
- Twelve ¼"-diameter bolts at least 1" long, with matching washers and nuts**
- Four ⅜" carriage bolts at least 1-½" long, with matching washers and nuts
- Two 1" conduit clamps for holding the stationary bike to the plywood platform; if your stationary bike's feet are not steel

tube or a different size, adjust the size or style of the clamps as necessary
- Four ½"-long wood screws

*This assumes that the perforations in your steel angle are at least ⁵⁄₁₆" in diameter. If yours are different, change the size of your bolts and matching washers and nuts accordingly.

**This assumes that your bench grinder's base contains four mounting holes that are ¼" in diameter. Adjust the number and size of bolts to suit your bench grinder.

Tools
- Workbench
- Screwdriver
- Safety goggles
- Allen wrench for tightening the pulley's set screw
- Open-ended wrenches
- Metal file
- Marking pencil or pen
- Drill with ⁵⁄₁₆" and ⁷⁄₁₆" bits plus ¾" countersink bit

Steps for Making a Pedal-Powered Tool Sharpener

1. This plan uses the same drive type as the pedal-powered grain mill described in Chapter 3. Thus, to prepare your stationary bike to power your bench grinder, first follow Steps 1 through 10 in the plan for converting a hand-cranked grain mill to be pedal-powered.
2. Now you should have a pulley belt around your stationary bike's front wheel, whose tire has been removed and to whose rim you've added friction tape. You're ready to

modify your bench grinder to be pedal-powered.

Note: For safety's sake, do not allow the bench grinder to be plugged in or turned on at any point during this process!

3. This plan adds a pulley to one side of the bench grinder's shaft. Therefore, to pedal-power the bench grinder's abrasive disk you'll want to remove the opposite disk, whether it's a wire wheel, buffer or finer abrasive. Grinders vary, but you'll probably have to remove a nut and washer, and perhaps a shaft collar or spacer, before you can remove the disk. If the shaft and attachment are rusty, try applying some penetrating oil and leaving it overnight to help loosen the connection.

4. Most bench grinders have a guard, or shield, around each disk, fastened to the base with screws. Remove the guard from

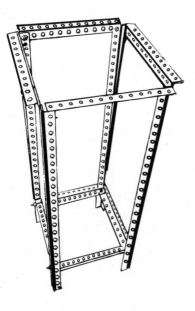

Figure 6.10 Tool Sharpener Stand

the end of the shaft where you intend to put a pulley.

5. Now that the shaft is free, slide the pulley onto it until the pulley is positioned roughly the same place as the disk you removed in Step 3. (Loosen the pulley's set screw first, if necessary.) If the end of the shaft is threaded, position the pulley's edge within the threaded area or closely against it.

6. Tighten the set screw on the pulley until it's firmly set in place.

7. If you removed a nut and washer in Step 3 and your pulley is next to or within the threaded area, replace the nut and washer so that they're close against the side of the pulley, then tighten the nut.

8. Now you're ready to make the stand that will hold your bench grinder. If you haven't cut your perforated steel angle to length, do so. Use a file to remove any burrs from the cut edges.

9. The four 36"-long pieces of perforated steel angle will serve as the stand's legs. The eight 15"-long pieces of perforated steel angle will serve as braces between the legs. Four will be bolted between the legs at the very top of the stand. The other four will be bolted between the legs near the bottom of the stand, as shown in Figure 6.10.

10. To begin, arrange four of the 15"-long pieces of perforated steel angle in a square around the far edge of the legs. Each brace should be oriented on the outside of the legs with one flat side perpendicular to the legs. These braces at the top of the stand will create a flat plane on which

the mounting base for the bench grinder can rest.

11. Use the ⁵⁄₁₆" carriage bolts to bolt the top braces to the last perforation in the legs and tighten the nuts only as much as is necessary to keep the braces in place.

12. At approximately 6" from the end of the legs *opposite* the braces you bolted in the previous step, you'll insert the remaining four braces on the inside of the legs. In other words, arrange the braces so that one flat side is flush with the inside flat edge of each leg. Bolt the braces to the legs, tightening the nuts only as much as is necessary to keep the braces in place.

13. Next, you'll add feet to the stand. Bolt one of the 3"-long pieces of perforated steel angle to each of the stand's legs. Orient the small pieces so that one flat side rests on the floor while the other is flush against the outside edge of the leg. Tighten the nuts only as much as is necessary to keep the feet in place.

14. Now set your stand upright on the floor. Jiggle or adjust the braces and feet until the stand is square and stable. Then tighten all 12 nuts firmly.

15. Center the 15" × 15" piece of ¾" plywood on the stand's top. From below, use a marking pen or pencil to indicate the center of a hole about 2" in from each corner on each side, as shown in Figure 6.11.

16. Place the bench grinder on the stand's top and arrange it so that the pulley hangs over the left edge of the stand as the pedaler would see it. (Be careful not to move the top out of place while doing so.) With this arrangement, the belt drive will spin the pulley and the bench grinder's shaft in the correct direction for a person sharpening tools to set up on the opposite side of the stand from the pedaler. Leave a few inches between the center of the pulley and the edge of the stand's top. Also align the bench grinder so that the pulley is parallel to the top's edge.

17. Mark where the bench grinder's mounting holes fall on the stand's top. Depending on your bench grinder, you might have two or four of these holes.

18. Now remove the top from the stand and, using the drill and ⁵⁄₁₆" bit, drill holes in each of the places you marked in the previous steps. (This assumes that the holes in your bench grinder's base are ¼". If yours are smaller or larger, change your drill bit to match when you drill the grinder's base mounting holes.)

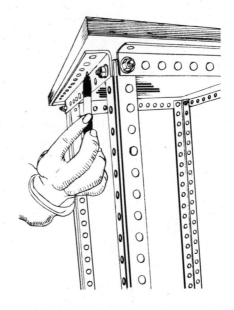

Figure 6.11 Marking Holes in the Top

19. Set the top back on the stand, aligning the holes you just drilled near the outside edges of the stand's top with holes in the stand's braces. Use eight ¼" bolts and their matching washers and nuts to bolt the top to the stand.

20. Use four ¼" bolts and their matching washers and nuts to bolt the bench grinder to the stand's top. (This assumes that the holes in your bench grinder's base are ¼". If yours are smaller or larger, change your bolt and matching washer and nut size to match the grinder's base mounting holes.)

21. Next, you'll arrange the bench grinder on its stand near the pedal drive to determine their best positions before fixing them in place. Put the stand on the 28" × 28" piece of plywood.

22. Set the front of the stationary bike on the same plywood platform so that the bike's wheel is to the left of the stand from the pedaler's perspective.

23. This is the time to determine where the stationary bike needs to be in order for the pulley to remain taut and provide the most efficient transfer of motion. Pull the stationary bike near the stand and guide the open end of the V-belt over the pulley on the bench grinder's shaft. Then push the stationary bike away until the belt is taut. Make sure that the bike's wheel is directly in line with the pulley and that the belt doesn't veer left to right. (You might need to adjust the stand's position on the plywood, too.) Verify that the belt is as tight as you can make it. You might even want to mark this position, then add up

to a half inch of distance between your stationary bike and the stand later to ensure the connection will not be loose.

24. For the best stability, you'll want to bolt the stand to the plywood platform. Mark where the center of the holes in the stand's feet fall on the platform. Also trace the outline of the stationary bike's feet or front support on the platform, so that you can later reposition everything just as you have it now.

25. Remove the belt from the bench grinder's pulley, then set aside the stationary bike and stand. Put the plywood platform on a workbench and, using the ⁷⁄₁₆" drill bit, drill the holes you marked in Step 24.

26. On the underside of the plywood (the side that does not show the outline of your stationary bike's front feet) use the ¾" countersink bit to remove space around each of the holes you drilled in the previous step.

27. Insert the ⅜" carriage bolts through the holes you drilled in Step 25 from the underside of the plywood, then set the plywood on the floor.

28. Replace the stand and insert the carriage bolts through the stand's feet. Fasten the matching washers and nuts to secure the stand to the plywood platform.

29. Next, you'll fix the stationary bike to the platform in a similar manner. Reposition the stationary bike to match the outline you drew in Step 24. Place a conduit clamp over the steel tube on either side of the stationary bike's front feet and use the wood screws to screw them into place. If your stationary bike has a base that's flat

or made of a different sized steel tube, adjust your style and size of clamp accordingly. Or, if you judge that the weight of the bike and a rider is sufficient to prevent it from moving, you can skip this step.

30. Now you can attach the open end of the V-belt to the pulley on the bench grinder's shaft. Get on the stationary bike and pedal to test and use your bench grinder.

Figure 6.12 shows a two-person human-powered tool sharpener in use in Chennai, India. Note the very large flywheel and resulting gear ratio. Though this crank might be challenging to turn, it would deliver high rpm to the grinding wheel.

Commercially Available Plans and Devices for Recreation and Emergency Preparedness

The category "recreation" is applied broadly here. Recreation could, for example, include sewing, food preparation and gardening, whose human-powered aspects are covered elsewhere in this book. But for many people it involves something electric or electronic — a TV, video game, laptop or portable MP3 player. The following sections describe devices you can purchase for pedal-powered and hand-cranked electricity generation, which can also be considered part of emergency preparedness.

At the other end of the spectrum from electronic forms of recreation are traditional skills and folk arts. Many people have returned to these pursuits in their spare time, perhaps as a response to the fast pace that all our electronic gadgetry compels. The second

half of this chapter describes foot-powered woodworking tools popular in the late 19th century, some of which are experiencing revived interest today. You'll learn how you can find or make one of these devices for use in your own shop.

Pedal-Powered Electrical Generators

When it comes to generating electricity, you might, understandably, feel more comfortable leaving the circuitry to the experts and using something that's tested and guaranteed

Figure 6.12 Hand-Cranked Tool Sharpener in Chennai, India

to work. If you prefer to buy a pedal-powered electrical generator, you can choose from two products, one made by Windstream Power LLC and the other by Convergence Tech.

Windstream Power LLC was founded in 1974 by physicist and electrical engineer Colin Kerr. Colin hadn't planned to make pedal-powered electrical generators. His company

Figure 6.13 Windstream Power's Human Power Trainer

grew from a novel wind turbine he designed. With his wind power systems came a "tiny, affordable" permanent magnet DC generator, and by 1978 some customers, namely ocean-going yachters, had found uses for the generator besides the transformation of wind power to electricity. They were attaching the generators to bicycles on stands and pedaling on deck to make power. Next, the yachters requested special sprockets to use on the chain drives they'd rigged up to the generators. So Windstream sold the sprocket and the generator as a bike-adapter kit. Finally, in response to growing demand, Windstream gave customers exactly what they wanted: a human-powered electrical generator. At the time it was the only such device available commercially. Full-page ads in *Popular Science* and *Popular Mechanics* fueled interest further.

Now Windstream makes two human-powered electrical generators. One, called simply the Human Powered Generator, is a rectangular base with crankarms that can be mounted on a tabletop or floor. Pedals or handles can be attached to the crankarms to make it foot- or hand-powered. The other generator, called the Human Power Trainer and pictured in Figure 6.13, consists of a permanent magnet DC generator in a trainer stand that can accept any bicycle. The bike's rear tire rubs against a spindle on the generator's shaft in a friction drive arrangement, thus turning the shaft and creating current. Power generated is directed to Windstream's Portable Power Pack, which contains a battery and inverter and has receptacles for both AC and DC connectors. As you pedal, you can send electricity directly to any appliance or you can let the

Power Pack store it for later use. At the time this was written, the Human Power Trainer cost $595, the Power Pack was an additional $475, and the Human Power Generator sold for $550. For more information, see the company's Web site at windstreampower.com.

During the oil crisis of the late 1970s, teachers became interested in Windstream's generators. Colin told me, "It became very fashionable in education to introduce renewable energy, and human power is a very good way to reflect just what it takes to produce the energy to do a particular thing."[2] More recently foresters stationed in remote areas of Siberia ordered hundreds of them, presumably to power radios. Now, once again, education and environmental awareness have prompted renewed interest in the generators. Colin's daughter Sheila, who succeeded her father in 2005, told me that the company's latest human-power invention is a metal light box that holds two bulbs: one incandescent and one compact fluorescent. Kids pedal the Human Power Generator to light one bulb, then the other. Of course, the incandescent bulb, which requires 60 watts, taxes the muscles much more than the compact fluorescent, which needs only 23 watts to generate the same amount of light. Sheila said, "We have tried it out with schools and other local organizations that promote energy efficiency. It's designed to be a learning tool and is a lot of fun."[3]

Meanwhile, although Colin no longer oversees Windstream Power's engineering efforts, he remains engaged in the renewable energy field. If he were founding a human-power technology company today, he said

he'd focus on "integrating power generation into human motion without necessarily having external apparatus," that is, devising "a method of generating the electricity that doesn't involve any large, heavy things, like conventional generators." He suggested that smaller and more efficient generators combined with new, energy-efficient consumer electronics would make human power more practical for modern users. He also imagined that human power could be generated from wearable or implanted devices. But, true to his physicist's training, he cautioned, "There's one thing you have to remember. If you're getting energy from something, no matter how passive that appears, it's nevertheless a load being put on whatever system is giving it out, and so if you're getting power out of a chemical reaction in the bloodstream, for instance, that power is coming from somewhere. Basically it's the same thing as doing exercise, only it doesn't appear to be. What you take out has to come from somewhere. It's not magic."[4]

Recently, five of Windstream's Human Power Trainers were used in series to run a supercomputer. Members of the MIT cycling team pedaled for about 20 minutes and sent 1.2 kW to the computer, which was running a fusion modeling program. Their next goal is to convince Guinness to make "Human Powered Computation" an official category, for which they would have set the world record.

Another company that supplies pedal-powered electrical generators is Convergence Tech, headed by Bill Gerosa and his wife, Kim Andersen. Bill told me he developed the pedal electrical generator after years of interest in alternative energy, particularly solar power.

Also an avid cyclist, he used to ride his bike on an indoor trainer during the cold, northeastern winters. However, he regretted that the power he generated was merely dissipated as heat, and so he devised a way to channel that energy into his home's battery bank, part of his solar power system. He began selling the pedal-powered generator in 1999. In 2007, with increased awareness of environmental issues, interest in his product spiked. Sales that year quadrupled compared to the previous year. Many of his customers are individuals, some are corporations using the generator in promotional events, and others are schools and museums.

Convergence Tech's pedal electrical generator, called the Pedal-A-Watt, is similar in design to the one sold by Windstream Power. It uses a bike in a trainer stand and a friction drive to rotate the shaft on a DC generator.

Figure 6.14 Convergence Tech's Pedal-A-Watt Generator

Bill pointed out that one difference between his product and Windstream's is that his costs significantly less — $339 for the generator, plus an additional $365.95 for the PowerPak, which includes a battery and inverter and outlets for AC or DC power. The Pedal-A-Watt is manufactured in the US and comes with a lifetime warranty. His company also sells a wattmeter, DC generator, and DC power center separately, along with plans and parts for making your own pedal electrical generator. At the time this was written Bill was developing a battery charger that could be clamped to the rear wheel of a bike so that the rider could charge electronic devices while in motion.

Bill said he welcomes other manufacturers and do-it-yourselfers bringing more human-powered electrical generators to life. He emphasized the need to increase consumer awareness of energy use and conservation. To that end, he's established a program that helps schools obtain Pedal-A-Watt generators at reduced cost. Comments from customers who purchased his product, he said, have been overwhelmingly positive, although a few who held unrealistic expectations have been disappointed. "They want to have their seven-year-old pedal for 30 minutes and be able to watch TV all afternoon." When he demonstrates his generator at schools, he tries to balance realism with the kind of idealism that fuels invention. "You can make energy from all kinds of crazy things. I try to convey this to kids, who see what's possible. You just have to keep at it, keep thinking about it until you find a way to implement it."[5]

In addition to the pedal-powered electrical generators featured in this chapter,

Jason Moore's Pedal-Powered Laptop Desk

Jason Moore, a PhD student in mechanical engineering at University of California-Davis, had originally planned to concentrate his research efforts on pedal-powered machines. But, not finding a subtopic with sufficiently technical depth, he instead chose to delve into the details of bicycle handling. Yet his passion for pedal-powered devices, prompted when an undergraduate advisor handed him a copy of the book *Pedal Power In Work, Leisure, and Transportation*, persisted.

In the spring of 2007 Jason turned his passion into a class for undergraduates at UC-Davis. The nine-person team decided to build a pedal-powered device for the campus community and began by interviewing people to define what type of machine was most desirable. Consensus pointed to a stand-alone pedal-powered laptop desk that anyone could pedal to charge and use. By the end of the semester, the group had built a working prototype. It uses a bike's chain drive and sprocket to turn the shaft of a cast-off permanent magnet DC motor that Jason found. (For optimal efficiency, Jason strongly recommends using chain drives over belt or friction drives.) The motor, acting as a generator, is connected to an ultracapacitor, which is, in turn, connected to an inverter. Along the way, a diode prevents current leakage. Because anyone might use the pedal-powered laptop, the team incorporated a voltage regulation method that disconnects the generator when the user's output hits 15V. In addition, the circuit includes meters so that users can see how much power and voltage they're generating. The entire apparatus is encased in plastic so that moving parts pose no dangers.

Jason spent the summer of 2007 in Guatemala volunteering with Maya Pedal and helping them make bicimáquinas. When he returned in autumn, he decided to refine the pedal-powered laptop desk's function and form. The result, shown in Figure 6.15, was entered into Specialized Bicycle's "Innovate or Die" pedal-powered machine competition in December 2007. Then it was installed in the student commons at UC-Davis. Jason said that although it might seem like a novelty, the pedal-powered laptop desk is a vital tool for educating students about energy use.[6]

Figure 6.15 Jason Moore's Pedal-Powered Laptop Desk

Chapter 2 describes those built by inventors Bart Orlando, Nate Byerley, Lee Ravenscroft and others. In Chapter 1 you'll find information about the pedal-powered electrical generators that David Sowerwine's organization, EcoSystems, supplies to villages in Nepal. And as mentioned earlier in this chapter, you can also buy plans for making your own pedal-powered electrical generator from Convergence Tech or David Butcher.

Human-Powered Consumer Electronics

Chapter 1 outlined the evolution of human-powered electricity generation, from an 18th-century treadle electrostatic generator to a 21st-century bio-nano generator that circulates in the bloodstream. Although the electrostatic generator is a relic and passive energy harvesting isn't yet ready for retail, today's consumers can take advantage of technologies in between. This section describes human-powered radios, flashlights and small electronics chargers that incorporate those innovations.

A unique confluence of old and new technology has made human-powering such devices practical. Old technology, involving muscles, cranks and dynamos, still generates the power. Newer technology stores and releases it. Traditionally, mechanical flywheels, springs, and later, lead-acid or alkaline batteries, captured the muscle power we generated. But today's batteries and ultracapacitors offer greater storage in smaller forms. They also last longer and in some cases, charge and discharge more quickly. For example, most hand-cranked radios rely on nickel-metal hydride (NiMH) batteries, the same type used in most hybrid gas-electric cars (new types are under development). Compared to rechargeable alkaline batteries with the same voltage rating, NiMH batteries can withstand up to ten times as many charging cycles. Other devices, like MP3 players, flashlights and cell phones, typically depend on lithium-ion batteries, which are known for their high energy density. They, too, remain viable much longer than rechargeable alkaline batteries.

Advances have also reduced the amount of energy necessary to power devices that play music, transmit pictures and sound, or project light. A compact fluorescent bulb using approximately 15 watts issues the same amount of light as an incandescent that uses 60 watts. An LED bulb equal to a 60-watt incandescent requires only 2.5 watts. It's true that you could human-power a 60-watt light bulb with a pedal-powered generator, probably for a limited time. Yet it's well within your power to power the compact fluorescent or LED bulb with either your leg or arm muscles for an extended period. (Or better, fully charge a battery, as described in this chapter's plan for a pedal-powered electrical generator, then connect the bulb to the battery.) Even laptops that use special, low-power processors can be hand-powered, as evidenced by the One Laptop Per Child (OLPC) XO laptops described in Chapter 1.

Powering the devices described in this section isn't physically challenging. However, there are some "best practices" to follow when using them. Avoid charging a device while it's switched on. Though it's possible to do, it's not optimal for the battery. (And it will be more taxing than charging when the device is switched off.) Also, if yours uses a lithium-ion battery, don't let the battery become fully depleted. It might lose its ability to hold a charge or become difficult to charge in the future. If it uses a NiMH battery, cycle it at least once a month by discharging it, then charging it completely, to maximize its life.

Manufacturers sometimes offer guidance on how many minutes of cranking will lead to a certain period of operation or a full charge. Of course, this depends on several variables, including your cranking speed, the battery's viability, and what the device is doing. As examples, however, one hand-cranked radio manufacturer claims that 2 minutes of cranking will give you 15 minutes of playing time. A maker of cell phone chargers claims that 2 minutes of charging gives you 6 minutes of talk time and even more standby time. Cranking a human-powered LED flashlight for 30 seconds ought to give you about 10 minutes of light at a low-to-moderate intensity.

When choosing a hand-cranked electrical device, look for one with quality construction. In particular, examine the handle, the component that will take the most stress over time. If it's made of flimsy plastic, be wary. Although it hasn't happened to me, other users report having the small handles snap off in their hands. Also bear in mind that a tiny handle will be more difficult to turn than a more substantial one and therefore less effective at transferring your muscle power. And look for a device that can be firmly held or supported by your nondominant hand as you crank. Finally, if it matters to you, scour reviews to find which brand is quietest. All of the dynamos

make a whirring noise as you crank, but some are louder than others.

Several types of hand-cranked radios (often combined with flashlights — and sirens!) are on the market now. As described in Chapter 1, the Freeplay Foundation supplies hand-cranked radios to people in sub-Saharan Africa. The aid agency's partner, Freeplay Energy Plc, sells similar (but not the same) human-powered radios and flashlights in Western countries. At the time this was written, Freeplay's hand-cranked radios, which are also capable of being solar powered, sold for between $40 and $80.

Etón's FR1000 Voicelink is marketed as a multipurpose emergency radio and endorsed by the American Red Cross. Shown in Figure 6.16, it includes a AM/FM radio, weather

Figure 6.16 Etón's FR1000 Voicelink Emergency Radio

radio, 2-way transmitter, flashlight and siren. It also comes with a cell phone charger jack, though the cable to connect your phone to the radio is not included. At the time this was written it sold for about $150. It's the latest of such devices from this company. Etón makes several other hand-cranked emergency radios under its name and distributes the German Grundig brand radios in the US.

Vector, now owned by Black and Decker, makes hand-cranked multipurpose devices under the brand name Storm Tracker. Their gadgets include a radio tuner, a digital alert display (which can receive text messages from a weather service), flashlight and a small TV. The TV, however, cannot be human-powered. At the time this was written Storm Trackers, depending on the model, sold for between $40 and $90.

RusTek is another of a handful of companies that makes hand-cranked radio/flashlight combinations. Its Apollo 2, shown in Figure 6.17, is smaller and lighter weight than the Etón, Vector or Freeplay models discussed here, but like the others, is cased in rubberized plastic and includes a siren and a cell phone charging outlet. At the time this was written the Apollo 2 sold for as low as $25. A RusTek spokesperson told me that the company, which also makes hand-cranked coffee mills and cell phone chargers, plans to expand its line of human-powered devices.

At least a dozen companies make hand-cranked flashlights, also known as dynamo flashlights, alone. Some use NiMH batteries while others use lithium-ion. Those made by Freeplay Energy garner the best reviews. Its Sherpa Xray, shown in Figure 6.18, relies on a NiMH battery and sells for about $30. It contains an ultrabright cluster of seven LEDs with variable light intensity. On a full charge and at low intensity, Freeplay claims the Xray can shine for 20 hours. Another Freeplay dynamo flashlight is the Jonta. Larger and designed for durability, it sells for about $50. It features a light indicating optimal cranking speed and

Figure 6.17 RusTek's Apollo 2 Radio/Flashlight

Figure 6.18 Freeplay's Sherpa Xray Dynamo Flashlight

another that warns of a low battery condition. A typical, less expensive model, such as those that sell for about $15, wouldn't include these features, would probably be made of cheaper materials, and would likely use a lithium-ion battery.

Also on the market are several stand-alone hand-cranked cell phone chargers. These devices are small enough to fit in your pocket or briefcase and, minus their carrying pouch and cable, weigh less than 3 ounces. The drawback to their size is that the hand cranks are also very small. Your hands might get cramped after more than a minute of holding and winding. Because adapters vary widely among mobile phone models, be sure your charger comes with the right plug for your phone. Figure 6.19 shows one popular hand-cranked cell-phone charger, the Sidewinder, and this model also includes an LED so it can act as a flashlight. At the time this was written, it sold for about $20. The manufacturer recommends cranking at a rate of two turns per second and advises that 2 minutes of hand cranking will result in 6 minutes of talk time. One further note: it's been my experience, and that of others, that this and similar cell phone chargers will not work if your phone's battery is completely discharged.

Dynamos, the mechanisms behind the hand cranks in the aforementioned devices, have long been used to light bicycle headlights. Mark Hoekstra lives in the Netherlands, where bikes are ubiquitous and most have dynamos. A few years ago he decided to modify the dynamo on his bike so it could charge his iPod as he rides. After several refinements he was successful. In case you're in-

Figure 6.19 Sidewinder Mobile Phone Charger

terested in doing the same, he's kindly posted details about his invention on his Web site geektechnique.org. (The same instructions were published in condensed form in Volume 11 of *Make* magazine.)

If you prefer to buy a human-powered music player, those have finally reached consumers. Trevor Baylis, inventor of the clockwork radio, has gone on to nurture new inventors through his Trevor Baylis Brands group. From that venture, in late 2007 emerged a new type of hand-cranked device, the Eco Media Player, shown in Figure 6.20. The most feature-rich human-powered consumer product available to date, it combines a music player, video player, voice recorder, flashlight, text reader, photo viewer, radio and cell phone charger. It can play music, for example, for 40 minutes

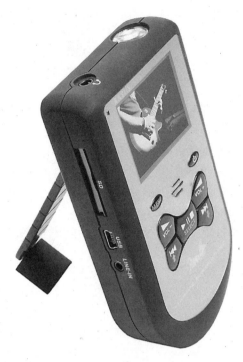

Figure 6.20 Trevor Baylis Brand's Eco Media Player

Figure 6.21 Shake Flashlight

after one minute of cranking. At maximum charge, it could play for 20 hours. (That's after 30 minutes of cranking!) Early reviews noted a few drawbacks to the device, some of which are related to the hand-cranking capability. It's larger than most portable music and video players, for example. In addition, it came with only 2 GB of memory and some users found its buttons less responsive than they'd prefer. At the time this was written, it sold for about $350 and sales outlets were limited.

Human-powered consumer electronics aren't limited to dynamo-driven devices, however. If a gadget takes little enough energy, inventors can dream up all kinds of ways to run it. For example, there are flashlights, like the one shown in Figure 6.21, which are charged through shaking. A half dozen companies make these, including Hummer, Dura Light, Rayovac and Applied Innovative Technologies. All operate the same way. As you shake the flashlight, magnets oscillate within a coil and induce a voltage on the coil. The resulting electricity is directed to a capacitor for storage. Most provide up to 5 minutes of light after 30 seconds of shaking. (Though one manufacturer claims its will provide 20 minutes of light for the same amount of work. Also, Dura Light's Freedom brand uses a nickel-metal hydride battery, rather than a capacitor, and its manufacturer claims it provides 2 hours of light after 30 seconds of shaking.) Some people prefer the shake flashlights over hand-cranked flashlights because they contain fewer moving parts and therefore have fewer things to break. At the time this was written, prices for shake flashlights ranged from $12 to $40.

More whimsical human-powered consumer electronics include: a camera that resembles a rotary pizza cutter and is powered by rolling the wheel over a hard surface; a camera that's powered when you spin it; a yo-yo-powered MP3 player; a pull-cord-powered MP3 player; and perhaps strangest, the Firefly, an LED nose ring driven by a tiny fan that hangs from your nostril and, being spun by your exhalation, transmits current to illuminate the LED. Although some of these products are still in the conceptual phase, consumers will no doubt have an increasing choice of unique human-powered electronics in coming years.

Human-Powered Woodworking Tools

Opposite the human-power spectrum from consumer electronics are the heavy-duty, belt- and gear-driven woodworking tools that came along in the mid-19th century. While working on this book I visited with several people who prefer human-powered woodworking machines to their motorized counterparts. Some appreciate that the tools are relatively quiet. Others claim that they enjoy better control over their work when the tool is foot- or hand-powered. Those who work in developing countries can't count on having electricity, and so the tools must have an alternate power source. Human power, portable and always available, suits the need well. In the case of most scroll saws (or jigsaws) and formers, the effort required to operate the tool is relatively light. In part, this is due to the ingenuous design of those 19th-century models. But when it comes to table saws (or rip saws), band saws and very large lathes, the effort can be strenu-

ous, and in some cases, calls for two or more people.

However, choices for woodworkers who want to use foot-powered lathes, scroll saws, formers and other tools are limited. You can construct one yourself or find an antique version, and those in good condition are relatively expensive. Perhaps they're out there, but my research didn't turn up any companies that make new treadle woodworking tools, nor any shops that would build one on request. The good news, however, is that some devoted woodworkers have written excellent plans for making your own tools. This section describes the best of them.

Serious woodworkers likely know about Roy Underhill, host and co-producer of the PBS show "The Woodwright's Shop." Roy began introducing viewers to traditional tools and craftsmanship over 20 years ago. Along with Windsor chairs and wooden puzzles, he has also taught viewers to make treadle lathes, spring pole lathes, and foot-powered scroll saws. By searching PBS's Web site (pbs.org), you can find which episodes cover these topics. In episode number 1806, for example, Roy builds a reproduction "Colonial Williamsburg" treadle lathe. Many of the shows can be viewed online, or you can order a video copy. If you want a more permanent and detailed reference, Roy's books *The Woodwright's Workbook* and *The Woodwright's Shop* contain plans.

Individuals less famous than Roy Underhill have also published detailed instructions for making foot-powered tools. One of the best comes from Steve Schmeck, who lives in the Upper Peninsula of Michigan and carves spoons, bowls and wooden sculptures. Steve became interested in treadle lathes when he saw a giant one at a historical demonstration over 20 years ago. Soon after that he built a modest-sized version for his shop, shown in Figure 6.22. It's made of maple lumber culled from his wood lot, plus pulleys, bearings and other hardware, including the Pitman rod from a treadle sewing machine base. The lathe's belt consists of two treadle sewing machine belts that he stitched together with nylon thread after finding that the metal clips normally used to cinch the belts prevented smooth operation on the lathe.

As Steve and his wife Sue exhibited at art fairs in the 1980s and 1990s, demonstrating the treadle lathe drew customers to their booth. Many people asked Steve how he built the lathe, so he decided to write plans. The instructions, which are clearly written and well illustrated, are available for download, on CD, or in print from his Web site manytracks.com. His site also features photos of lathes people have built based on his plans (some of which, he told me, bear little resemblance to his lathe, but display great creativity!). If you follow his plans and make a treadle lathe, I'm sure he'd appreciate hearing from you. Steve said that

Figure 6.22 Steve Schmeck and His Treadle Lathe

he still uses the treadle lathe daily, though not necessarily as a lathe. He's fitted it with a drill chuck that can accept various sanding disks, thereby turning it into a treadle sander, which he uses to sand his hand-carved spoons.[7]

Treadle scroll saws, or jigsaws, are probably even simpler to make than treadle lathes. One source of plans comes from Rick Hutcheson. For more than 15 years, Rick has made his career working with scroll saws and writing articles on the topic for magazines such as *Wood* and *Decorative Woodcrafts*. Though he uses mainly motorized scroll saws to make his Victorian patterns, he also col-

lects, designs and builds foot-powered ones. In his collection of nearly 200 scroll saws, about 60, he told me, were foot-powered. In addition, Rick sells plans for making a treadle scroll saw, as well as a pedal-powered version, via his Web site at scrollsaws.com. Over 700 people have purchased his plans, and many have sent him photos of their finished projects. Rick said he came up with his designs after studying his favorite antique scroll saws, adopting their best features, and then using trial and error to arrive at a design that worked well. He also aimed to make his design simple for an average woodworker to

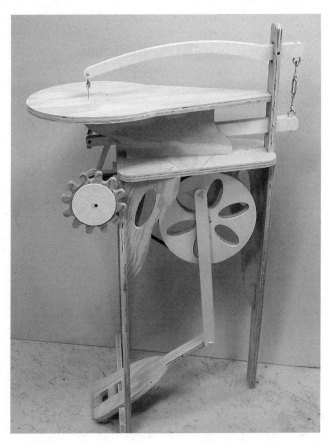

Figure 6.23 Rick Hutcheson's Treadle Scroll Saw

construct.[8] Figure 6.23 shows Rick's home-made treadle scroll saw.

Another plan for making a treadle scroll saw, called the Parker Treadle Jigsaw, was published in the March/April 1976 *Mother Earth News*, which is available online from their Web site, motherearthnews.com. In this version, the author made a jigsaw that sits on top of a treadle sewing machine base. The treadle belt is looped over the jigsaw's flywheel, rather than the sewing machine's handwheel. In fact, this technique is also used by some woodworkers in the developing world.

For more information on antique foot-

Eric Hollenbeck and Blue Ox Millworks

In 1973, with a $300 bank loan and a love of machinery, Eric Hollenbeck founded Blue Ox Millworks, a company that specializes in custom reproduction millwork. Ever since, his business has been financed by cash flow — which typically meant trading for, refurbishing or building his own equipment. Using human-powered tools was a necessity in many cases. Eric told me, "It's way cheaper and way easier to manufacture something human-powered than it is to try and manufacture something that is motorized." Eric also believes in the quality of older, human-powered tools. When I visited his Eureka, California workshop, he demonstrated a Portland picket pointer, a machine that makes slats of wood into pickets for fences. After one pull of the lever, the wood came out tapered to a perfect arc at one end. "There isn't a modern machine built that can out-produce it for either quickness or quality," he said.

Blue Ox Millworks houses hundreds of human-powered machines, from treadle-powered and pedal-powered scroll saws, lathes, shapers and table saws to printing presses and a homemade compo press. The woodworking tools, manufactured mainly in the late 1800s by firms such as W. F. and John Barnes Co. and Millers Falls Co., especially intrigue Eric. He pointed out that these companies brought the industrial age to the craftsman and made their work lightning fast compared to working with hand tools.

"These guys had it down pat, and they were doing phenomenal things."

The machines at Blue Ox Millworks are not display pieces, however. All are still in use, by his staff and also by students. Eric established a school where teens can learn the traditional arts of blacksmithing, woodworking, ceramics and bookmaking. In this way, Blue Ox Millworks acts as a preserve for traditional knowledge. Eric worries that in the age of electronics, we're losing our mechanical know-how. "The information that

Figure 6.24 Eric Hollenbeck of Blue Ox Millworks

powered tools, the following books, both by Kenneth Cope, make excellent references: *American Foot Power and Hand Power Machinery* and *American Lathe Builders: 1810–1910*. In addition, you'll find a vast repository of information, including photos and a forum for traditional woodworking enthusiasts, at the Old Woodworking Machines Web site, owwm.com. If you want to discover the value of your antique treadle lathe, learn how to replace its bearings or research the history of its manufacturer, this is the place to start.

[we] are throwing away is the information it took us 25,000 years to glean: how do you live on this planet comfortably with what's around you? We may not want to do that, because it's tied to so many different things, and every little part of the puzzle is holding the whole puzzle together. You take any one part out and the whole puzzle falls apart, and that's a fairly fragile position to be in. And it's amazing, you can't back up. It's a hell of a deal to try and back up and think mechanically again."

Further, he suggested that society's current emphasis on speed might be the cause of our environmental crisis. "I just don't think that the forest and the planet can sustain our kind of throwaway society. If you make things right and make things to last, then you don't have to make a million of them in a short period of time. You can make a few in a period of time and they're passed on generation to generation. It's that mentality that's going to have to be the driving force, and there are people out there that are willing to pay and are willing to invest in something. I say invest because you pay a lot more for it as the original buyer, but then your grandkids' grandkids are still using the product, so then stretched out over that length of time all of a sudden the product is pretty inexpensive. A lot less expensive than the junk that each generation had to buy."

A story he told me about making his own varnish illustrates his philosophy of creation. He had scraped off the pitch from some damaged pine trees miles away, collected it in a jar, then carefully boiled the pitch until it became the right consistency and color. The process took about half a day. When woodworking friends chided him, pointing out that he could buy a *quart* of varnish for less than $7.00, he said, "You know, you're absolutely right, except there's a hidden cost in that 7 dollars. And the hidden cost is knowledge. You have just traded knowledge for convenience. You don't know what that stuff in that can is made of, you don't know how to manipulate it, you don't know how to do anything at all with it, only what the manufacturer on the can says – do this and this and this – and that's what you know how to do."[9]

Eric and Blue Ox Millworks are the subject of a book, *Tales from the Blue Ox*, written and illustrated by Dan Brett, and he's renown in the US as an expert on old woodworking tools. Strangers regularly send him photos of equipment they've found at an auction or flea market and ask him to identify it. His curiosity seems endless. Chances are, he'll long find ways to mix old-world knowledge with new experiences and come up with clever solutions – even if they're not speedy.

FURTHER RESOURCES

Historically Human-Powered Devices:

American Artifacts. americanartifacts.com/smma/index.htm

American Precision Museum. americanprecision.org/

American Textile History Museum. athm.org/

Batory, Dana M. 1997. *Vintage Woodworking Machinery: An Illustrated Guide to Four Manufacturers.* The Astragal Press.

Berto, Frank. 2004. *The Dancing Chain: History and Development of the Derailleur Bicycle,* 2nd rev. exp. ed. Van der Plas Publications.

Bicycle Museum of America. bicyclemuseum.com/

Brett, Dan. 2003. *Tales From the Blue Ox.* The Astragal Press.

Candee, Richard M. 2005. *The Hand-Cranked Knitter and Sock Machine.* Cottonwood Hill Publishing (also available as a CD-ROM).

Carter, Constance. The History of Household Technology with Constance Carter (Journeys and Crossings, Library of Congress Digital Reference Team). loc.gov/rr/program/journey/household.html

Circular Sock Knitting Machines. angoravalley.com/csm.html

Cooper, Grace Rogers. 1976. *The Sewing Machine: Its Invention and Development.* Smithsonian Institution Press (also available online at sil.si.edu/digitalcollections/hst/cooper/).

Cope, Kenneth L. 2001. *American Foot Power and Hand Power Machinery.* Martin J. Donnelly Antique Tools.

Cope, Kenneth L. 2001. *American Lathe Builders: 1810–1910.* The Astragal Press.

Derry, T. K. and Trevor I. Williams. 1993. *A Short History of Technology,* Dover.

Herlihy, David V. 2004. *Bicycle: The History.* Yale University Press.

Hollenbeck, Eric. Blue Ox Millworks. blueoxmill.com/

Hounshell, David. 1985. *From the American System to Mass Production 1800–1932: The Development of Manufacturing Technology in the United States.* The Johns Hopkins University Press.

King, Stuart. History of the Lathe: part one — reciprocal motion. stuartking.co.uk/index.php/history-of-the-lathe-part-one-reciprocal-motion/

Maxwell, Lee. Washing Machine Museum. oldewash.com/

International Sewing Machine Collectors' Society (ISMACS). ismacs.net/home.html

Old Wood-Working Machines. owwm.com/

Pedaling History Bicycle Museum. pedalinghistory.com/PHmuseum.html

Sharp, Archibald. 2003. *Bicycles & Tricycles: A Classic Treatise on Their Design and Construction.* Dover Publications.

Tiller's International. tillersinternational.org/

Thornton, Don. 1997. *Apple Parers.* Thornton House Publishing.

Thornton, Don. 1999. *The Eggbeater Chronicles.* Thornton House Publishing.

Union Hill Antique Tools. tooltimer.com/index.html

Viney, Mike. The Virtual Apple Parer Museum. appleparermuseum.com/index.htm

Wightman, Dick. Welcome to Treadle On! treadleon.net/

White, Lynn. 1962. *Medieval Technology and Social Change.* Oxford University Press.

Human Power in Appropriate Technology:

Allen, Hugh and Carl Bielenberg. 1995. *How to Make and Use the Treadle Irrigation Pump.* Practical Action.

Bielenberg, Carl. Better World Workshop. RFD 1, Marshfield, Vermont, 05658 USA.

Campus Center for Appropriate Technology (CCAT), Humboldt State University. humboldt.edu/~ccat/

CTARA: Centre for Technology Alternatives for Rural Areas. iitb.ac.in/~ctara/index.html

EcoSystems Pvt. Ltd. EcoSystems — EcoPower. ecosystemsnepal.com/ecopower.php

EnterpriseWorks/VITA. enterpriseworks.org/

Freeplay Foundation. freeplayfoundation.org/

Full Belly Project. fullbellyproject.org/

IDEI: International Development Enterprises (India). ide-india.org/ide/index1.shtml

KickStart: The Tools to End Poverty. kickstart.org/home/index.html

Legacy Foundation. legacyfound.org/index.html

Malnutrition Matters: Food Technology Solutions. malnutrition.org/

Maya Pedal. Asociación Maya Pedal. mayapedal.org/

MIT D-Lab. web.mit.edu/d-lab/

One Laptop Per Child. laptop.org/

PlayPumps International. playpumps.org/

Practica Foundation. practicafoundation.nl/

Practical Action — Intermediate Technology Development Group (ITDG). itdg.org/

Shannon, Larry and Jim Sylivant. Build Your Own Treadle Pump. treadle.pump.googlepages.com/buildyourowntreadlepump

Smillie, Ian. 2001. *Mastering the Machine Revisited: Poverty, Aid and Technology.* Intermediate Technology Development Group Publishing.

Village Earth: The Consortium for Sustainable Village-Based Development. villageearth.org/index.php

Weisman, Alan. 1999. *Gaviotas: A Village to Reinvent the World.* Chelsea Green Publishing.

Human Power Potential:

Alexander, Robert McNeill. 1992. *The Human Machine.* Columbia University Press.

Burke, Edmund R., ed. 2003. *High-Tech Cycling,* 2nd ed. Human Kinetics.

Human Power Institute. *Human Power eJournal.* hupi.org/HPeJ/index.htm

Lawyer, David. Human Energy Accounting. lafn.org/~dave/energy/human_energy .html

McCullagh, James C., ed. 1977. *Pedal Power In Work, Leisure, and Transportation.* Rodale Press. (Out of print, but available used.)

Vogel, Steven. 2000. *Cat's Paws and Catapults: Mechanical Worlds of People and Nature.* W. W. Norton & Company.

Vogel, Steven. 2001. *Prime Mover: A Natural History of Muscle.* W. W. Norton & Company.

Wilson, David Gordon. 2004. *Bicycling Science,* 3rd ed. The MIT Press.

Human-Powered
Machine Inventors and Users:

Andrews, Richard. PEDAL (Pedal Energy Development Alternatives). pedalpower .org

Brandis, Jock. Full Belly Project. fullbelly project.org/

Breeden, Frederick. Just Soap. justsoap.com/

Butcher, David. David Butcher: Pedal Powered Generator — DIY Plans. los-gatos .ca.us/davidbu/pedgen.html

Bulthaup, Colin. Potenco: Powering Endless Possibilities. potenco.com/

Byerley, Nate. The Juice Peddler. bikeblender .com/

Carter, Bill. footpowered.com/

Corbett, Graham and Michael Sacco. ChocoSol Traders. chocosoltraders.com/

Delft University of Technology. io.tudelft.nl (Search for "human power").

Ebenezer, Job. Standard Bicycle with Pedal Power Attachment (Dual Purpose Bicycle). technologyforthepoor.com/Pedal PowerReport/PedalPowerReport.htm

Gadsden, Alex. Cyclean: The pedal powered washing machine. cyclean.biz/

Hartman, Albert. High Tide Associates. hightidelabs.com/

Hoekstra, Mark. geektechnique.org/

Homeless Dave. HD Clothes Washin' Man. homelessdave.com/hdwashingman.htm

Hutcheson, Rick. Rick's Scrollsaws. scroll saws.com/

International Human Powered Vehicle Association (IHPVA). ihpva.org/

Kusilek, Anne. Finely Finished. finely-finished.com/

Maya Pedal. Asociación Maya Pedal. mayapedal.org/

MIT D-Lab. web.mit.edu/d-lab/

Moore, Jason. Pedal Desk Project 2007. mae.ucdavis.edu/~biosport/jkm/ped_ desk.htm

Orlando, Bart. Pedal Powered Innovations, Designed and Built by Bart Orlando, Assisted By HSU Students At CCAT.

humboldt.edu/~ccat/pedalpower/inventions/frames_final_htm.htm

Parker, Woody Roy. juicycle info. juicycle.com/

Polito, Ben. Five Islands Orchard — Cider Equipment. fiveislandsorchard.wordpress.com/category/cider-equipment/

Ravenscroft, Lee. Working Bikes. workingbikes.org

Schmeck, Steve. Make Your Own Treadle Lathe. manytracks.com/lathe/default.htm

Shannon, Larry and Jim Sylivant. Build Your Own Treadle Pump. treadle.pump.googlepages.com/buildyourowntreadlepump

Sowerwine, David. EcoSystems Pvt. Ltd. EcoSystems — EcoPower. ecosystemsnepal.com/ecopower.php

Underhill, Roy. The Woodwright's Shop. pbs.org/wws/

Weir, Alex. cd3wd.com/

Whaley, Brad. scienceshareware.com/

Commercially Available Human-Powered Devices

American Lawn Mower Company. reelin.com/

Brill. Brill Cylinder Mowers. brill.de/produkte.php?produktgruppe=6&language=EN

Byerley Bicycle Blender. The Juice Peddler. bikeblender.com/

Clean Air Gardening. Push Reel Mowers. cleanairgardening.com/reelmowers.html

Convergence Tech., Inc. econvergence.net/

Country Living Grain Mill. countrylivinggrainmills.com/

Etón Corporation. etoncorp.com/

Freeplay Energy Plc. freeplayenergy.com/

Gaiam. gaiam.com/

GSI Outdoors. gsioutdoors.com/

Haaga. Products. haaga-gmbh.de/en/produkte.html

Happy Valley Ranch. Our Products: Cider and Wine Presses. happyvalleyranch.com/products.php.

Homestead Harvest. homesteadharvest.com/index.html

Industrial Revolution. Play and Freeze Ice Cream Maker. icecreamrevolution.com/

Lehman's. lehmans.com/

The Pedal Power. thepedalpower.com/

Pleasant Hill Grain. pleasanthillgrain.com/family_grain_mills.aspx

Red Hill General Store. redhillgeneralstore.com/

Rustek. rustekonline.com/

Schnitzer. Stone grain mills and flakers. schnitzer.com.au/

Sidewinder Emergency Cell Phone Charger. sidewinder.ca

Temple, David. People-Powered Machines. peoplepoweredmachines.com/index.php

Thomas Stuart Wheels. Potter's Wheels, Kick Wheels. thomasstuart.com/

Trevor Baylis Brands Plc. trevorbaylisbrands.com/tbb/home/home.asp

Walton Feed. Grinder Introduction. waltonfeed.com/self/grinder.html

Windstream Power LLC. Pedal Power Generators. windstreampower.com/

NOTES

Introduction

1. Lorraine Lanningham-Foster, Lana J. Nysse and James A. Levine, "Labor Saved, Calories Lost: The Energetic Impact of Domestic Labor-saving Devices." *Obesity Research* 11, no.10 (October 2003), 1178–1181.
2. Garry J. Egger, Neeltje Vogels and Klaas R. Westerterp, "Estimating Historical Changes in Physical Activity Levels," *The Medical Journal of Australia* 175, no. 11 (December 2001), 635–636.

Chapter 1
The Evolution of
Human-Powered Devices

1. Lynn White, Jr., *Medieval Technology and Social Change* (Oxford University Press, 1962).
2. Ibid., 105.
3. Ibid., 108–110.
4. Ibid., 115.
5. Daniela Lazarová, "Man Powered Medieval Crane at Prague Castle," interview by Ondrej Protiva, *Current Affairs*, Radio Praha (9 May 2006) radio.cz/en/article/82857 (accessed January 28, 2008).
6. T. K. Derry and Trevor I. Williams, *A Short History of Technology: From the Earliest Times to A.D. 1900* (Oxford University Press, 1960).
7. H. G. Wells, *A Short History of the World* (The Macmillan Company, 1922).
8. R. J. Forbes, *A History of Technology*, ed. Charles Singer (Oxford University Press. 1958).
9. David H. Shayt, "Stairway to Redemption: America's Encounter with the British Prison Treadmill," *Technology and Culture* 30, no. 40 (October 1989): 908–938.
10. Ibid., 911.
11. Jeannie Duckworth, *Fagin's Children: Criminal Children in Victorian England* (Hambledon and London, 2002).
12. Shayt, "Stairway to Redemption," 914.
13. "The Treadmill Coldbath Fields," *The New York Times*, February 15, 1885.
14. Shayt, "Stairway to Redemption," 929.
15. "50 best British summer holiday breaks,"

TimeOut London, May 29, 2007, timeout
.com/london/features/2944/5.html (accessed November 4, 2007).

16. Brendan O'Neill, "Is carbon offsetting just
eco-enslavement?," *spiked*, September 3,
2007, spiked-online.com/index.php?/
site/article/3788/ (accessed November 4,
2007).

17. "To cancel out the CO_2 of a return flight
to India, it will take one poor villager
three years of pumping water by foot. So
is carbon offsetting the best way to ease
your conscience?" *Times Online,* August
28, 2007, timesonline.co.uk/tol/news/
world/asia/article2337485.ece (accessed
November 4, 2007).

18. Climate Care, "Benefiting farmers
and their families–truth about treadle
pumps," September 21, 2007, climatecare
.org/news/benefiting-farmers-and-their
-families-truth-about/ (accessed November 4, 2007).

19. "To cancel out the CO_2 of a return flight
to India, it will take one poor villager
three years of pumping water by foot. So
is carbon offsetting the best way to ease
your conscience?" *Times Online,* times
online.co.uk/tol/news/world/asia/article
2337485.ece, August 28, 2007 (accessed
November 4, 2007).

20. Angela Lakwete, *Inventing the Cotton Gin:
Machine and Myth in Antebellum America*
(Johns Hopkins University Press, 2003).

21. Todd Timmons, *Science and Technology
in Nineteenth-Century America* (Green-
wood Press, 2005).

22. David A. Hounshell, *From the American System to Mass Production, 1800–1932*
(The Johns Hopkins University Press,
1984).

23. Carrie Brown, *Industrial Revolution in
the Upper Connecticut River Valley: An
Overview* (American Precision Museum,
2007).

24. Grace Rodgers Cooper, *The Sewing Machine: Its Invention and Development*
(Smithsonian Institution Press, 1976).

25. Ruth Brandon, *Singer and the Sewing
Machine: A Capitalist Romance* (Kodan-
sha America, 1996).

26. Ibid., 126–127.

27. Hounshell, *From the American System to
Mass Production, 1800–1932,* 89–91.

28. Singer Sewing Company, singerco.com/
company/history.html (accessed January
30, 2008).

29. Kenneth L. Cope, *American Foot Power
and Hand Power Machinery* (Martin J.
Donnelly Antique Tools, 2001).

30. Mrs. Lynn Linton, "Cranks and Crazes,"
The North American Review 161, no. 469
(December 1895), 667–674.

31. David V. Herlihy, *Bicycle: The History*
(Yale University Press, 2004).

32. Archibald Sharp, *Bicycles & Tricycles: A
Classic Treatise on Their Design and Construction* (Dover Publications, 2003).

33. Herlihy, *Bicycle: The History,* 31–32.

34. Ibid., 86–90.

35. Ibid, 84.

36. A. Ritchie, *King of the Road* (Ten Speed
Press, 1975).

37. Carrie Brown, *Pedal Power: The Bicycle in
Industry and Society* (The American Precision Museum, 1997).

38. Herlihy, *Bicycle: The History,* 251.

39. Brown, *Pedal Power: The Bicycle in Industry and Society*, 18.

40. W. Rybczynski, *Paper Heroes* (Anchor Press/Doubleday, 1980).

41. E. F. Schumacher, *Small Is Beautiful: Economics as if People Mattered* (Harper and Row, 1973).

42. "People and Technology, Transforming Lives," Practical Action, practicalaction.org/docs/about_us/practical_action_strategy_2007-12.pdf (accessed November 10, 2007).

43. R. Whiticombe and M. Carr, *Appropriate Technology Institutions: A Review* (ITDG, 1982).

44. Ian Smillie, *Mastering the Machine Revisited: Poverty, Aid, and Technology* (Practical Action Publishing, 2006).

45. Carroll Pursell, "The Rise and Fall of the Appropriate Technology Movement in the United States, 1965–1985" *Technology and Culture* 34, no. 3 (July 1993), 629–637.

46. Amy Smith, interview with author, February 15, 2007, Cambridge, Massachusetts.

47. Ibid.

48. Ken Weimar, telephone conversation with author, October 11, 2007.

49. Ibid.

50. Ibid.

51. Ibid.

52. Ibid.

53. Richard Andrews, telephone conversation with author, July 7, 2007.

54. Weimar, telephone conversation with author.

55. The 2nd UN World Water Development Report, March 2006, unesco.org/water/wwap/wwdr2/table_contents.shtml (accessed November 10, 2007).

56. S. S. Wilson, "Pedaling Foot Power for Pumps," World Water, 1983 (As referenced in Peter Fraenkel, "Water Lifting Devices," (Food and Agricultural Organization of the United Nations, 1986).

57. "Treadle Pump Programme," IDEI, ide-india.org/ide/treadlepump.shtml (accessed November 11, 2007).

58. Weimar, telephone conversation with author.

59. Alan Weisman, quoted in "Utopia Rises Out Of the Colombian Plains," *All Things Considered*, NPR, transcript no. 1589, segment no. 06, August 29, 1994.

60. Alan Weisman, *Gaviotas: A Village to Reinvent the World* (Chelsea Green, 1998).

61. Marissa Valdez, telephone conversation with author, July 24, 2007.

62. Ibid.

63. PRACTICA Foundation, "Rope Pump Manual Ethiopia," 2006.

64. Netherlands Water Partnership, "Smart Water Solutions," 2006.

65. "Peanut Power," *Popular Mechanics* (November 2006).

66. International Labour Office and the United Nations Industrial Development Organization, "Small-scale oil extraction from groundnuts and copra," Technical Memorandum No. 5, Technology Series (1983).

67. *The Appropriate Genius*, directed by Rob Hill, Common Sense Films, (in progress).

68. Alison Hynd and Amy Smith, "Meeting a Pressing Need: Project Appraisal of the Oilseed Ram Press and Approaches

to Implementation," Fall 2005, web.mit
.edu/d-lab/DlabI05/Readingsfall05/oil
seed_press_cs_version2_highres.pdf (accessed February 2, 2008).

69. Ibid.

70. KickStart: The Tools to End Poverty,
kickstart.org/tech/technologies/oilpro
cessing.html (accessed February 2, 2008).

71. Frank Daller, telephone conversation
with author, November 20, 2007.

72. Michael B. Schiffer, *Draw the Lightning
Down: Benjamin Franklin and Electrical
Technology in the Age of Enlightenment*
(University of California Press, 2006).

73. Drill Regulations for Field Companies of
the Signal Corps (Provisional), early
radiohistory.us/1911pak.htm (accessed
January 21, 2008).

74. John Behr, "Traeger, Alfred Hermann
(1895–1980)," in Australian Dictionary of
Biography, vol. 12 (Melbourne University
Press, 1990).

75. Albert Hartman, telephone conversation
with author, November 27, 2007.

76. "The Pedal Power: Pedal Power FAQs,"
thepedalpower.com/Pedal%20Power%20
Website/070911%20Pedal%20Power%20
Website%20FAQ.html#Q2 (accessed January 22, 2008).

77. Susan E. Stein and Jennie Lane, "A Legs-
on Approach to Energy Education Then
and Now: A Longitudinal Study" (paper
presented at the North American Association for Environmental Education
(NAAEE) Conference, 2006).

78. David Sowerwine, telephone conversation with author, September 27, 2007.

79. Freeplay Energy Plc:History, freeplay

energy.com/about/history (accessed January 22, 2008).

80. Freeplay Foundation, freeplayfoundation
.org/ (accessed January 22, 2008).

81. Colin Bulthaup, telephone conversation
with author, October 16, 2007.

82. Ibid.

83. Raj Pandian, telephone conversation
with author, August 15, 2007.

84. Thad Starner, "Human Generated Power
for Mobile Electronics," *Low Power Electronics Design*, ed. Christian Piguet (CRC
Press, 2004).

85. Ibid.

86. Joe Kullman, "Backpack Power: Energy
Harvesting Made Easy," fulton.asu.edu/
fulton/news/page.php?sid=401 (accessed
January 23, 2008).

87. Thad Starner, "Human-Powered Wearable Computing," *IBM Systems Journal*
35:3–4 (1996), 618–629.

88. Ibid.

89. Roy Kornbluh, e-mail communication
with author, July 10, 2007.

90. Lawrence C. Rome et al., "Generating
Electricity While Walking With Loads,"
Science 309, no. 5741 (9 September 2005),
1725–1728.

91. J. M. Donelan et al., "Biomechanical Energy Harvesting: Generating Electricity
During Walking With Minimal User Effort," *Science* 319, no. 5864 (8 February
2008), 807–810.

92. "Power From Blood Could Lead to Human Batteries," *The Sydney Morning Her-
ald*, August 4, 2003.

93. Ricky K. Soong et al., "Powering an Inor-
ganic Nanodevice with a Biomolecular

Motor," Science 290, no. 5496 (24 November 2000) 1555–1558.

94. Brian Noer, "The Promise of Biomolecular Motors," *Nanowerk* (September 20, 2006), nanowerk.com/spotlight/spotid=844.php (accessed January 24, 2008).

95. John Roach, "Urine Battery Turns Pee Into Power," *National Geographic News* (August 18, 2005), news.nationalgeographic.com/news/2005/08/0818_050818_urinebattery.html (accessed January 23, 2008).

Chapter 2
Putting Human Power to Work

1. Richard Andrews, telephone conversation with author, July 7, 2007.

2. Ibid.

3. Vaclav Smil, *Energies: An Illustrated Guide to the Biosphere and Civilization* (The MIT Press, 1999).

4. David Gordon Wilson, *Bicycling Science,* 3rd ed. (The MIT Press, 2004).

5. Steven Vogel, *Prime Mover: A Natural History of Muscle* (W. W. Norton and Company, 2001).

6. Wilson, *Bicycling Science,* 3rd ed., 64, 75.

7. Ray Browning, telephone conversation with author, October 24, 2007.

8. Edmund Burke, *High-Tech Cycling* (Human Kinetics, 2003).

9. C. R. Kyle, V. J. Caizzo and M. Palombo, "Predicting Human Powered Vehicle Performance Using Ergometry and Aerodynamic Drag Measurements," (paper presented at conference Human Power for Health, Productivity, Recreation and Transportation, Technology University of Cologne, September 1978).

10. Richard Powell and Tracey Robinson, "The Bioenergetics of Power Production in Combined Arm-leg Crank Systems," *Human Power* 6, no. 3 (1987): 8–18.

11. J. Y. Harrison, "Maximizing Human Power Output by Suitable Selection of Motion Cycle and Load," *Human Factors* 12, no. 3 (1970): 315–329.

12. Peter Slob, "The Human Power Chart: Sustained Comfortable Cranking," (PhD diss., Delft University of Technology, April 2000).

13. M. Pater, "A Human Powered MP3 Player," (graduation report at the Sub-faculty of Industrial Design Engineering, Delft University of Technology, 2000).

14. Vogel, *Prime Mover: A Natural History of Muscle,* 136–137, 151.

15. Roy Kornbluh, "Power from Plastic: How Electroactive Polymer 'Artificial Muscles' Will Improve Portable Power Generation in the 21st Century Military" (presentation at Tri-Service Power Expo, July 2003).

16. Thad Starner, "Human Generated Power for Mobile Electronics," in *Low Power Electronics Design*, ed. Christian Piguet (CRC Press, 2004).

17. D. Zuidema, "Design of a Human Powered Product for O₂ France" (Delft University of Technology, 2001).

18. Arjen Jansen and Ab Stevels, "Human Power, a Sustainable Option for Electronics," Delft University of Technology, 1999.

19. Arjen Jansen and Peter Slob, "Human Power: Comfortable One-Hand Cranking," (paper presented at the International

Conference on Engineering Design, Stockholm, 2003).

20. Wilson, *Bicycling Science,* 3rd ed., 44–46, 83.

21. Vogel, *Prime Mover: A Natural History of Muscle,* 158–167.

22. David Gordon Wilson, "Understanding Pedal Power," (Volunteers in Technical Assistance [VITA], 1986).

23. David B. Perry, *Bike Cult* (Four Walls Eight Windows, 1995).

24. Vogel, *Prime Mover: A Natural History of Muscle,* 216.

25. H. J. Hopfen, *Farm Implements for Arid and Tropical Regions,* Paper no. 91 (FAO Agricultural Development, 1969), 10. (Conversion to English units by author.)

26. Smil, *Energies: An Illustrated Guide to the Biosphere and Civilization*, xvi.

27. Keith E. Holbert, Associate Professor, Arizona State University, "Hydro-Tidal Power," eas.asu.edu/~holbert/eee463/HydroTidalPower.pdf (accessed February 7, 2008).

28. Keith E. Holbert, Associate Professor, Arizona State University, "Nuclear Power Plants," eas.asu.edu/~holbert/eee463/NuclearPowerPlants.pdf (accessed February 7, 2008).

29. US Department of the Interior, "Reclamation: Managing Water in the West, Hydroelectric Power," July 2005, usbr.gov/power/edu/pamphlet.pdf (accessed February 7, 2008).

30. Browning, telephone conversation with author.

31. Union of Concerned Scientists, "The Hidden Cost of Fossil Fuels," August 10, 2005, ucsusa.org/clean_energy/fossil_fuels/the-hidden-cost-of-fossil-fuels.html (accessed February 7, 2008).

32. Andrews, telephone conversation with author.

33. Nate Byerley, telephone conversation with author, July 6, 2007.

34. Bart Orlando, interview with author, March 11, 2007, Arcata, California.

35. Ibid.

36. S. S. Wilson, "Bicycling Technology," *Scientific American* 228, no. 3 (March 1973), 81–91.

37. David S. Lawyer, "Bicycle Energy," September 2007, lafn.org/~dave/trans/energy/bicycle-energy.html (accessed February 7, 2008).

38. Allan V. Abbott and David Gordon Wilson, *Human Powered Vehicles* (Human Kinetics Publishers, 1995).

39. Slob, "The Human Power Chart: Sustained Comfortable Cranking," 27.

40. J. Spicer et al., "Effects of Frictional Loss on Bicycle Chain Drive Efficiency," *Journal of Mechanical Design* 123, no. 4 (2001); and Phil Sneiderman, "Pedal Power Probe Shows Bicycles Waste Little Energy" *The Johns Hopkins Gazette* 29, no. 1 (August 30, 1999).

41. "Guatemalan Indigenous Pedal Their Way to Mechanization," NotiCen: Central American & Caribbean Affairs (June 23, 2005).

42. Doña Ana, interview by MIT student Victoria Tai, May 27, 2005, web.mit.edu/teresab/www/Bicilavadora/Testimonio.doc.

43. Don Santiago, interview by MIT student Victoria Tai, May 27, 2005, web.mit.edu/

teresab/www/Bicilavadora/Testimonio .doc.

44. Carlos Marroquin Machàn, interview by MIT student Victoria Tai, May 27, 2005, web.mit.edu/teresab/www/Bicilavadora/ Testimonio.doc.

45. Adam Summers, "Meddling with Pedaling," *Natural History* 113, no. 2 (March 2004), 42–43.

46. David Weightman, "Design for a Pedal Driven Power Unit for Transport and Machine Uses in Developing Countries" (Volunteers in Technical Assistance [VITA], 1976).

47. Job Ebenezer, telephone conversation with author, September 21, 2007.

48. Alex Gadsden, telephone conversation with author, October 3, 2007.

49. Colin Kerr, telephone conversation with author, September 26, 2007.

50. Jeffrey P. Broker, "Cycling Biomechanics: Road and Mountain" in *High-Tech Cycling*, ed. Edmund R. Burke (Human Kinetics, 2003).

51. Scott Cooper, "St. Earth Pottery: [Process]: Throwing," St. Earth Pottery (September 19, 2007), negentropic.com/clay/ process/throwing.shtml, and e-mail correspondence with author.

52. J. P. Modak, "Human Powered Flywheel Motor Concept, Design, Dynamics, and Applications," in Proceedings of the World Congress in Mechanism and Machine Science IFToMM 2007, Besancon, France, June 17–21, 2007.

53. Ibid.

54. David Sowerwine, e-mail correspondence with author, October 3, 2007.

55. Wilson, *Bicycling Science,* 3rd Ed., 85.

56. Alex Weir, "Pedal Thresher and Grain Mill," cd3wd.com/thresher/default.htm (accessed September 30, 2007).

57. Diana Branch, in *Pedal Power In Work, Leisure and Transportation* (Rodale Press, 1977).

58. Eric Hollenbeck, interview with author, Eureka, California, March 8, 2007.

59. *Mayan Territory*, dir. Victoria Tai, Develop, September 18, 2007, truveo .com/Develop-Mayan-Territory/id/ 335084412.

60. US Environmental Protection Agency (EPA), "Basic Information: Municipal Solid Waste (MSW)," January 3, 2008, epa.gov/garbage/facts.htm (accessed February 7, 2008).

61. National Bicycle Dealer's Association (NBDA), "Industry Overview 2006," nbda.com/page.cfm?PageID=34 (accessed February 7, 2008).

62. Wilson, *Bicycling Science,* 3rd ed., 399.

63. Orlando, interview with author.

Chapter 3
Human-Powered Devices
For the Kitchen

1. Karen Baar, "In Kitchen Tools, Old Friends Are Best Friends," *New York Times*, August 27, 1997.

2. Frederick Breeden, telephone conversation with author, June 28, 2007.

3. Nate Byerley, telephone conversation with author, July 6, 2007.

4. Graham Corbett and Michael Sacco, telephone conversation with author, September 25, 2007.

5. Michigan Apple Committee/Michigan State University Product Center, "How to Make Cider," productcenter.msu.edu/documents/cider/makecider.pdf (accessed January 17, 2008).

6. Woody Roy Parker, telephone conversation with author, November 30, 2007.

7. Ben Polito, fiveislandsorchard.wordpress.com/category/cider-equipment/ (accessed: January 16, 2008).

8. David Lebovitz, "Making Ice Cream Without a Machine," July 30, 2007, davidlebovitz.com/archives/2007/07/making_ice_crea_1.html (accessed December 24, 2007).

Chapter 4
Human-Powered Devices
For Lawn and Garden

1. Gene Logsdon, *Homesteading: How to Find New Independence on the Land* (Rodale Press, 1973).

2. Larry Shannon and Jim Sylivant, telephone conversation with author, January 6, 2008.

3. US Environmental Protection Agency, "Beneficial Landscaping," August 16, 2006, epa.gov/greenkit/landscap.html (accessed January 19, 2008).

4. Andrew W. Lee, *Backyard Market Gardening: The Entrepreneur's Guide to Selling What You Grow* (Good Earth Publications, 1993).

5. Associated Press, "Manual Lawn Mowers are Making a Comeback," May 27, 2007.

6. Felicity Barringer, "A Greener Way to Cut the Grass Runs Afoul of a Powerful Lobby," *The New York Times*, April 24, 2006.

7. Roger Westerholm, "Measurement of Regulated and Unregulated Exhaust Emissions From a Lawn Mower With and Without an Oxidizing Catalyst: A Comparison of Two Fuels," *Environmental Science and Technology* 35, no. 11 (June 2001), 2166–2170.

8. David Temple, telephone conversation with author, December 9, 2007.

9. Richard Ehrlich, telephone conversation with author, January 18, 2008.

10. David Gordon Wilson, *Bicycling Science,* 3rd ed. (MIT Press, 2004).

11. David Gordon Wilson, interview with author, February 12, 2007, Cambridge, Massachusetts.

12. Wilson, *Bicycling Science,* 3rd ed., 404.

13. Kevin Blake, telephone conversation with author, December 20, 2007.

Chapter 5
Human-Powered Devices
for Housework

1. Curt Wohleber, "The Vacuum Cleaner," *Invention and Technology Magazine* 21, no. 4 (Spring 2006).

2. David Butcher, telephone conversation with author, December 7, 2007.

3. Anne Kusilek, telephone conversation with author, April 25, 2007.

4. Bart Orlando, interview with author, March 11, 2007, Arcata, California.

5. Janome Customer Relations, e-mail correspondence with author, January 15, 2008.

6. Amy Smith, telephone conversation with author, July 19, 2007.

7. Janome Customer Relations, e-mail correspondence with author.

8. Homeless Dave, "HD Clothes Washin' Man (A Pedal-Powered Alternative to Wringing)," homelessdave.com/hdwashingman.htm (accessed January 14, 2008).

9. Katherine T. Durack, "It All Comes Out in the Wash: Persuasion in Technical Proposals — Nineteenth Century Washing Machine Proposals to the U.S. Patent Office," *Proposal Management* (Fall 1999), 37–44.

10. Alex Gadsden, telephone conversation with author, October 3, 2007.

Chapter 6
Human-Powered Devices for Recreation and Emergency Preparedness

1. David Butcher, telephone conversation with author, December 7, 2007.

2. Colin Kerr, telephone conversation with author, September 26, 2007.

3. Sheila Kerr, e-mail correspondence with author, October 4, 2007.

4. Kerr, telephone conversation with author.

5. Bill Gerosa, telephone conversation with author, January 8, 2008.

6. Jason Moore, telephone conversation with author, December 29, 2007.

7. Steve Schmeck, telephone conversation with author, January 15, 2008.

8. Rick Hutcheson, telephone conversation with author, January 16, 2008.

9. Eric Hollenbeck, interview with author, March 8, 2007, Eureka, California.

IMAGE CREDITS

A1 Cable Solutions, 47

Alex Gadsden, 200

Allison Jones Photography, 36

All-Clad, 139

American Textile History Museum, 10

Bakken Library, Minneapolis, 44

Bart Orlando, 106

The Bicycle Museum of America, New Bremen, Ohio, 26, 27, 28

BRILL GLORIA Haus- und Garten-geräte GmbH, 175

Christopher Soghoian, 225

Clipper International/Rustek, 138, 232

Convergence Tech, Inc., 228

Country Living Products, 133

David Butcher, 216, 217

David Sowerwine/EcoSystems, 49, 100

The Day, New London, Connecticut, 29

DK images, 9

Earthway Products, 171, 173

Etón Corporation, 231

The Full Belly Project, 41

Frank Daller, Malnutrition Matters, 42, 92

Frederick Breeden, 122

Freeplay Energy, 51, 232

Freeplay Foundation, 50

Gary Roberts, 21 (Fig. 1.11)

George Austin, 108

GSI Outdoors, 130

Guildhall Library, City of London, 13

Gwyndaf Jones, 83

Haaga® Kunststofftechnik GmbH, 177

Happy Valley Ranch/Ray & Wanda Stagg, 143

High Tide Associates, 46

"Homeless Dave," 201

Industrial Revolution, Inc., 147

Jason Moore, 229

Kevin Blake, 178

KickStart, 33

Larry Shannon, 156

Lee Ravenscroft, 129

Lehman's, 197, 199, 234

Mathieu McFadden, ChocoSol Traders, 136

Max Davis, 145

Mel Serow, University of Michigan-Flint, 52

Michael Middleton (drawing). From *Gaviotas* by Alan Weisman. With permission of the publisher, Chelsea Green Publishing, 37

Mike Viney, 88

Nate Byerley, 74, 132

The Nelson-Atkins Museum of Art, 9

Norwell Crane/Handshouse Studio, 11

PlayPumps International, 37

Potenco, 51

Pragotrade, Inc., WestonSupply.com, 140, 144

Randy Roeder, 20

Red Hill General Store, 146

Richard Ehrlich, 176

Rick Hutcheson, 237

Saris Cycling Group, Inc., 104

Sidewinder, 233

SRI International, Menlo Park, CA, 56

State Library of South Australia, 45

Steve Schmeck, 236

Steven Gray, 39, 43, 82, 98, 189

Stuart King, 8

Tamara Dean, 238

Thomas Stuart Wheels, 96

Trevor Baylis Brands, 234

Tribest Corporation, 141

Wilson, David Gordon, *Bicycling Science*, 3rd edition, © 2004 Massachusetts Institute of Technology, by permission of The MIT Press., 65 (figure 2.9), 66 (figure 2.4), 77 (figure 4.16)

Windstream Power LLC, 226

Woody Roy Parker, 142

All illustrations by Nick Reitenour

All photos not credited are in the public domain

INDEX

ABOUT THE AUTHOR

TAMARA DEAN is a writer with varied interests whose published work includes bestselling technical books, stories, and essays. She lives in Wisconsin with her partner David in an eco-friendly home they built from compressed earth blocks and reclaimed timbers. They routinely use human-powered devices in the home and garden while experimenting with new contraptions in the workshop.

If you have enjoyed *The Human-Powered Home*, you might also enjoy other

BOOKS TO BUILD A NEW SOCIETY

Our books provide positive solutions for people who want to
make a difference. We specialize in:

Sustainable Living ◆ Ecological Design and Planning

Natural Building & Appropriate Technology

Environment and Justice ◆ Conscientious Commerce

Progressive Leadership ◆ Resistance and Community ◆ Nonviolence

Educational and Parenting Resources

New Society Publishers

ENVIRONMENTAL BENEFITS STATEMENT

New Society Publishers has chosen to produce this book on recycled paper made
with 100% post consumer waste, processed chlorine free, and old growth free.
For every 5,000 books printed, New Society saves the following resources:[1]

42	Trees
3,779	Pounds of Solid Waste
4,158	Gallons of Water
5,424	Kilowatt Hours of Electricity
6,871	Pounds of Greenhouse Gases
30	Pounds of HAPs, VOCs, and AOX Combined
10	Cubic Yards of Landfill Space

[1]Environmental benefits are calculated based on research done by the Environmental Defense
Fund and other members of the Paper Task Force who study the environmental impacts of the
paper industry.

For a full list of NSP's titles, please call 1-800-567-6772 or check out our web site at:

www.newsociety.com

NEW SOCIETY PUBLISHERS